No distinction of sex?

Women's History

General Editor
June Purvis
Professor of Sociology, University of Portsmouth

Published
Carol Dyhouse
No distinction of sex? Women in British universities, 1870–1939

Bridget Hill
Women, work and sexual politics in eighteenth-century England

Linda Mahood
Policing gender, class & family: Britain, 1800–1940

June Purvis (editor)
Women's history: Britain, 1850–1945

Forthcoming
Lynn Abrams and Elizabeth Harvey (editors)
Gender relations in German history

Shani D'Cruze
Sex violence and working women in Victorian and Edwardian England

jay Dixon
The romantic fiction of Mills & Boon, 1909–95

Ralph Gibson
Women, faith and liberation: female religious orders in nineteenth-century France

Wendy Webster
Women in the 1950s

Barbara Winslow
Sylvia Pankhurst: a political biography

No distinction of sex?
Women in British universities, 1870–1939

Carol Dyhouse

University of Sussex

UCL
PRESS

First published in 1995 by UCL Press

UCL Press Limited
University College London
Gower Street
London WC1E 6BT

The name of University College London (UCL) is a registered trade mark used by UCL Press with the consent of the owner.

British Library Cataloguing-in-Publication Data
A catalogue record for this book is available from the British Library.

Library of Congress Cataloging-in-Publication Data
Dyhouse, Carol, 1948–
    No distinction of sex? : women in British universities, 1870–1939
/ Carol Dyhouse.
        p.   cm. —Women's history
    Includes bibliographical references and index.
    ISBN 1-85728-458-5 (HB). —ISBN 1-85728-459-3 (PB)
    1. Women—Education (Higher)—Great Britain—History—19th
century. 2. Women—Education (Higher)—Great Britain—History—20th
century. 3. Women college students—Great Britain—History—19th
century. 4. Women college students—Great Britain—History—20th
century. 5. Women college teachers—Great Britain—History—19th
century. 6. Women college teachers—Great Britain—History—20th
century. I. Title. II. Series.
LC 2046D94 1995
376'.65'0941—dc20   95-875
                                                                                              CIP

Typeset in Sabon.
Printed and bound by
Biddles Ltd, Guildford and King's Lynn, England.

Contents

For my Mother, in memory

Acknowledgements

I want to express my thanks to the British Academy for the small personal award in 1991 that enabled me to begin work on this project. The opportunity to complete the collection of data through an extensive programme of visits to university archives throughout the country came with a grant from the Spencer Foundation in Chicago in 1992. It is difficult to see how this book could have come into being without the support of the Spencer Foundation, and the courtesy and generosity I have experienced from its officers at all times has been an added encouragement. At the same time I must emphasize that the responsibility for material presented in this study, together with the conclusions reached, remain my own.

A study that depends so heavily on archival source material has been made possible through the co-operation and advice of university librarians and archivists across Britain, all of whom gave unstinting support even when they were experiencing unprecedented demands on their time. I would like to thank Chris Penney and Dr Benedict in Birmingham, Mike Richardson and Nicholas Lee in Bristol, and Roger Norris in Durham. Joan Kenworthy took time and trouble to guide me round the archives of St Mary's College in Durham. Mary Forster and Rosemary Stephens introduced me to the archives in Leeds. Adrian Allan and Michael Cook helped me to sift through material in Liverpool. Adrian Allan, with his extensive knowledge of the archives of university bodies throughout the country, has been a continuing source of information and advice throughout the period in which I have been working on this project. I am grateful for the help of Dr Nockles and Dr McNiven in Manchester, and Elizabeth Healey was extremely co-operative in allowing me access to the records housed in Ashburne Hall in Manchester. John Richards and John Briggs guided me through archival material in Nottingham, and Dr Helen Mellor introduced me to papers relating to Florence Boot Hall. I would like to thank Michael Bott in Reading, Peter Carnell and Peter Linacre in Sheffield, Jenny Ruthven and Chris Woolgar in Southampton. My work in the archives of University College, London, was greatly facilitated by Elizabeth Gibson, in the Records Office, and Gillian Furlong, in the Manuscripts Room. Patricia Methven was an infallible guide to the archives in King's College, London, and Angela Raspin to those at the London School of Economics. Richard Williams and Anne Barrett helped with inquiries in Birkbeck and at Imperial College, respectively.

In Wales, I want to thank Richard Brinkley for his friendly support in Aberystwyth; Tomos Roberts, in Bangor, and Sheila Buckingham, who was welcoming and memorably hospitable in introducing me to the archives of Aberdare Hall in Cardiff. In Scotland, Jo Currie and Jean Archibald tirelessly supplied me with material in Edinburgh. Robert Smart guided me through material on the history of St Andrews, and Lorna Walker helped with the history of University Hall in St Andrews. Lesley Richmond and Kate Hutchison were informative and helpful in supplying material relating to the history of the University of Glasgow.

The primary focus of this book is on universities outside "Oxbridge", but the status of the women's foundations in Oxford and Cambridge carried important implications for the rest of the university "system" and their archives house a wealth of material relevant to the study. Pauline Adams introduced me to the archives of Somerville College, in Oxford. Dr Carola Hicks and Mrs Anne Bull helpfully allowed me access to material in Newnham College, Cambridge. Kate Perry was a knowledgeable guide to material in Girton, and our mutual interest in the history of the early generations of women graduates led to some stimulating exchanges of ideas.

Outside of the archives of individual universities and colleges, I want to acknowledge the help I received from Richard Storey, in the Modern Records Centre housed at Warwick University, who introduced me to the use of documents relating to the early history of the Association of University Teachers, the Clara Collet papers, and the records of the Headmistresses' Association. I am grateful to Beryl Roper and to May Hynd, who allowed me access to the archives of the British Federation of University Women, then housed in Crosby Hall, and to Evelyn Haselgrove, who produced material relating to the history of the University Women's Club in Audley Square. Mrs Rosemary Everidge kindly made space for me to consult the records of the Gilchrist Educational Trust in London. In the University Library at Sussex, the staff were unfailingly helpful in tracking down a mass of obscure references and in procuring material via the Inter-Library Loans Service. I particularly want to thank Joan Benning and David Kennelly, whose goodwill I fear I always take for granted.

There are many others who have helped, either by supplying material and references, or by discussing various aspects of the project with me over the last few years. Dulcie Groves has kindly volunteered information on a number of issues. Barbara Lees talked to me about hall life in Reading (from the students' point of view) and in Manchester (from the perspective of a warden). Elspeth Huxley also shared memories of Reading between the wars. Elsie Duncan Jones was eloquent about her experiences in Cambridge, Southampton and Birmingham. I am grateful to Keith Snell, who kindly arranged access to Margaret Miller's papers. Gerry Webster pointed me in the direction of information about women scientists. I have benefited from discussions with all these and a number of other people. Thanks particularly to Jennifer Carter, Di Drummond, Alison Gaukroger, Chris Heward, Jane Lewis, Roy Lowe, Lindy Moore, Sybil Oldfield, Penny Summerfield and Pat Thane in this context. There are several people whose support for this work goes back a number of years now, and my thanks to Rosemary Deem, Sara Delamont, Harold Perkin, June Purvis, Jenny Shaw and Brian Simon, all of whom have given encouragement over the long term.

I am grateful to the University of Sussex, and especially to Alun Howkins and Terry Diffey, for supporting my request for leave of absence from teaching in 1994-5. I owe a special debt of gratitude to Nick von Tunzelmann, for the phenomenal tact with which he has suggested apparently minor revisions in the text. Margaret Ralph put the text on disk with extraordinary speed and competence: her encouragement has been an added bonus. My thanks also to Steven Gerrard and his colleagues at UCL Press for their friendly and efficient support. My close friends and family have endured much with a tolerance that was generally more than I deserved.

Alexandra and Eugénie were ingenious in suggesting alternative titles for this book, one of which ("Scholars and Amazons") I jettisoned with considerable reluctance.

‚ò†

Introduction

A report published by the Hansard Society in 1990 argued that women suffered from a double disadvantage in British university life.[1] The writers of the report cited figures showing that women still constituted a minority (14 per cent) of full-time, tenured university academic staff, and pointed out that this minority was concentrated in lower grade posts.[2] The Hansard Commission contended that it was "wholly unacceptable that British universities should remain bastions of male power and prestige". Oxford and Cambridge, particularly, were singled out for censure:

> The barriers facing women at Oxford and Cambridge can be summarised quite succinctly: in two overwhelmingly male-dominated institutions, women simply are not *good chaps* . . .[3]

But they conceded a need for more investigation:

> There is little empirical evidence available about the processes at work which bar women's progress at Oxford or Cambridge, or at any other university: academics have only just begun to research themselves.[4]

Academics are indeed beginning to "research themselves", and questions about gender and equal opportunities have been widely discussed in recent years. But there is nothing new about the concern with the male exclusiveness of the older universities. Ruth Deech, Principal of St Anne's College, Oxford, was reported in *The Guardian* in 1992 as being "appalled" to discover herself barred from entering the library of the Oxford and Cambridge Club.[5] She can hardly have been that *surprised*. We can all too easily recall Virginia Woolf's eloquent protest in *A room of one's own* half a century earlier, and her haunting images of being shooed off the grass and out of the library by

Beadles and Fellows in flapping gowns.[6] Oxford allowed women to take degrees in 1920, Cambridge withheld full membership of the university from them until 1948. Most colleges in Oxford and Cambridge now admit both sexes; women can walk on the grass as well as the gravel. However, sexual politics remain a live issue, and continue to nurture a rich vein of feminist protest.[7] But what of Britain's other universities? We have recently witnessed the upgrading of large numbers of erstwhile polytechnics and colleges of higher education to university status. This book is concerned with what we now designate the older universities, those institutions founded and chartered in the main before the Second World War, which can be said to have set the pattern. The group includes the four Scottish universities, all of ancient foundation, Durham (established in 1832), and London (1836). It also comprises the provincial or civic universities founded after 1850: Birmingham, Manchester, Liverpool, Sheffield, Leeds and Bristol. Reading, which acquired full university status in 1926, is included in this study, as are the colleges of the University of Wales. I have also made some reference to the university colleges of Nottingham, Southampton and Leicester.

Contemporaries saw the creation and development of the then newer, civic universities as a movement of crucial importance in national history and the development of British social life. In particular, they singled out the fact that by the end of the century these institutions all admitted women. Writing in the *Sociological Review* in 1939, Charles Grant Robertson argued that:

> The new universities have, indeed, made a notable, perhaps the most decisive, contribution to the revolutionary "emancipation of women"; they have been both pioneers and registers of a profound movement in thought, feeling and ideals.[8]

There were prominent women educationalists who would have agreed with him. Sarah Burstall's contribution to the *Directory of women teachers* in 1913 included the following:

> The Archbishop of York recently stated that when the history of the last twenty years came to be written, it would seem that few social phenomena were of greater national importance than the rise of the new universities. As women enjoy in all these an equality with men as to degrees, scholarships and fellowships, appointments to staffs, access to teaching, laboratories, libraries, etc., and almost universally participate in government

through Court, Senate, Convocation and similar bodies, the new universities must, *a fortiori*, be of great importance and value in girls' education.[9]

The contrast between Oxbridge and Britain's other universities in respect of the treatment accorded to women was much remarked upon, often with acerbity. Cambridge might preserve "the old fantastic arrogance of the youthful male", remarked a writer in *The Woman's Leader* in 1922, and men would no doubt continue to be "miseducated" in its precincts but the women could now go elsewhere.[10]

Even before the end of the nineteenth century, some universities outside Oxbridge were advertising themselves as making "no distinction of sex". Perusing the pages of the feminist Christina Bremner's detailed survey and handbook, *The education of girls and women in Great Britain*, which was published in 1897, we frequently stumble across this or a similar claim. The University of London is heralded as "the first academic body in the United Kingdom to throw open its degrees, honours, prizes to students of both sexes, *on terms of perfect equality*" (my italics).[11] In the University of Wales: "Men and women are on an absolute equality as regards degrees, entrance to classes, and what is equally important, social life".[12] Bremner quotes from the prospectus of Firth College, Sheffield, which states that its "doors are open to all, without distinction of sex or class".[13] She is somewhat tight-lipped over provision in the Victoria University (then a federation of Manchester, Liverpool and Leeds), since the attitude to women at that time at Owens College, Manchester could "hardly be styled as cordial".[14] But she comments on the achievement of Bristol, egalitarian except for the medical school, and celebrates the arrangements made by the university colleges of Nottingham, which made "no distinction of religion . . . or of sex", and, particularly, Reading: "Every class in the College, and every society, is open to men and women *without distinction*; women also sit on the governing body" (my italics).[15]

The phraseology entered promotional literature. By the 1920s, Manchester can be seen as trying to mend its reputation somewhat. Contributing to a series of articles on "Women in the universities", published in the *Journal of Careers* in 1928, Manchester's adviser to women students claimed that there were "the same opportunities for women as for men to enjoy the facilities which the University offers; there is *no distinction* between them".[16]

What did this mean? The sceptical feminist may be forgiven for wondering whether the claim is analogous to that made so frequently at the bottom of job advertisements today: "the University of X is an equal opportunities employer". How much substance is, or was, there in the rhetoric? Or even, what do equal opportunities or identical provision mean in a system of deeply entrenched inequality or difference?

Was it just a question of relativism? Mary Stocks was shocked by Oxford after studying at the London School of Economics in the early years of the present century:

> London, or rather the School of Economics, and indeed London University, was an egalitarian world. Women played an equal part in it, equal in status if not in numbers, and were in no sense conscious of being second-class citizens. From no academic activity were they excluded by virtue of their sex. No avenue of academic promotion was closed to them. And, so far as I was aware, no learned society excluded them either from its deliberations or from its social festivities.
>
> But Oxford was quite otherwise. Its women's colleges were there on sufferance. . . . The centre of University social life was in the male college common rooms. No woman could share that life . . .[17]

Similarly, Rachel Trickett, Principal of St Hugh's, Oxford, noted as recently as 1986 that

> The older provincial universities have a more liberal history with regard to accepting women than Oxford or Cambridge, and have always been generous in appointing them. The eight years during which I taught at the then University College of Hull revealed no trace of prejudice against women as students or as lecturers.[18]

It is by no means difficult to find comments of this kind, but they undoubtedly provoke further questions. How do we reconcile the claims of equality or the argument that the provincial universities were devoid of prejudice against women, with the structures of inequality almost taken for granted by the authors of the Hansard Report? On the face of it, it seems unlikely that the patterns of access, provision and attitudes to women students and teachers in universities other than Oxbridge were more liberal in 1914, or 1939, than in the 1980s.

Let us turn to the historians. There has been little research into the development of British universities as social institutions, let alone into patterns of gender differentiation within their walls. There are a number of histories documenting the struggle of pioneer women in Oxford and Cambridge,[19] and more recently feminist historians have turned their attention to the role of the separate women's colleges, both in Oxbridge and in the University of London. Sara Delamont has contributed greatly to our awareness of the strategies and predicaments of women who sought acceptance in male-dominated elites.[20] Martha Vicinus has illuminated our understanding of the female cultures and friendship networks that flourished in Girton and Newnham, Somerville and Lady Margaret Hall, Royal Holloway and Westfield Colleges.[21] But few historians have looked in detail at the experiences of women in Britain's other universities.

The subject has not been ignored entirely. In 1941 Mabel Tylecote wrote a history of women's education at the University of Manchester.[22] Studies of women's experiences in the University of Wales and in Aberdeen University appeared in 1990 and 1991,[23] and in 1987 Sheila Hamilton completed a doctoral dissertation on women students in Scottish universities between 1869 and 1939.[24] Most recently, Julie Gibert has focused attention on the civic universities before the Second World War with research on women students in the Universities of Manchester, Bristol and Birmingham.[25] At the risk of doing violence to the detail of these works, Sheila Hamilton's conclusion suggests that women students moved towards a position of formal or academic integration in the universities of Edinburgh, Glasgow, St Andrews and Aberdeen, while remaining rather segregated in social life.[26] Julie Gibert's thesis is rather different. Generalizing on the basis of her study of three universities, she argues that the civic universities readily opened their doors to women, making little attempt to segregate the sexes either academically or socially. Women were not driven to form gender-based subcultures, because "at the red bricks, the cause of female education succeeded quickly, and with relatively little controversy".[27] Gibert's conclusions contrast rather strikingly with those of Mabel Tylecote, 40 years earlier, and also with those of Lindy Moore, whose study of women students in Aberdeen emphasizes their position as a "muted" group,[28] rather than as the "powerful and visible" section of the community depicted in Gibert's account. Once again, a number of questions formulate themselves: on the basis of what kind of evidence are these conclusions arrived at? To what extent are generalized conclusions possible?

These writers have paid little attention to the role of women on the staff of universities in the period before 1939. Gibert concerned herself solely with women students. The writers of the Hansard Society report were particularly concerned with "women at the top", but took it as self-evident that women teachers and academics would act as role models and exemplars for female students. If women academics were thin on the ground and of lowly status, then "women undergraduates may feel that academic life is not for them".[29] Two early studies of women academics in Britain by Ingrid Sommerkorn and Margherita Rendel both commented on the poverty of historical data relative to the numbers and experience of women teachers in universities before 1939.[30] More recently a study by Fernanda Perrone set out to investigate the careers of women academics in Oxford, Cambridge and London, arguing that some progress, albeit limited, was made by this group in establishing themselves as part of a newly emerging profession of university teachers before the Second World War.[31] There have not, to the best of my knowledge, been any studies of the historical position of women academics and teachers in civic universities in the period with which this book is concerned. Rendel's impression was that the proportions of women holding posts in the younger civic universities earlier this century were higher than the national average.[32] She tentatively suggested that the proportions and position of these women did not change much, and may even have declined in certain subject areas, between 1912 and 1976.[33]

Again, a number of important questions suggest themselves. The lack of historical studies of women academics in Britain can be contrasted with the situation in the USA, where feminist scholars have paid closer attention to historical trends. Susan B. Carter has focused on changing patterns of women's employment as college and university faculty through the period 1890 and 1963, deftly pinpointing long-term tendencies and suggesting useful explanations for the declining representation of women between 1930 and 1960.[34] Her arguments have called into question Jessie Bernard's earlier contention that the falling numbers in the interwar period reflected women's own preferences for domestic rather than academic life.[35] A series of essays brought together by Geraldine Jonçich Clifford, exploring the experiences of academic women in co-educational universities in the United States between 1870 and 1937, highlighted the fact that women generally entered these institutions through a separate, gender-based labour market. Women were employed as "lady principals", "deans of women", or special "tutors to women students".[36] Integration could entail the disappearance of such posts, making it more difficult for women to secure positions. One of the tasks of this book will be to find out whether a similar situation obtained in Britain.

Segregation as opposed to integration could guarantee a protected space, or what might almost be seen as a form of positive discrimination for women. It is the recognition of this that has historically buttressed, and to some extent continues to underlie, feminist support for single-sex women's colleges. It has often been argued that the representation of women on university staffs has declined alongside the demise of single-sex institutions.[37] But feminists have always been divided over questions of segregation, separate spheres and protected women's spaces. It is never easy for an observer to interpret the meanings of patterns of gender segregation such as those found in many universities earlier in this century. Where we find separate societies for men and women students, this may reflect policy on the part of university authorities; it may also have represented student choice, a pattern of normative expectations about the ordering of social life. It might have been the consequence of male exclusiveness, or perhaps it should be seen as an index of feminist awareness or self-consciousness among the women. I would argue that there is a crucial need for historical awareness here, for the patterns and forms of separation between the sexes are complex and shifting and can only be understood fully in relation to their changing historical context.

Women constituted only a small minority of students, around 15 per cent, in British universities at the beginning of the present century. By 1939 this minority had swelled to about 23 per cent.[38] The proportion of women varied considerably between individual universities, within their faculties and through time. Women academics and tutors constituted only a tiny minority of university staff. In her recent work on industrial corporations and bureaucracies in America, Rosabeth Moss Kanter has argued persuasively that the lives and experiences of women in corporate structures are governed by the proportions in which they find themselves.[39] In organizations where men preponderate, women tend to be seen as tokens rather than as individuals; their position is characterized by conflict and difficulty; they fear visibility;

and their presence functions to *underline* rather than to *undermine* the dominant culture. Where a skewed distribution of the sexes becomes less extreme and the proportion of women increases from around 15 per cent to around 35 per cent of the corporate body, the female minority becomes much more powerful, women are less isolated, and can form coalitions or even create a counterculture within the organization. This kind of analysis can certainly supply insights into the experiences of women in university communities during the period with which this book is concerned. Women can hardly be described as powerful in these communities, but they were by no means completely *powerless*. Where their numbers allowed, they did indeed form coalitions and support networks, and they managed to carve out and to defend important cultural spaces.

Universities are clearly different from industrial corporations, however. Universities need students. Partly because historians of women's higher education in Britain have concentrated their attention on Oxford and Cambridge, we have vivid and enduring images of women battling for access into sacred portals, and of authorities reluctant to extend privilege. This picture must be balanced by an awareness of the fact that many of Britain's other universities were concerned with the difficulties of recruiting enough students to keep their recently established departments going. They could not afford *not* to enrol women, particularly in arts, humanities and education. In any materialist analysis, this was an important source of women's power. So too, were the donations of women benefactors, often made with the intention of strengthening provision for women students specifically within the co-educational university.

This book concerns itself with the experiences of women, as both students and teachers in British universities before 1939, paying particular attention to patterns of distinction and discrimination; separation and integration; feminist strategies and gendered institutions; subcultures and social forms. In Chapter 1 I look at patterns of provision: the chronology of women's access to the universities and the characteristics of their accommodation within them. This latter theme is explored further in Chapters 2 and 3, which look at the superintendence of women students and the establishment of halls of residence and hostels. Chapter 4 focuses on the careers of women academics, and Chapter 5 on gender, student experience and feminism.

Notes

1. Hansard Society Commission, *Women at the top* (London, 1990), p. 65.
2. *Ibid.*
3. *Ibid.*, p. 67.
4. *Ibid.*
5. "In a class of her own", *Guardian*, 22 July 1992, p. 19.
6. V. Woolf, *A room of one's own* (Penguin, 1973), pp. 7–9.
7. See Cambridge University Women's Action Group, *Forty years on . . .* (Report on the numbers and status of academic women in the University of Cambridge, September 1988), A. Spurling, *Report of the women in higher education research project 1988–90* (King's College Cambridge, 1990) and "Opportunity Knocks", *Oxford Today* 4(2), p. 2, Hilary issue, 1992.
8. C. G. Robertson, "The provincial universities", *Sociological Review* 31 p. 253, 1939.
9. *The directory of women teachers and other women engaged in higher and secondary education* (London: The Year Book Press, 1913), pp. lii–liii.
10. "Women, politics and education", *The Woman's Leader and The Common Cause* (23 June 1922), p. 163.
11. C. S. Bremner, *Education of girls and women in Great Britain* (London, 1897), p. 140.
12. *Ibid.*, p. 151.
13. *Ibid.*, p. 155.
14. *Ibid.*, p. 149.
15. *Ibid.*, pp. 154, 155, 161.
16. P. Crump, "Women students at the universities: IV, Manchester University", *The Journal of Careers* (November 1928), p. 28.
17. M. Stocks, *My commonplace book* (London, 1970), pp. 99–100.
18. R. Trickett, "Introduction" in *St Hugh's: one hundred years of women's education in Oxford*, P. Griffin (ed.) (Oxford, 1986), p. 13.
19. See A. M. A. Rogers, *Degrees by degrees* (Oxford, 1938), V. Brittain, *The women at Oxford: a fragment of history* (London, 1960) and R. McWilliams-Tullberg, *Women at Cambridge: a men's university, though of a mixed type* (London, 1975).
20. S. Delamont, *Knowledgeable women: structuralism and the reproduction of elites* (London, 1989). See also the same author's essay "The contradictions in ladies' education", in *The nineteenth-century woman: her cultural and physical world*, S. Delamont & L. Duffin (eds) (London, 1978), and J. S. Pedersen, *The reform of girls' secondary and higher education in Victorian England: a study of elites and educational change* (New York & London, 1987).
21. M. Vicinus, *Independent women: work and community for single women, 1850–1920* (London, 1985). See also the same author's "'One life to stand beside me': emotional conflicts of first generation college women in Eng-

land", *Feminist Studies* 8, pp. 602–28, 1982.

22. M. Tylecote, *The education of women at Manchester University, 1883–1933* (Manchester, 1941).

23. G. Evans, *Education and female emancipation; the Welsh experience, 1847–1914* (Cardiff, 1990); L. Moore, *Bajanellas and semilinas: Aberdeen University and the education of women, 1860–1920* (Aberdeen, 1991).

24. S. Hamilton, *Women and the Scottish universities c. 1869–1939: a social history*, PhD thesis (University of Edinburgh, 1987).

25. J. S. Gibert, *Women at the English civic universities 1880–1920*, PhD thesis (University of North Carolina at Chapel Hill, 1988).

26. Hamilton, *Women and the Scottish universities*, p. 160.

27. Gibert, *Women at the English universities*, p. 8.

28. Moore, *Bajanellas*, p. 136.

29. Hansard Society, *Women at the top*, p. 66.

30. I. Sommerkorn, *On the position of women in the university teaching profession in England: an interview study of 100 women teachers*, PhD thesis (London School of Economics, 1967), p. 14; and M. Rendel, "How many women academics, 1912–76?" in *Schooling for women's work*, R. Deem (ed.) (London, 1980), pp. 142–61.

31. F. Perrone, *University teaching as a profession for women in Oxford, Cambridge and London, 1870–1930*, DPhil thesis (Oxford, 1991).

32. Rendel, "Women academics", p. 145.

33. *Ibid.*, p. 154ff.

34. S. B. Carter, "Academic women revisited: an empirical study of changing patterns in women's employment as college and university faculty, 1890–1963", *Journal of Social History* 14, pp. 675–99, 1987.

35. J. Bernard, *Academic women* (Pennsylvania, 1964).

36. G. J. Clifford (ed.), *Lone voyagers: academic women in co-educational universities, 1870–1937* (New York, 1989), p. 11ff.

37. See, for instance, Rendel, "Women academics", p. 145.

38. R. D. Anderson, *Universities and elites in Britain since 1800* (Basingstoke, 1992), p. 23.

39. R. M. Kanter, *Men and women of the corporation* (USA: Basic Books, 1977), pp. 206–12.

Chapter One

❧

Patterns of provision: access and accommodation

Admitting women

Josephine Kamm, an early historian of women's education, observed that in the long struggle to obtain university degrees for women "Britain blazed no trail".[1] In this respect British universities lagged behind their American counterparts, as well as the universities of the Commonwealth.[2] Access came later, and accommodation was often rather more meagre. Phoebe Sheavyn, who was Senior Tutor to Women Students at Manchester University in the early 1920s, compiled a brief survey for the International Federation of University Women around 1924, in which she contrasted the poverty of provision for women in British universities with the dignified and spacious arrangements that she had seen in the United States.[3]

Dr Sheavyn was well placed to comment on educational provision and social opportunity; she came from a relatively poor social background, and as a young woman she had taught in a Board School in the Midlands, allegedly "after her hemming had passed the scrutiny of a male inspector with a magnifying glass".[4] Following some depressing teaching experiences she became a governess in the family of an architect who had encouraged her to sit for the Oxford Local Examinations. This had led to a scholarship at the new College of Aberystwyth. She was awarded a first-class honours degree in English by the University of London in 1889, her master's degree in 1894, and a D.Litt. in 1906. Between 1894 and 1896 she held posts as Reader and then Fellow of Bryn Mawr in Pennsylvania, where she was able to acquire first-hand knowledge of American provision for the higher education of women, before returning to England as Tutor and Lecturer

11

at Somerville. In 1907 she left Oxford to take up an appointment as Senior Tutor to Women Students and Warden of Ashburne Hall in Manchester.[5] Sheavyn's life history was extraordinary in terms of her social mobility, variety of experience, and sheer longevity (she lived to be 102), but these were some of the qualities that rendered her a sharp social observer.

In Britain, the University of London was, in 1878, the first university to admit women to its degrees (with the exception of medicine), and University College London (UCL), which opened most of its classes to women in the same year, has laid claim to being the first co-educational university institution.[6] But the pattern is complex, and much depends on definitions. Neat chronological lists of dates of entry are not easy to draw up and can often be misleading. Women were frequently allowed access to classes before, or in some cases after, being allowed to sit degree examinations. There were sometimes special qualifications for women: St Andrews University in Scotland had offered a higher certificate (the LA, later LLA or "Lady Literate in Arts") to women students from 1876.[7] Students in the newer university colleges prepared for the degrees of the University of London before these colleges obtained their separate charters. Women were cautiously admitted to classes in Owens College, Manchester, in 1883, for what was originally designated as a trial or probationary period of five years. Access to degrees in Manchester (then part of the "Victoria University" federation of Manchester, Liverpool and Leeds) came slowly and in instalments.[8] At first, only the pass degree and four honours schools in the Faculty of Arts were open to women, although by 1897 they were admitted to all degree examinations except those in engineering and medicine.[9] Apart from Oxford and Cambridge, Durham was the last university in England to admit women to its degrees. In Durham a supplementary charter licensing their admission to all courses and degrees (with the exception of divinity) was obtained in 1895, although women were excluded from membership of Convocation until 1914.[10] None of the charters granted to the new civic universities in England excluded women. In Scotland, legislative changes of 1889 and 1892 empowered the four Scottish universities to admit women to classes and degrees.[11] The charter of the University of Wales, granted in 1893, stipulated women's eligibility for degrees and also offices, stating specifically that they should be treated as full members of the university.[12]

However, as stated above, much depends on definitions. Women students were often admitted to classes in colleges that later became part of chartered institutions of full university status. The College of Science in Newcastle, originally part of the University of Durham, accepted women students before Durham did.[13] Mason College in Birmingham, Firth College in Sheffield, the Yorkshire College in Leeds, and the university colleges in Nottingham, Reading and Bristol all admitted women students to some or all of their classes before they received their charters. The pattern is blurred further by arrangements for instruction in medicine: almost everywhere it was opposition from faculty in the medical schools, and their links with senior staff and managers of local hospitals and infirmaries, that delayed the universities' formal provision for the full acceptance of women students to classes and examinations. In Edinburgh, the bitter struggles between, on the one hand, Sophia Jex-Blake and the group of women who battled to obtain a medical education in the 1870s, and, on the other, the medical faculty, led by Professor Robert Christison, arguably produced a backlash, which left the university authorities confused and wary about the rights of women to full access to university facilities, particularly the women students of medicine.[14] In Glasgow, the existence of a separate medical school for women in Queen Margaret College delayed the university's sense of any need to open its own medical classes to women, even after the incorporation of Queen Margaret College into the university in 1893.[15] Even in University College London, with its proud tradition of pioneering co-educational provision, women were not admitted into the Faculty of Medicine until 1917.[16]

The Ladies' Educational Associations

If medical schools served to delay the full admission of women, female students were often admitted to classes taught at least partly under the aegis of university authorities before their admission to degrees. This was not only in connection with the separate qualifications or certificates offered to women students such as the St Andrews' LA mentioned above. Here we have to consider the work of the Ladies' Educational Associations founded, for the most part, in the 1860s and 1870s. There were a large number of these associations, and they were originally founded for a number of purposes.[17] Following the opening of the Oxford and Cambridge and other university Local Examinations to women in the second half of the nineteenth century, these associations frequently supervised the arrangements whereby girls and women sat for these examinations, also acting as support groups for women teachers. Others were more specifically concerned to promote the higher education of women, to which end they organized classes and lecture series, sponsored scholarships and bursaries, and lobbied their local institutions of higher education for access and facilities. There were Ladies' Educational Associations in almost all the larger towns and many of the smaller ones too: some of these were relatively informal and have left little documentation, others were highly organized, long lived and powerful. The best known was the North of England Council for Promoting the Higher Education of Women, founded in 1867 to unite the local educational associations in Manchester, Liverpool, Leeds, Sheffield and Newcastle.[18] The activities of Anne Jemima Clough and Josephine Butler in connection with the council, together with its role in pioneering the University Extension Movement and its influence on the foundation of Newnham College, have received a good deal of attention from historians. Twelve towns were represented on the council between 1867 and 1874.[19]

Negley Harte has illuminated the role played by the London Ladies' Educational Association in facilitating the process whereby University College came to admit women in 1878. The London Association, founded in 1868–9, was modelled to some extent on the North of England Council. With the key support of Henry Morley, Professor of English, and other sympathetic professors from University College, the London Ladies' Educational Association began to organize "lectures for ladies" originally outside college premises. Gradually these lectures were introduced into the college, although for propriety's sake the classes were kept strictly separate from the men's classes. Gradually a number of mixed classes were introduced: after 1878 these came to predominate and as the college came formally to accept women students the London Ladies' Educational Association disbanded.[20]

This pattern was echoed, with local variations, elsewhere in Britain. In Yorkshire the Yorkshire Ladies' Educational Association arranged for Cambridge Extension lectures, which effectively developed into the arts departments of the Yorkshire College, later the University of Leeds. Indeed, in 1882 the Yorkshire Ladies presented Edward

Baines, as representative of the college, with a cheque for a thousand guineas, in recognition of the college's role in facilitating women's access to higher education in the area.[21]

Ladies' Educational Associations were also important in Scotland, particularly in Edinburgh and Glasgow. Sheila Hamilton has looked in detail at the work of the Edinburgh Ladies' Educational Association (ELEA), founded in 1869.[22] Like the London Association, this was a highly respectable body which worked closely with university professors who were sympathetic to the need for higher education for women, and in particular with David Masson, Professor of English Literature and Rhetoric. Lecture series organized by the association were well attended and of a wholly reputable standard: they were all given by professors wearing gowns. This made it comparatively easy for the university authorities to agree, in 1872, to offer a special certificate for women who had qualified to a certain standard in literature, philosophy and science.[23] In 1874 the first three ladies, Flora Masson, Margaret Mitchell and Charlotte Carmichael, later to be the mother of Marie Stopes, received their certificates.[24]

The institution of a special certificate for women fell short of the aspirations of many feminists, and it is hardly surprising to learn that Emily Davies wrote to the Edinburgh Ladies' Education Association in 1872 expressing her alarm over the injurious effects of setting up a separate standard for women.[25] However, as Sheila Hamilton has argued, the comparatively cautious, accommodating strategies of the ELEA helped to soothe some of the tension and controversy generated in Edinburgh by the campaigns of the women bent on studying medicine. As Professor Masson observed, the ELEA effectively developed into a kind of female Faculty of Arts, the students of which were taught by university professors, but not yet entitled to sit examinations for degrees.[26] In 1879, the ELEA renamed itself the Edinburgh Association for the Higher Education of Women, the role of professors on its Council and executive committee was strengthened, and the new association began to issue an annual calendar similar in format to the university's own.[27] The association continued to petition for full access to degrees.

In Glasgow, similarly, there was co-operation between the Glasgow Association for the Higher Education of Women and the university. John Caird, the Principal of Glasgow University, presided over the large public meeting at which the association was formally constituted in 1877.[28] Again, a pattern developed whereby sympathetic professors lectured and provided accommodation for classes organized by the women's association. In 1883 a gift from Mrs Isabella Elder, a wealthy local widow, allowed the Glasgow Association to open its own college close to the university. Queen Margaret College was incorporated in 1884. The college was not at the outset formally affiliated to the university, although the Senatus elected two members of its governing body, and there were teaching links.[29] The college developed on the periphery of the university, opening its own medical school in 1890, and the Glasgow Association continued to campaign for the admission of women to degrees. Following the ordinance of 1892, the college became formally a part of the university; in effect, the "women's department", although women students continued to be known as "Queen Margaret students".[30]

The Ladies' Educational Associations, then, played an important part in facilitating women's access to the universities. They had powerful patrons and supporters of both sexes. The president of the Glasgow Association was Princess Louise, Marchioness of Lorne, and the executive committee of the Edinburgh Association in 1878 was headed by the Duchess of Argyll. Some of the office holders and many of the subscribers to these associations were the wives and daughters of wealthy local citizens, or widows and unmarried daughters with considerable wealth at their disposal, who were in a position to make significant educational endowments. This is an important theme that will be returned to later in the chapter. Supporters and subscribers also included a large number of professors' wives and daughters. (We have seen that Flora Masson was one of the first to receive a certificate in Edinburgh in 1874.) The support of university professors and teachers sympathetic to the cause of women's education was crucial in fostering academic links, and in ensuring that the educational work of the associations was of an appropriate standard. This meant that when the universities opened their degree examinations to women, there were women whose previous attendance at classes enabled them to qualify almost immediately, without much further study. In Edinburgh, for instance, the "first eight ladies" who graduated in arts in 1893 had all been students of the Edinburgh Association for the Higher Education of Women,[31] and in Glasgow, the medical classes at Queen Margaret College had been carefully arranged so that in 1892 attendance at these classes qualified students to proceed immediately to university examinations. Marion Gilchrist, a student at Queen Margaret College, became the first woman to obtain a Scottish medical degree in 1894.[32]

Women students: numbers and social composition

Compared with the number of women who had attended lectures organized by the local Educational Associations in university towns, the number of women graduates was at first small. In Glasgow, three more Queen Margaret College students received their medical degrees in 1894, and arts degrees were awarded to two women in the following year.[33] In Aberdeen, the first four women graduates were capped in 1898.[34] In England, four women students obtained their BA degrees from the University of London in 1880;[35] degrees were conferred on four women students in Manchester in 1887.[36] The sight of these early women students graduating was still unusual enough to provoke public interest and merriment at the turn of the century. When Birmingham University mounted its first degree day procession in July 1901, and the first female student was presented to Joseph Chamberlain, it is recorded that the male undergraduates shouted out "Go on, Sir, kiss her", although Chamberlain did not oblige.[37]

From around 1900, however, the number of women students rose steadily, especially in arts departments, all over Britain. In London in 1927, over 500 women students graduated.[38] Figures from the University Grants Committee (UGC) show that women represented 16 per cent of the student population of Great Britain in 1900: this proportion rose to 24 per cent in 1920 and 27 per cent in 1930, falling again to 23 per cent on the eve of the Second World War.[39] The proportion of women was higher in the Scottish universities and in the University of Wales. By 1899 one quarter of the students in Aberdeen's Faculty of Arts were women, and by 1913 nearly half.[40] In St Andrews, women students represented 40 per cent of the total student population as early as 1907–8. The proportions were 31 per cent in Aberdeen, 24 per cent in Glasgow, and 18 per cent in Edinburgh for the same year.[41] By 1937–8 the UGC figures show a total of 11,299 full-time women students enrolled in British universities (including Oxford and Cambridge but excluding Ireland). There were 37,890 men, so women represented nearly one quarter of the total.[42]

17

Writing about what he saw as the revolutionary changes that higher education had effected in the status and aspirations of women, Charles Grant Robertson observed that by 1939 women graduates were "as plentiful as tabby-cats, in point of fact, too many".[43] There were indeed a number of educationalists and social observers who argued that the network of provision for women students had been spread widely enough by that date. This was not least because the increase in career opportunities for educated women had not kept pace with their supply. Teaching remained the major occupational outlet for women graduates.[44] Margaret Tuke, Principal of Bedford College, complained that the universities "were apt to be regarded, as far as women were concerned, as institutions for the training of teachers", noting that the figures at her disposal indicated that between half and three quarters of all women graduates were destined to enter the profession.[45] As early as 1914, Edith Morley lamented the fact that too many girls committed themselves to teaching because it appeared to be the only route to obtaining a grant for higher education, and there were few other professions to which they might aspire.[46] R. D. Anderson has argued that women's access to higher education was intimately related to the fluctuating market for teachers.[47] The decrease in the proportion of women students over Britain as a whole in the 1930s, although accounted for to a considerable extent by a decrease in their numbers in Scotland, can be related to the Depression and a falling off in the demand for schoolteachers during that decade.[48]

Those who petitioned for women's access to the universities in the 1870s almost invariably emphasized the need for improving the education of women teachers. We have already noted the close connections between the Schoolmistresses' Associations of the 1860s and 1870s, and the Societies for the Higher Education of Women. The Edinburgh Ladies' Educational Association, in pressing the Universities Commission in Scotland to consider women's entitlement to degrees in the 1870s, pointed to the fact that both Edinburgh and St Andrews universities had instituted Chairs in Education, and argued that since the majority of teachers were women, they could be seen as having an obligation to attend to their needs.[49] Similar arguments were made elsewhere. In 1885 the Edinburgh Association established its own college, St George's, for the training of women teachers in connection with the Teachers' Training Syndicate of the University of Cambridge.[50] The Cambridge Syndicate had been set up in 1879: it made provision for lectures in the theory, history and practice of education, conducted examinations that could be prepared for in Cambridge or elsewhere, and issued certificates to candidates who were successful in these examinations.[51] The Cambridge Day Training College for Women, with Miss E. P. Hughes as Principal, was founded a few years later in 1885. The Cambridge certificate was keenly supported by Miss Clough, and by Frances Buss of the North London Collegiate School, and it became widely respected among headmistresses across the country. In 1883 the University of London established a postgraduate diploma in education, and the Victoria University followed with a similar qualification in 1895.[52] By 1900 there were secondary training departments in 21 universities and university colleges in Britain.[53] As has often been observed, training for teaching at the secondary level was more popular among, and taken much more seriously by, women than men at this time.[54]

The universities' involvement in teacher education generally grew rapidly after the 1890s, and followed the foundation of the "day training colleges", which were the ancestors of the modern university departments of education.[55] In 1890 the government drew up regulations for the administration of grant aid to day training colleges in connection with the universities and university colleges. Students were to receive their general education in the ordinary classes of the university, while their professional training was to be the responsibility of the day training college. Academic and professional work could be fitted into a two year course of training, although students might also remain for three years if they wished, and were able to take a degree. A number of universities responded immediately to the invitation to establish day training departments, seeing this as an opportunity to expand student numbers. Day training colleges were established in 1890 in Manchester, Newcastle, Nottingham, Birmingham, Cardiff and King's College London. Similar institutions were set up in Sheffield, Cambridge, Liverpool and Leeds in the following year. Oxford, Bristol and Aberystwyth followed in 1892, Bangor in 1894 and Reading and Southampton in 1899. Exeter's day training college was established in 1901; University College London instituted a day training college in 1892, but this was shortly afterwards disbanded.[56] Experience eventually showed the combination of academic and professional study in a concurrent course to be an arduous undertaking, particularly for the weaker students, and after 1911 a three year academic course, followed by one year of training, became the preferred pattern.[57]

After 1910 the Board of Education's scheme for training secondary teachers allowed students who pledged their intention to teach to be eligible for grant support over four years, which covered tuition fees for three years of degree work and a last year in the education department.[58] The grant also included a maintenance allowance. The intake of students bent on a career in either elementary or secondary school-teaching was of crucial importance to the new universities. W. H. G. Armytage argued in 1955 that

> it is not too much to say that the civic universities in their struggling years, and the university colleges all along, owed the very existence of their arts faculties and in many cases their pure science faculties to the presence of a larger body of intending teachers whose attendance at degree courses was almost guaranteed by the State.[59]

In the University of Wales around the turn of the century, we find that in Bangor in 1897, 98 out of a total of 258 students were in the day training college; in Cardiff and Aberystwyth teachers in training constituted about a quarter of the student body.[60] P. H. Gosden notes that in the University of Leeds the number of students holding teacher training grants represented about a quarter of the entire student body through the inter-war years.[61]

Large numbers of these intending teachers were women. Gosden notes that it was as "King's Scholars", as grant-aided trainee teachers were called, that women students first became a visible presence in the University of Leeds.[62] The day training colleges in Bristol and in Nottingham were originally set up for women only. J. B. Thomas has calculated that in Bristol in 1895–6, 42 per cent of all students in the Faculties of Arts and Science were day training college girls, and they even represented 35 per cent of those reading mathematics.[63] Mabel Tylecote observed that the advent of the day training college in Manchester in 1892 greatly strengthened the "women's department" in the university, effectively doubling the number of women degree students between 1891–2 and 1892–3.[64] From 1899–1914 one third, or in some years approaching a half, of all Manchester's women students were members of the day training college, and as a result women were beginning to outnumber men in the Faculty of Arts as early as 1904–5.[65]

The term "day training college" is somewhat misleading because, as J. B. Thomas has pointed out, from very early in their history these departments or colleges attracted students from beyond their immediate localities and the question of residence had to be considered.[66] This was seen to be a particularly important matter where women students were concerned. University authorities were not easy about allowing their female charges to live in unsupervised lodgings: parents might not approve. More importantly, the Board of Education did not approve, and allocated grants for maintenance, education and training only to students living in recognized colleges and hostels. The Board of Education regulations were crucial in spurring the provision of supervised hostels and halls of residence for women, the development of which will be discussed in a later chapter. These early halls and hostels involved careful chaperonage, limiting the extent to which female student teachers interacted with the rest of the student body. The potential for such interaction was further limited by the tendency of other students and some academic departments to look down on the teacher-training contingent, who were often from somewhat more humble social origins. In Durham Miss Roberts, who was appointed as first Principal of the University Women's Hostel in Claypath in 1899, remembered that "the Training College Girls had a few acquaintances among the townsfolk, but none of the students under my care ever had undergraduate friends".[67] This informal social apartheid seems to have continued for some time. Even though Durham was such a small city and considerable numbers of the students at the training colleges sat for university degrees and certificates, by the 1920s, C. W. Gibby, who was appointed to a lectureship in chemistry at the university in 1926, recalled a pattern of segregation:

> Social life in Durham was very pleasant, and I received great kindness from people, many of whom were more than a generation older than myself. People connected with the Castle, Hatfield, St Mary's and the Cathedral mixed with one another, but in an orbit which hardly touched St Chad's and St John's, and entirely ignored the training colleges. . . . I don't think there was any animosity; it was probably a kind of snobbery, a feeling that the members of the new colleges were "not quite, don't you know".[68]

The women university students at St Hild's College in the 1920s formed their own society separate from the central Women's Union

Society in Durham.[69] Similarly in Bristol, Marian Pease, who was appointed Mistress of Method to the new day training college in 1892, remembered that she had been "anxious not to swamp" the small body of about 20–30 women students who were preparing for London degrees in Bristol at that time with her group of 60 teacher trainees.[70] It was no doubt partly her social tact that disinclined her to encourage social intercourse between these two groups of students. In Bristol women trainee teachers lived in separate, and often substandard hostels, a situation that the Board of Education viewed with "grave concern" and found objectionable by 1918.[71]

In other universities, such as Birmingham or Manchester, there appears to have been much less segregation between intending teachers and the rest of the student body, and in some women's hostels the perceived advantages (both social and educational) of mixing the two groups were emphasized from the outset. In any case, the institution of the four-year, consecutive pattern of training after 1911 served to reduce the differences and to facilitate the integration of teacher trainees with the rest of the student body. Phoebe Sheavyn commented in 1924:

> In some Universities, and particularly in those which still offer a two-year training course for teachers in Elementary Schools, the "training students" form a class somewhat apart from the other, regarded as to some extent socially, and perhaps also intellectually, inferior. In others no distinction whatever exists, except that the "training" student has to satisfy the fairly stringent regulations of the Board of Education, in regard to making satisfactory progress year by year.[72]

In 1928 Margaret Tuke asserted that a university education was by then an option for "the average woman", or even a necessity, "sometimes an unwelcome necessity", for those who needed to earn their own living and could not rely on their parents for support. In her opinion standards had declined somewhat from the "pioneer" years at the end of the nineteenth century. "The number of women students in the universities in England has increased during the last fifty years from seventy-one to more than 9,000", she wrote, "and if the keenness for learning today cannot be compared with that of the seventy students of 1877, we cannot be surprised".[73] It is clear from her article that Tuke was more sympathetic towards women who sought knowledge as "an end in itself" and were in pursuit of "a tradition of taste and culture which cannot be gained in one generation", than she was towards those who looked upon their university education as "mere training for a career".[74]

In the last quarter of the nineteenth century attendance at university lectures had indeed been characterized by the presence of large numbers of ladies of leisure, many of them married, who were in pursuit of general culture: some of them seeking perhaps to make good the deficiencies of their earlier education, others looking for entertainment or some kind of social purpose. Many women enrolled for classes without any intention of sitting examinations or working towards degrees. Focusing on evidence mainly from the Oxford women's colleges, Janet Howarth and Mark Curthoys have suggested that there was a "dual market" for women's higher education in the late nineteenth and early twentieth centuries.[75] Women students in Oxford came overwhelmingly from the professional, commercial and industrial middle class, but within this category there were wide variations in status and income. The majority of women went on to engage in paid work at some time in their lives, but a significant minority – around one in eight – did not. The majority of the early cohorts of women students at Oxford – around 70 per cent – did not marry, although this pattern changed after the war, and particularly by the 1930s marriage became more common. Howarth and Curthoys argue that although most women who went up to Oxford in the early days probably envisaged teaching as a career, a sizeable number had no specific vocational objectives, nor did they have any real need to contemplate such objectives. This was because either they were possessed of sufficient independent means, or their chances of making "good" marriages were high.

Did this "dual market" persist elsewhere? Most university towns had their affluent suburbs, and the daughters of the civic bourgeoisie from Clifton in Bristol, from Edgbaston in Birmingham, from Alderley Edge in Manchester and from the elegant squares and terraces of Edinburgh's New Town, may have continued to attend their local universities in pursuit of general culture rather than through vocational aspiration. Tylecote estimates that about half of the students in the Women's Department in Manchester between 1886 and 1891 were "ladies" who attended a single course, in English literature perhaps, or in German. Others worked at several subjects, but only a small proportion aimed at a degree:

The "ladies" were not registered students, but possessed cards admitting them to certain lectures. The registered students were termed "women".[76]

However, the number of students attending classes without any intention of sitting for degrees undoubtedly declined fairly sharply before 1914. In Glasgow the proportion of women graduating represented 24 per cent of the total of women entrants in 1895–6: by 1910–11 this proportion had risen to 71.8 per cent.[77] Sheila Hamilton has pointed out that the numbers of what were often referred to, rather deprecatingly, as "debutante attenders" fell off steeply before 1911, and this pattern seems to have been common in most institutions. Phoebe Sheavyn observed in the 1920s that "English girls of aristocratic or wealthy parentage do not as yet go to the University in large numbers; most of the students come from homes of limited means".[78] It seems likely that the great majority of the women who attended universities, particularly outside Oxbridge, by around 1914, did so in the hope that it would improve their opportunities of earning a living, either before marriage, or in the event of their not marrying at all.

Of course, many women may have hoped that the wider social networks of university life would extend their choice of marriage partner. From the 1890s onwards, satirical features in *Punch* magazine regularly mocked the courtship aspirations of women students. A cartoon in the *Morning Leader* in July 1905 was headed "Don't crush", and depicted a queue of women purchasing railway tickets to Bangor in response to announcements "that at least six professors at Bangor University" had "married lady students" in that year.[79] Winifred Peck, a student at Lady Margaret Hall in Oxford just before the First World War, recorded that no girl who became engaged while in the college was allowed to stay, since a student who needed a degree for her livelihood was felt to be more deserving of the room.[80] There are endless examples of women tutors' hostility to the idea of girls' getting engaged while at university: Marjorie Schofield (née Woodward), a student at St Mary's, Durham from 1921 to 1924, recalled that Miss Donaldson, the Principal, disapproved strongly when she became engaged to a fellow student at the Castle, insisting that she must have "broken the rules" in order to do so.[81] But chaperon regulations and restrictions on social intercourse between the sexes had relaxed considerably by the 1930s. Barbara Lees (née Brockman) who studied at

Reading University in that decade records that

> Reading in my time was known as the matrimonial university
> because so many students found their marriage partners there –
> in fact there was a joke in those days about naming a new Hall
> Wedmore (one of King Alfred's famous battles), and I remem-
> ber well an Economic History lecture given by Dr Peyton when
> a student asked "What *is* husbandry?" When the lecturer had re-
> covered from his astonishment he replied "What most young
> ladies come up to this university for". I met my husband at
> Reading – as my daughter also met hers.[82]

Judith Hubback, whose study *Wives who went to college* was published in 1957, noted a popular belief that university was "the best
possible marriage market for an intelligent girl", because there she
would "meet such a high concentration of her mental equals".[83]
Hubback's study was based on completed questionnaires from over
one thousand women who had graduated in English universities between 1930 and 1952: 36 per cent of these women reported having
met their husbands while at university.

The evidence we have on the social class origins of students in Britain's universities after 1914 is often fragmentary and much depends,
of course, on categorization. Most authorities agree, however, that
women students came from the same social background as the majority of male students: broadly speaking from the middle and lower-
middle classes. There were regional variations however, and in universities where costs were lower there was a larger representation of
what might be regarded as working-class students. Lindy Moore has
argued that this was, for instance, the case in Aberdeen.[84] Glasgow,
Birmingham, the Welsh university colleges, Nottingham, Liverpool
and Leeds may also have had larger proportions of working class students than elsewhere.[85] However, as R. D. Anderson has cautioned
from his study of Scottish university students in the early twentieth
century, "the non-middle-class element in universities was not primarily working class, but a stratum that brought together children of
skilled workers, shopkeepers and small farmers".[86] There were, in
any case, fewer women from the working class than there were men,
because here "both the scholarship machinery and the psychology of
motivation traditionally favoured boys".[87]

Women medical students came from significantly more affluent social backgrounds than did university women as a whole, not least be-

cause medicine involved a longer and more expensive course of study. Wendy Alexander has looked closely at the backgrounds of early women medical students in Glasgow and she calculated that the number of these students who came from professional backgrounds was approximately double the university average for all women students, while those from intermediate or working-class backgrounds were about half.[88] She cites an article from "the ladies' newspaper" *The Queen* in 1894, which estimated the total cost of a medical education for a woman living away from home at around £600. The cost of studying medicine in Glasgow was relatively cheap by contemporary standards but, even so, Alexander estimates that it cannot have been less than around £400 (including class and examination fees, lodging, equipment and textbooks) by around the turn of the century.[89] She suggests that if we follow F. Musgrove's analysis of middle-class incomes at this time, professional men, well-to-do clergy, superior tradesmen, lesser gentry and industrial managers might have expected (as the middle-middle class) to earn £200–£1,000 p.a.; whereas upper-middle class men would have commanded above £1,000 p.a.[90] The fathers of Alexander's sample group of women were divided fairly evenly between upper-middle and middle class groups, but with some from the lower-middle class. Clearly the strain of supporting a daughter's medical education at around £100 p.a. would have been difficult or nigh impossible for these groups without some form of external support.

Elizabeth Bryson's autobiography, *Look back in wonder* (1966), is the story of an exceptional woman and can hardly be considered representative, but it nevertheless illustrates some of the strategies adopted by someone from a background of material deprivation but firm educational purpose.[91] Dr Bryson (née Macdonald) was born in Dundee in 1880, the fourth child of a family of nine, of whom seven managed to acquire a full university education. From an early age, inspired by stories of Sophia Jex-Blake in Edinburgh, Elizabeth dreamed of studying medicine. With the support of a determined mother (who pieced together an income by giving music lessons) and the help of bursaries, Elizabeth enrolled as a student at St Andrews University in 1896. She learned that the authorities would not permit her to begin studying medicine until she was 19 years old (she was only 16 in 1896), and so she read for an arts degree first, graduating MA with first-class honours in English a few months before her nineteenth birthday. She had been spurred in her motivation to do well in these examinations by the hope that she might win a scholarship of £100 p.a. for two years, and indeed,

> When the results were posted up there was only one name in the list for First Class Honours and, believe it or not, that name was mine. My first thought – I had won the Scholarship! Joy unbelievable![92]

The following day however Elizabeth was summoned to a meeting of the university Senate, and congratulated on her success in the examination, but the Principal

> went on in a somewhat subdued tone – to say how sorry they all were that they could not award me the Scholarship that I had undoubtedly earned. Why? Because I was a woman! It would require an Act of Parliament to alter the terms before the award could be made to a woman. I was completely silent, dumb with disappointment.[93]

The coveted scholarship went to a man with second-class honours in the examination: Elizabeth was given a bursary of £30 p.a. Undeterred, she went on to five years more study at the Bute Medical School in St Andrews and the new University College in Dundee. She continued to live at home and to support herself with the bursary and by working as assistant dispenser in a local chemist's shop for £1 a week during vacations. Matters for her family were greatly eased by the Carnegie bequest in 1901–2, which guaranteed the fees for students of Scottish birth or extraction in the universities of Scotland. Elizabeth Macdonald completed her medical training in 1905, her distinction in the degree examinations helped to secure her one of the first Carnegie research scholarships, and she proceeded to advanced work in gynaecology. Her work was considered quite outstanding, but as a woman she was barred from hospital appointments in the area, so in 1908 she emigrated to New Zealand.

Scholarships, grants and costs

In 1914 Edith Morley collected details of the costs of tuition and residence for women students in British universities, which showed that tuition fees for an arts degree ranged from around 10 guineas p.a. (Aberdeen, St Andrews) to around £20 p.a.[94] Fees for courses in science were slightly higher. The cost of residence in university halls or hostels for women students at this time ranged rather widely from £32 to £60 p.a. The fees for students in the Oxford and Cambridge women's colleges were then around £105 p.a. (including tuition, examination fees and residence). By the 1920s Phoebe Sheavyn estimated the cost for Oxbridge women students at £135–£150 p.a., again including tuition, board and lodging, but not including the cost of books or personal expenditure. Next in order of expense came London, where the fees for residence in college were higher than elsewhere, at around £90–£100 p.a. In the larger towns and cities in England, Sheavyn estimated the cost of university residence for women at around £70 p.a., whereas in the smaller civic institutions and in Wales and Scotland it was between £40 and £50 p.a. Tuition fees, according to Sheavyn's estimates, ranged from around £15 to £45 p.a. in arts subjects, with the cost of science subjects again rather higher.[95]

The question of women's eligibility for university scholarships and bursaries arose almost as soon as they enrolled as students in the civic universities. Most accounts of the stormy years when women fought to enter medicine in Edinburgh give prominence to the affair of the Hope Scholarship in 1870.[96] Edith Pechey's outstanding performance in the chemistry class in Edinburgh in that year theoretically entitled her to this scholarship, which gave the holder free admission to laboratories for research purposes. Pechey's moral claim to the scholarship was strengthened by the fact that its endowment fund derived from the profits that Charles Hope, Professor of Chemistry 50 years earlier, had made from a series of lectures he had delivered to the ladies of the community. Pechey was given a bronze medal, but the scholarship on this occasion was awarded to the male student who had come second in the examination on the grounds that the women students, who had been taught separately, could not be considered to have been full members of the class. The decision was not a popular one, and the whole affair helped to exacerbate sexual politics in Edinburgh.[97]

In Manchester the question of women's eligibility for Owens College Scholarships arose in the 1880s, provoking much discussion about what the wishes of the founders of these scholarships would have been, could they have foreseen the admission of women. A test case arose when a woman applied for the Victoria Scholarship in classics, but evidently she was not allowed to compete for it as the legal position was doubtful.[98] However, Mr Thomas Ashton responded by endowing a special Victoria Scholarship for Women, and after 1885 some of the older scholarships and prizes were in fact opened to women. The institution of scholarships for women in Manchester owed much to local benevolence, particularly to the strong network of supporters for the Women's Department, who had close links with Manchester High School for Girls. Several annual scholarships of £20 p.a. were offered by this group between 1883 and 1892.[99] In Durham, similarly, the 1890s brought considerable debate over women's eligibility for entrance scholarships. It was generally agreed that "it would not be convenient that the scholarships now open to men should be taken away from them or thrown open equally to women students", and this resulted in the foundation of a new scholarship for women, available from 1897.[100] In many towns the local Ladies' Educational Associations and their supporters were active in setting up special scholarships for women. In Edinburgh Miss Houldsworth and Sarah Mair of the ELEA both provided funds for bursaries in each of their names in the 1870s and 1880s.[101] In Bristol the Catherine Winkworth Scholarship Fund was set up in 1879 to provide scholarships for women as a memorial to Catherine Winkworth; the subscriptions included a significant donation by the committee of the Clifton Association for the Higher Education of Woman.[102] Several of the scholarships established by the local educational associations were attached to the women's halls of residence that were built in the last years of the nineteenth century.

Many of the new scholarship schemes in universities were open to men and women equally. In St Andrews, the Taylour Thomson Bequest of £30,000 in 1883 stipulated the donor's desire that bursaries should be made available to students of both sexes, in equal numbers, and in the case of women, used to assist them in qualifying for the medical profession.[103] (It was a Taylour Thomson bursary that enabled Elizabeth Macdonald to begin her studies in St Andrews in the 1890s.) Scholarships in the newer universities were less likely to be exclusively for men. Marjory Fry noted in 1909 that all Birmingham's scholarships were open to women.[104] However, informally awards to women might still provoke comment: Birmingham's Professor of German, H. G. Fiedler, wrote to Charles Harding, who had founded a scholarship in modern languages (and incidentally was Fiedler's father-in-law), informing him that in 1903 the scholarship had gone to a woman student from the local high school, and commenting that "she seems decidedly a bright girl . . . though I would rather have commenced work with a man".[105]

Another noteworthy source of funding for women students in the late nineteenth and early twentieth centuries was the Gilchrist Educational Trust founded in 1865, and originating from the bequest of the eccentric but liberally inclined Dr John Borthwick Gilchrist (who had died in 1841).[106] A considerable proportion of the income from this bequest of £70,000 went into scholarships and fellowships for women in Oxford, Cambridge, London and at several of the newer universities. Recipients of Gilchrist awards included Sara Burstall (later headmistress of Manchester High School), Clara Collet, Alice Zimmern, Enid Starkie, Helen Wodehouse and E. M. Butler (both of these last two women were destined to become professors) and a number of women who rose to prominence in the educational world.[107] The trustees of this bequest included men of liberal views in education and also, before 1939, three women: Dr Sophie Bryant (headmistress of the North London Collegiate School), Margaret Tuke of Bedford College, and Lynda Grier of Lady Margaret Hall. They prided themselves, with some justification, on being one of the first public bodies to make significant provision for women in higher education.[108]

Apart from Board of Education grants to teachers in training, and the scholarships and bursaries attached to particular universities, the main source of support available to women students before the First World War came from local authority grants. Local authority scholarships were the biggest single source of support to university students generally: in the two years 1911 and 1912 their total cost amounted to £56,893, the average value of an award being around £43–4 p.a.[109] However, the system of awards was extremely patchy: local education authorities (LEAs) differed widely in their practices, some (around one third in 1911–12) making no awards to university scholars at all. Girls were almost everywhere at a disadvantage.[110] In 1911–12, of the 464 university scholarships made by LEAs in England, 373 went to boys and only 91 to girls.[111] In 1916 the Board of Education's Consultative Committee Report on scholarships for higher education pointed out that since there were fewer endowed schools for girls, the proportion of girls who received their full secondary education in grant-aided schools was conspicuously greater than that of boys, "yet the provision of scholarships to take such girls to the universities is even more conspicuously less".[112] Few authorities reserved special awards for women, and some of them gave their few successful girl scholars around £20 less p.a. than the boys.[113]

The 1916 committee strongly recommended that more scholarships should be made available to girls. According to G. S. M. Ellis, whose report on the scholarship system, *The poor student and the university*, was published in 1925, by 1914 "the supply of public scholarships for women was lagging behind the demand for higher education in a most alarming manner".[114] By 1922–3, Lord Haldane noted that local authority expenditure on grants had increased to £220,000,[115] but many believed the amount continued to be inadequate, and girls were still failing to secure anything like their equal share of awards. There were energetic appeals to private benefaction in the localities. In Manchester, for instance, a public meeting in the town hall was held in 1918 "with the object of raising a fund to provide a more adequate supply of University Scholarships for Women", and through the efforts of Mrs Hope Hogg, Warden of Ashburne Hall of Residence for Women, C. P. Scott and other sympathizers, nearly £7,000 was raised within a few months. By 1936, when administration of this fund passed to the university, about 57 entrance scholarships had been made available by the Manchester committee.[116]

In 1920 state scholarships (originally 200 in number) were introduced by the Board of Education, partly as a result of the recommendations of the Consultative Committee report of 1916. These covered fees and offered up to £80 maintenance p.a. in case of need. They were suspended as a result of economy measures in 1922 but reintroduced in 1924.[117] It is interesting that the Board of Education was immediately embroiled in a controversy about the proportion of scholarships that should go to girls. Originally they were divided equally, with half going to boys and half to girls. However, many more boys reached the required standard in School Certificate examination than did girls, and there was pressure from headmasters to allocate more scholarships to boys. When the number of state scholarships was increased from 200 to 300 in 1930, it was decided to allocate 188 scholarships to boys, leaving 112 for girls. There were bitter complaints from headmistresses and from teachers in girls' high schools who pointed out that boys had many more sources of funding available to them than girls. Board of Education officials were uncertain as to how to handle the situation. They observed that:

> The Regulations as they stand would not prevent us from making a larger allocation to girls at the expense of boys, if the argument is considered a determining one. Apart, however, from the question of policy which the argument involves, it is probable that anything short of a substantial addition to the number allocated to girls would not satisfy the Headmistresses, and that anything which satisfied them would raise a protest from the Headmasters.[118]

Officials also argued that as future teachers, girls had other sources of funding open to them, and observed that, in any case, were the girls to be judged in open competition with the boys (a notion that the 1916 Consultative Committee had clearly argued *against*, on the grounds that adolescent girls were subject to particular strains during their school years[119]), girls would gain many fewer awards than boys. The matter remained contentious throughout the 1930s.

The amount of controversy generated by this debate indicates just how coveted state scholarships were. In 1928 Margaret Tuke estimated that "a considerable proportion of women students (certainly not less than 50 per cent of the whole number) hold scholarships drawn from public funds".[120] Nevertheless, any ladder of opportunity from elementary school to university was harder to find, and offered fewer footholds, for girls than for boys. In Birmingham, societies offering loans to women students were said to be swamped by applications, and the archives of women's halls of residence everywhere contain evidence of wardens making heroic efforts to piece together small loans and bursaries for students who found themselves in acute financial difficulty.[121] The annual report of the Central Employment Bureau for Women in 1924 drew attention to the extraordinary number of requests for loans towards the cost of university fees and training received from individuals in that year, noting that:

> Many parents belonging to the professional and middle classes are passing through a time of exceptional hardship and strain. Out of their small incomes it is impossible for them to meet the expense of training their daughters and yet it is essential that these girls should be prepared for work in which they may be self-supporting.[122]

The loan fund that had been established by the bureau in 1910 was considered quite inadequate, and attempts were made to seek co-operation and support from benevolent and trust funds elsewhere.

Between 1910 and 1925 loans were found for 225 needy female students in universities and teacher training. Cases of individual difficulty rose steeply in the 1930s, when the evidence suggests that expense increasingly debarred many women from embarking upon a university education in the first place.

Making space for women

What sort of accommodation did the universities make for their first women students? Provision was usually rather meagre, and given the social mores of the late nineteenth century, women were carefully secluded from the men. There are many stories of broom cupboards, of poky rooms in dingy basements and of side doors and separate entrances at this time.

Negley Harte, celebrating University College London's early admission of women students, nonetheless observes that women were treated as "second-class citizens in all manner of ways".[123] Mary Adamson, studying science at UCL in the 1880s, recalled a distinctly "chilly" rather than a "cheery segregation" between men and women students.[124] Adamson was enrolled as a student at Bedford College but sought access to teaching at UCL when she found that Bedford was unable to provide advanced teaching in science. She was allowed to join the physics and botany classes at UCL, but allegedly was told that admission to the chemistry class was unthinkable, as the women students would be "scarred for life and have their clothes burnt off them as the men threw chemicals around". Adamson was not allowed to enter the physics lecture theatre through the main door. She remembers being obliged to use a little door at the back. She had to sit high up and well back from the men. In the botany class, she was also made to arrive well beforehand and to sit quite separately from the men. The only other room that the women might frequent in college

> was a vast, semi-dark cloak room stretching under the portico and entered from the open air. It had hat pegs all round and some big, bare tables and a nondescript female was seated permanently by the fireplace. Quite a number of women students frequented it, largely Slade students who were all very lively and friendly with one another and the fireside woman. I think this

33

must have been the only room available to women and that they had not then access to the dining room, for they had to take snacks of food in it, and occasionally a seedy waiter would hasten in with a covered plate of food, dab it on a table, and beat a hasty retreat.[125]

Similar conditions prevailed elsewhere. The Women's Department in Brunswick Street, Manchester, was in "a depressingly small and dark" house, "gloomy and dingy, full of draughts and smoking chimneys". This afforded few social opportunities, although there was a reading room, "redeemed from utter dreariness only by photographs of Michael Angelo's Sistine prophetesses placed there by Miss Wilson" (the first Tutor to Women Students).[126] Tylecote records that women's admission to classes in Owens College was marked by the acquisition of an umbrella stand:

> So it came about that the first property the women held in Owens was the famous umbrella stand acquired in 1886. Next year came the cession of "a little room under the roof, approached by a small staircase behind an iron gate" with loopholes in the staircase walls. Mummies occupied the neighbouring museum, and stuffed lions, tigers and gorillas lurked in the corridor outside. The room was "transformed into a common room and each student" (writes one of them) "did her part in contributing something towards its furniture and decoration".

The women were again required to use separate entrances, and a maid-of-all-work was obliged to fetch any books they might need from the library. Another small common room was provided in 1888, but when the students asked if they might make tea in it the Principal forbade this on account of the risk of fire. "The fact that the teacups were washed in the fire buckets no doubt emphasized the apparent irresponsibility".[127] Women medical students did not fare much better. They were originally allocated one small room

> which had to serve them as a dissecting room and cloak room, and the exigencies of the timetable frequently compelled them to take their lunch there.[128]

One of the conditions of admitting women to medical classes had stipulated a separate women's dissecting room. According to Catherine Chisholme, one of the first women medical students, Miss Wilson was "much relieved that it was not necessary to smoke in the dissecting room".[129]

Conditions had improved slightly in Manchester, but by no means everywhere, by the time of the First World War. In Edinburgh, the women students in the Old Buildings occupied a "dungeon" in the basement with no natural light and "with toilet facilities of a very spartan, dingy kind".[130] In Aberdeen, at Marischal, the women students again rejoiced in the occupancy of a windowless room popularly known as "the dungeon", or "coffin".[131] At King's a room comfortable for 10 or 12 students was being used by 60 or 70 women by 1897. Alternative accommodation was provided in 1899 and again in 1904, but the situation remained unsatisfactory and during the war the women complained bitterly about the stultifying effect of inadequate, cramped facilities on social life: "the hideous crimson divan (of the broken springs) and the appalling array of hard, straight-backed chairs. . . . No power on earth could make the Ladies' Room an attractive or an inviting place".[132] Edna Rideout, who enrolled as a student in Liverpool University in 1912, remembered the tiny common room used by women students in the Victoria Building during her first term: the women's coats and hats being piled up on the balcony where they caused considerable obstruction, frequently falling down into the Victoria Hall, then "the inviolate stamping-ground of men students", below.[133] The novelist Storm Jameson, a student at Leeds University from 1909 to 1912, recalled the "sordidly shabby" common room used by the women students. As Secretary of the Women's Representative Council she decided to try to improve things through the acquisition of a new carpet, incurring the wrath of the Professor of Classics who was Treasurer of the Students' Union, and who inveighed that "in his very long experience no undergraduate, male or female, had ever behaved in so unprincipled a way".[134]

Benefactions and the shape of provision

The quality of accommodation offered to women students in these years depended a great deal on local benefaction. In Manchester the cost of running the Women's Department was estimated at £1,150 p.a. in the 1880s. The committee responsible for the department had agreed to make a grant of £500 p.a. to Owens College during the five year trial period of women's admission to the university, but income from fees was not sufficient to cover these expenses. A bequest of

£10,000 from the will of Mrs Abel Heywood, received in 1887, greatly eased the situation.[135] When it came to providing accommodation for the women's union, which was founded in Manchester in 1899, Mrs James Worthington of Sale stepped in with a grant of £5,000 "to provide a comfortable club house and refectory for the women students", the capital to be used towards the erection of a permanent building and the interest for the maintenance of a house that the Council had leased in Oxford Road. She and Mrs Tout worked indefatigably to furnish the house, Mrs Worthington

> completing her work by a gift of some Tanagra figures and a number of water-colour drawings from her own collection which were placed in the "exceedingly cheerful and pretty" drawing room.[136]

The local Ladies' Educational Associations played an important role in providing accommodation for women students. The Edinburgh Association for the Higher Education of Women moved from Shandwick Place to a flat in 8 Hope Park Square in 1893, and these comparatively spacious rooms accommodated the first women's union and societies, supplying the deficiencies of the drab premises offered by the university in the Old Quadrangle.[137] In Glasgow, the women students had their administrative and social headquarters in Queen Margaret College, originally donated by Mrs Elder and made over to the University Court by deed of gift after the admission of women in 1892. Mrs Carnegie, the wife of the Scottish benefactor, provided union facilities for the women at St Andrews and Dundee in 1904.[138] In Liverpool, Emma Holt, the unmarried daughter of a wealthy local shipowner and merchant, provided a house as a first hall of residence for women students, and gave liberally towards the cost of the women's wing of a new student union building, erected in 1913.[139] Almost everywhere the furnishing and decoration of women's common rooms depended on the generosity of local benefactors and well-wishers, some male, but mainly female, or the efforts of the women students themselves. In Southampton University College, the women expressed their gratitude to their fellow men students for the donation of a collection of photographs of the men's cricket and football teams, which graced the previously bare walls of the women's common room.[140] The women in Bristol were perhaps luckier – their reading room was brightened by "a delightful collection of photographs of eminent women", "including the 'advanced women' of medieval times who were not afraid to run the gauntlet of public opinion, and study both science and classics", and "the Pioneers in the Education of Women"; the collection having been donated by Miss Helen Blackburn in 1894.[141]

In *A room of one's own*, Virginia Woolf lamented at length on women's inability to endow the education of their daughters, and the long history of painful and difficult fund-raising that had characterized the foundation of the early women's colleges.[142] Writing in 1890, J. G. Fitch observed that any and all of the provision for the higher education of women in Cambridge by that time was attributable to private benefaction: women students had "neither asked nor received material aid in any form" from the university's resources, "the admission of women has not yet cost the university a shilling".[143] Feminist writing on education at this time was frequently spiked by a bitterness derived from the conviction that women had been historically swindled out of resources: the nunneries had been plundered for endowment of men's colleges; endowments for the education of children had been appropriated by boys' schools; the founders of the ancient universities had included wealthy women.[144] But the newer universities and university colleges rested on a very different financial footing. The state contributed practically nothing to the cost of these foundations, which depended almost entirely on voluntary contributions. Fees contributed only a small proportion of their income, let alone their operating costs, hence the observation of one recent historian who has described the civic universities as being "built on charity".[145] The stories of the male benefactors from wealthy industrial and commercial families who played such a key role in financing the new institutions, the Frys, Wills, Palmers and so forth, has often been told, but the part played by women benefactors has been less singled out for comment.

Women's benefactions were not on the same scale of course, since as W. D. Rubinstein has commented, "women in Britain were not often very wealthy in their own right".[146] But whether individually, as wealthy widows and unmarried daughters, or collectively, as subscribers to Ladies' Educational Associations or new foundations, women's contributions were still important in the developing network of provision for higher education. We have already observed the Yorkshire Ladies' Association presenting Edward Baines and the Yorkshire College with a thousand guineas in recognition of the college's contribution to women's higher education in 1882. Collective efforts from women continued to be very important well into the present century. The historian of Leicester University records that the foundation of a university college in Leicester owed much to the women of the city and country whose bazaar, organized in aid of the college funds in May 1922, raised an impressive £15,000.[147]

Some of the highly significant ways in which the outlook and intentions of individual benefactors could serve to shape the character of provision are apparent in the early history of the single-sex colleges for women. Bedford College, founded by the wealthy widow and feminist Elizabeth Reid, was possessed of a constitution and trust fund, the conditions of which had been carefully drawn up to ensure female governance.[148] Royal Holloway College, founded and endowed by Thomas Holloway in 1883 in memory of his wife, was bound by the terms of the founder's will, which stipulated that future trustees and governors of the college should all be male. The exclusion of women (and staff) from the governing body was a highly unsatisfactory arrangement, deplored by the Haldane Commissioners in 1909, but could not be changed until 1912.[149]

The wills drawn up by early benefactors of universities elsewhere in Britain similarly influenced the extent of women's access and provision. The will of John Owens, the founder of the college in Manchester that bore his name, had stated specifically the donor's desire to provide the means "of instructing and improving young persons of the male sex" in university subjects. This necessitated legal change in 1871 to circumvent the restriction.[150] The principal benefactor of University College Dundee was Miss Mary Ann Baxter of Balgavies, who originally donated £120,000 for the foundation of the new college (she later added another £10,000). Her co-benefactor and distant relative, John Boyd Baxter, also contributed sums of £5,000 on two separate occasions. These two benefactors did not always see eye-to-eye, but as a historian of Dundee has remarked, since Miss Baxter was giving nearly all the money, "she would dictate terms".[151] Dundee College, established on her conditions, was governed by a deed drawn up in 1881 stipulating that the college should promote the education of both sexes. There was to be no religious test, nor was any religious subject to be taught. Women students enrolled in Dundee well before they gained full access to the associated University of St Andrews. Seventy-five of the first students to be enrolled in Dundee were women, stimulating the local poet, William McGonagall, into an unforgettable eulogy of Miss Baxter – "Give honour to whom honour is due/Because Ladies like her are very few" – and her efforts – "For the ladies of Dundee can now learn useful knowledge/By going to their own beautiful college".[152]

Sometimes the generosity of local benefactors keen to promote the cause of women's education ran well ahead of the enthusiasm of university authorities. This appears to have been the case in Durham. Since Durham was a collegiate university with regulations requiring residence, the question of providing a college or hall for women students was an important issue. In 1881 the Senate in Durham agreed that women might be admitted to all the courses and degrees in the university (except in theology), but stipulated that they must reside in a college or hall licensed by the Warden and Senate, and under the control of the university. There the matter appears to have stood for some time: with the university expecting the Durham Ladies' Educational Association and other supporters to build and endow a college, and these supporters waiting for the university to provide one.[153] In 1886 the Senate rejected an offer made by Canon Brereton to convert Hatfield Lodge into a women's college: this may have been because it was having second thoughts about whether the university's charter did indeed empower it to grant degrees to women. In 1895 however, Senate petitioned the Crown for a supplementary charter giving the requisite powers, and this was granted in the same year.[154]

The university's "rather lukewarm attitude" towards women students continued to be apparent in its reluctance to settle the question of a women's college.[155] Senate had appointed a committee to investigate possibilities and this committee had recommended that the university make £5,000 available for a new building, provided that the same amount could be raised by the supporters of women's education. It was subsequently decided to reduce this contribution to £2,000, with £3,000 being made available on loan. By 1898 more than £6,000 had been promised to the "hostel fund", the enthusiasm of the women's supporters was high, and plans and builders' estimates for the construction of a new college were being invited in the hope that the foundations could be laid before the end of the year. Nothing came of these plans. Instead, the university agreed to rent a rather depressingly damp and dingy house at 33 Claypath, to accommodate the women students in 1899. By that time, many of those who had promised or actually donated money for a new college were becoming anxious and concerned about the lack of progress. Senate responded with some indifference, merely noting that the funds raised so far were not considered sufficient, and should they wish it, subscribers could have their subscriptions reimbursed.[156]

Laura Roberts, who had been appointed Principal to the women students in the far from salubrious accommodation in Claypath, has left us a full account of her experience of the university in these years. She recorded that from the very beginning she

> sensed the positive hostility or total indifference with which the residence of women students was regarded by most of the dwellers in the College, and by many of the University authorities; while the bachelor Bursar to whom the choice of a house, its decorations and its furnishings, had been committed, was said to dislike not only the movement, but the entire female sex.[157]

In her study of women scientists in America before 1940, Margaret Rossiter has remarked on the role of what she has called "coercive (or creative) philanthropy" – "the offering of large gifts with key strings attached" – in furthering opportunities for women in higher education.[158] Sometimes the strategy was successful, but in other cases the tactic could misfire: university authorities might accept a gift, but neglect its conditions or deflect it to other use. In other cases there might be endless controversy over the precise intentions of the benefactor, which could well end up by absorbing resources and frustrating the benefactor's general purpose. It is instructive to look at the difficulties raised in Glasgow by the Muirhead bequest of 1889 in this context.

In a will drawn up in 1889, Dr Henry Muirhead expressed strong feelings of indebtedness to the women in his life and his concern at how little "real, good solid and scientific education" had fallen to women's share. In view of these considerations he proposed to bequeath the greater portion of his savings for the purpose of erecting and endowing an institution or college for "the education of women by women, as far as that can practically and judiciously be carried out". The women students were "to receive education to fit them to become medical practitioners, dentists, electricians or chemists etc."[159] In a memorandum attached to the will Muirhead stipulated that he did not wish clergymen to have anything to do with the management of his proposed college, "for creeds are the firmest fetters to intellectual progress", nor did he want medical men as trustees, because "their trade unionism" was opposed to women entering the medical profession.[160] In 1892 agents of the Muirhead trustees wrote to the Secretary of the University Court in Glasgow enclosing excerpts from the will and offering to confer with the court in devising a joint scheme for the medical education of women. Interestingly, an earlier attempt at co-operation with Queen Margaret College seems to have come to grief because the two parties could not agree on terms. However, negotiations with the university foundered over a number of issues. The trustees' plan to establish a "Muirhead College" near Glasgow's Victoria Infirmary was not favourably regarded by the committee of the University Court, which argued that the university was not a mere examining body to test work done in affiliated colleges and emphasized its unwillingness to enter into any system of joint control.[161] Further, as the historians of the Victoria Infirmary have pointed out, the infirmary's constitution made it unable to provide exclusively for the clinical instruction of female students. The politics involved in these protracted and controversial negotiations were undoubtedly complex. In 1908, the trustees decided to use the money for scholarships, and more substantially for the endowment of two new university chairs at the Royal Infirmary.[162] Muirhead's vision of a college of science and medicine for women, governed by women, had failed to materialize.

The higher education of women in Glasgow suffered from another protracted controversy over the precise terms of a benefaction in the 1890s. In this case the benefactor in question, Mrs Isabella Elder, was still alive, and prepared to put up a spirited fight with the university authorities who, she maintained, had insulted her generosity and ignored her purposes. The controversy is interesting because it illuminates the complexities that surrounded the issue of "separate but equal" educational provision for women in these years. Mrs Elder was the wealthy widow of John Elder, a marine engineer and shipbuilder. It was her generosity that had largely brought about the establishment of the separate college for women in Glasgow, Queen Margaret College, with its own premises in North Park House (more recently the headquarters of BBC Scotland). From 1890–2 Mrs Elder had additionally met the costs of the associated medical school for women. Between 1892 and 1893 the university assumed responsibility for the college with its associated medical school, following a deed of gift from Mrs Elder. Correspondence between the latter and Principal Caird in 1892–3 makes it clear that Mrs Elder's understanding was that her gift of the college was made on certain conditions, the most important of which was that the college should continue in name and that its students should receive separate but equal teaching from the professors of the university.[163] Mrs Elder expressed her unease about newspaper reports that had unfavourably compared provision for women students in Glasgow with arrangements in Edinburgh. These reports had intimated that women in Edinburgh were to be taught by recognized teachers of the university, while in Glasgow the women would receive separate tuition from Queen Margaret tutors, who did not have the same standing. It seems that at this point Mrs Elder considered revoking her offer of Queen Margaret College, in favour of setting up an endowment fund for women students at the university. She decided against this on receiving an assurance from Principal Caird, who emphasized that women in Glasgow would be immeasurably better off than those in other universities in Scotland on account of their possession of a separate college. He pointed out that the university would not otherwise be able to afford any additional accommodation for women, that the university classrooms and laboratories were already full to overflowing with male students, and that since local opinion was so unfavourable to the idea of mixed classes in medicine, *without* the gift of the college, the medical education of women in Glasgow could not go any further. Correspondence from Mrs Elder makes it clear that at this stage she felt reassured about the situation.[164]

However, further difficulties soon arose in connection with the teaching offered to arts students in Queen Margaret College. As women came to be offered access to classes in Gilmorehill, university teachers became reluctant to organize what they saw as duplicate classes for the women in Queen Margaret College. When in 1894–5, it became apparent that there were to be no history classes organized in the college, and that any women students wanting to study the subject would have to join the men, Mrs Elder instructed her solicitors to write to Principal Caird indicating her view that this amounted to a breach of their agreement.[165] Matters were exacerbated when Richard Lodge, newly appointed to the Chair in History, wrote rather aggressively to the Secretary of the University Court expressing his strong disinclination to teach any extra classes in order for the women to be taught separately. He protested that he had been given no indication of any need for this at the time of his appointment and that he would regard any duplication as "an extraordinarily irksome and intolerable burden". In fact, if he had known that two sets of classes were to be part of his duties, he would not have applied for the post in the first place.[166]

Discontent rumbled on through solicitors' letters; the university authorities trying to placate Mrs Elder with various attempts at compromise, such as the teaching of some subjects in Queen Margaret College in alternate years. Eventually the University Court sought the opinion of Counsel, circulating this advice (in the form of a memorandum marked "Strictly private and confidential") to its members in 1896.[167] The legal advice received from John Rankine and J. B. Balfour was that Queen Margaret College no longer existed as a separate college, it was simply part of the university. More importantly, a deed of gift was not a contract, in that negotiations prior to its execution could not be "admitted to aid in its construction or to control its terms".

There the matter seems to have rested, at least as far as the University Court was concerned. Feelings in Queen Margaret College appear to have been divided. Undoubtedly many of the students were content to attend mixed classes, in spite of the inconvenient distances involved. However, another enduring problem stemming from the deed of gift of 1892–3 was that no provision had been made for the representation of the women of Queen Margaret College on the University Court. As Frances Melville, Mistress of the college from 1909 observed, this was "perhaps unfortunate, certainly significant" for the after conduct of college affairs.[168] Mrs Elder nursed her grievances over what she continued to consider an "unpardonable breach of faith". In 1899, frail with ill-health, she found an opportunity for revenge. The university wanted money for a chapel, a project with which (as she wrote to Principal Storey) she *might* have had every sympathy: but in view of the way in which they had treated her gift to the women students of the university, she felt wholly unable to contemplate any further benefaction.[169]

The advocates of university education for women in Glasgow in the 1880s and 1890s were, then, divided. Mrs Elder and Janet Galloway, the first Mistress of Queen Margaret College, were clearly in favour of "separate but equal" provision. However Frances Melville, who followed Janet Galloway as Mistress of Queen Margaret College, was more inclined to see the benefits of integration. Marion Gilchrist, the pioneer medical student at the college, reflecting in 1948 on the controversies of her youth considered that

> in Glasgow and Edinburgh, where special medical schools for women were started and paved the way for the entrance of women to the medical profession, these held back their progress and for a time prevented the women from getting equal teaching. St Andrews, including Dundee, and Aberdeen Universities opened all doors and had mixed classes. Now St Andrews has the first woman professor, Margaret Fairlie – distinguished in obstetrics and gynaecology.[170]

The most forceful objection to arguments for separate provision stemmed always from the conviction that separate would mean inferior, or be judged so. This conviction lay at the root of Emily Davies' thinking, and fuelled the arguments of what Sara Delamont has referred to as the "non-compromising" feminist advocates of women's higher education.[171] The belief that women's education should not be judged by a separate standard ensured the collapse of Thomas Holloway's plans for Royal Holloway College to develop into a fully-fledged university for women, with power to confer degrees on its own students. In a conference held at Royal Holloway in 1897, there was very little support for the idea of seeking a separate charter for the college.[172] This cleared the way for the scheme for its future development much preferred by Emily Davies and its recently appointed Principal, Emily Penrose, which was that Royal Holloway should aim at becoming a constituent college of any new teaching university of London. At the conference, Dr Sophie Bryant of the North London Collegiate School argued not only that there was no demand for a separate university for women, but that increasing numbers of girls were demanding "a university education of the established type". It was too late in her view, to say "that this type is, or was, established for men only".[173]

But Bryant's words were somewhat premature. The early years of the new century saw a number of influential educationists arguing precisely that the existing forms of higher education had been devised for men, and that women needed something different. This was an argument that could undoubtedly be made from a feminist as well as a non-feminist perspective. However, between 1900 and the outbreak of war, there was a significant strand of public opinion that favoured a more feminine, home-based curriculum for women.[174] This generated immense controversy, but profoundly affected the development of higher educational provision for women students in King's College London.

It is appropriate to conclude the foregoing discussion of patterns of endowment in women's education with reference to the history of King's College, because if elsewhere in the country provision for women was hampered by scarce resources, the history of King's College for Women was shaped by what was almost an embarrassment of riches in the years before the war.[175] This had certainly not been the case in the early years of what was originally the "Ladies' Department" of King's College in Kensington Square, which had come into existence in the 1880s, and developed into a vigorous academic community under the guidance of Lilian Faithfull, as Vice-Principal in the 1890s. Student numbers rose steadily in these years (to over 500 in 1906), and the department showed every sign of maturing into a fully-fledged college for women on the pattern of Bedford or Royal Holloway. Accommodation was cramped however, and the committee of management had begun to seek space for expansion.

In 1907 Lilian Faithfull was appointed headmistress of Cheltenham Ladies' College, her successor in what was now called the "Women's Department" in Kensington was Hilda Oakeley. Hilda Oakeley's appointment coincided with a period of curriculum innovation in the department that was ultimately to determine its whole future: this was the introduction, in 1908, of a new course in "home science". Enthusiasm for the new course brought together a group of women who sought to raise the status of domestic subjects, and who were genuinely convinced of the need for a more scientific and economically based study of the household with its associated concerns of nutrition, sanitation and hygiene. Proponents of this view included Mabel Atkinson, May McKillop, and several members of the Women's Industrial Council, as well as the growing numbers of women teachers of cookery and domestic subjects in the schools. The scheme drew further support from influential men in the universities such as Professor Arthur Smithells of Leeds, and Herbert Jackson, Professor of Chemistry at King's, who firmly believed in the need to foster a more feminine variant of science. The scheme was, of course, highly controversial, and for those women who adhered strongly to the belief that there was "no sex in intellect" it could appear as a highly retrograde development.[176] Hilda Oakeley's position was undoubtedly one of some ambivalence; she understood "the doubt, suspicion and dismay" with which many feminists greeted the proposal to educate women in home science, while on the whole publicly defending the scheme as an important educational innovation.[177]

Any lingering doubts about the intellectual validity of the home science course were soon to be swamped by a tide of public support and benefaction. While *Punch* was busy mocking the idea of girls matriculating on the basis of their culinary proficiency with apple dumplings and beef stew, enthusiasts for the scheme, firm in their belief that a university standard in home science would improve the efficiency of the nation's mothers, were actively canvassing the support of wealthy aristocratic patrons.[178] Lord Anglesey donated £20,000, the Dukes of Westminster and Devonshire, the Earl of Plymouth and Lady Wantage each gave £500. Mrs Wharrie added another £20,000, Sir Richard Garton the same amount. Thomas Dewey, Chairman of the Prudential Assurance Company, volunteered an astonishing £30,000. By 1912 over £100,000 had been raised. In conjunction with other developments, this munificence was to have a "cataclysmic" effect on "the Cinderella department" in Kensington.[179] In 1910, the London County Council asked Senate to consider "whether it would not be in the interests of the higher education of women generally that the College should aim at the development of the Home Science Department and should gradually abandon the other part of its work". The report of the Haldane Commission on the University of London in 1913 was of similar mind. In the teeth of opposition from Hilda Oakeley and the supporters of the Women's Department in Kensington Square, who "implored the Committee's permission to live and to retain the College's integrity", the recommendations were adopted, and King's College for Women disintegrated in all but name. The new department of Household and Social Science moved to spacious premises in Campden Hill in 1915 (a site originally intended for the women's college as a whole) while the rump of the staff and students from the arts and science departments in Kensington went to the Strand, inaugurating co-education in King's.

Oakeley records that there the women were welcomed by the student body "with striking openness of mind", a fine common room being allocated for their use.[180] She was clearly trying to make the best of things; as a woman with a self-confessed fear and dislike of controversy, she had found the last few years deeply traumatic. Reflecting on the events of 1908–15 twenty years later, she insisted that she had had no idea at the time of her appointment of the place that home science was to occupy: no-one at that time could have predicted its "sensational" growth. She confessed that, as public representative of the college, she felt bound to give the idea of home science a fair hearing, whereas had she *not* been in this position, she might well have aligned herself with the scheme's opponents:

> In part the contest was painful, because it brought me into opposition to women with whose general standpoint I was in essentials in agreement, and in whose camp I should have wished if possible to be.[181]

As things developed, she felt King's College for Women had been forced into playing the part of "Iphigenia for the University Agamemnon, a necessary sacrifice to the Olympian powers", and a victim of "forces too powerful for us to withstand".[182] It is important to remember that Oakeley had been attracted to King's precisely because it had begun to establish a tradition of high academic standards and seemed likely to develop into a fully independent women's college. She had found her previous post as Tutor to Women Students in the co-educational environment of Manchester University uncongenial.[183] But by 1915 she found herself in a similar position in the Strand, her title now being "Warden" rather than "Vice-Principal". In 1915, feeling that her work was "no longer essential", she resigned.[184]

Oakeley was replaced by Miss Eleanor Plumer, who took charge of the women students for the next two years. The Delegacy advertised the post as "that of the Head of the Women's side of a Co-educational College", believing that:

> While a strong corporate life for the College as a whole is desirable, opportunities must be provided for both men and women students to have certain activities in their separate common rooms, apart.[185]

The post was later designated that of "Tutor to Women Students". The experience of women in positions of this kind will be the subject of the next chapter.

The development in King's, like those in Glasgow, serves to illustrate the complexity of issues and motives surrounding decisions about whether the interests of female students were best secured by incorporating them in educational arrangements alongside men, or whether women's education should aim at separate or distinct forms of provision. The political implications of decisions of this kind could be decidedly ambiguous. Arguments over difference, which could depend either on the notion of women having special educational needs as women, or stem from the awareness of their vulnerable position as newcomers to higher education, less secure in their entitlement to resources, could be made equally from a feminist or from a conservative position. Mrs Elder's advocacy of separatism was based on her belief that this was the best way to earmark resources for women. The controversy in London was more concerned with divided perceptions about women's interests and the curriculum, although questions of resource allocation were by no means absent. Events in both London and Glasgow reveal a complex interplay between projects espoused by benefactors and the strategies of recipient institutions. The route towards securing women's best interests was rarely clear.

Notes

1. J. Kamm, *Hope deferred, girls' education in English history* (London, 1965), p. 268.
2. *Ibid.*, pp. 268–70.
3. P. Sheavyn, *Higher education for women in Great Britain* (London, n.d. (*c.*1924)), p. 19.
4. E. Huws Jones, *Margery Fry, the essential amateur* (London, 1966), p. 57.
5. *Ibid.*, see also "A greeting to Phoebe Sheavyn", *Yggdrasill* (the magazine of the Ashburne Hall Association, December 1966), and "A salute to Dr Phoebe Sheavyn", *Bryn Mawr Alumnae Bulletin* (1), 1966–7. (I am grateful to Dr Dulcie Groves for this reference.)
6. N. B. Harte, *The admission of women to University College London: a centenary lecture* (London, 1979), p. 3.
7. R. N. Smart, "Literate ladies: a fifty year experiment", *Alumnus Chronicle* (59) (University of St Andrews, June 1968), pp. 21–31.
8. M. Tylecote, *The education of women at Manchester University, 1883–1933* (Manchester, 1941), pp. 13, 26.
9. *Ibid.*, pp. 42–51.
10. C. E. Whiting, *The University of Durham 1832–1932* (London, 1932), pp. 147–54.
11. S. Hamilton, *Women and the Scottish universities c.1869–1939: a social history*, PhD thesis (University of Edinburgh, 1987), p. 140.

12. W. G. Evans, *Education and female emancipation, the Welsh experience, 1847–1914* (Cardiff, 1990), p. 210.
13. M. Hird (ed.), *Doves and dons: a history of St Mary's College, Durham* (Durham, 1982), n.p., *c*. p. 2.
14. Hamilton, *Women and the Scottish universities*, p. 162.
15. "Petition from women medical students concerning the opening of classes to women, 20 April 1904", *Minutes of Senate* 103 (University of Glasgow), p. 336.
16. Harte, *Admission of women*, p. 17.
17. R. D. Pope & M. G. Verbeke, "Ladies' educational organisations in England, 1865–1885", *Paedagogica Historica* 16(2), 1976, pp. 336–61: and N. Jepson, *The beginnings of English university adult education: policy and problems* (London, 1973), pp. 31–45.
18. S. Lemoine, *The North of England Council for Promoting the Higher Education of Women*, MA thesis (University of Manchester, 1968).
19. *Ibid.*, see also Kamm, *Hope deferred* p. 252ff; Pope & Verbeke, "Ladies' educational organisations", p. 346ff; S. R. Wills, *The social and economic aspects of higher education for women between 1844 and 1870, with special reference to the North of England Council*, MA thesis (University of London, 1951).
20. Harte, *Admission of women*, pp. 8–9.
21. D. R. Jones, *The origins of civic universities: Manchester, Leeds and Liverpool* (London, 1988), pp. 100–101. On the role of the Yorkshire Ladies' Association see also I. Jenkins, "The Yorkshire Ladies' Council of Education, 1871–91", *Publications of the Thoresby Society Miscellany*, 16(134), 1978.
22. Hamilton, *Women and the Scottish universities*, Chapters 1 & 2; E. Boog Watson, *The Edinburgh Association for the University Education of Women, 1867–1967* (Privately printed, n.d.); K. Burton, *A memoir of Mrs Crudelius* (Edinburgh, 1879).
23. Hamilton, p. 76ff.
24. *Ibid.*, p. 86.
25. *Ibid.*, p. 85.
26. *Ibid.*, p. 79.
27. *Ibid.*, pp. 102–3.
28. *Ibid.*, p. 110ff.
29. F. Melville, "Queen Margaret College", *The College Courant* (Journal of the Glasgow University Graduates Association, Whitsun, 1949).
30. *Ibid.*, see also O. Checkland, *Queen Margaret Union, 1890–1980: women in the University of Glasgow* (Glasgow, 1980), and Hamilton, pp. 110–18.
31. W. N. Boog Watson, "The first eight ladies", *University of Edinburgh Journal* 23, 1967–8; Hamilton, p. 163.
32. Hamilton, p. 179.
33. *Ibid.*, p. 180.
34. *Ibid.*, p. 146.
35. M. Tuke, "Women students in the universities", *Contemporary Review*

133, p. 72, 1928.
36. Tylecote, *The education of women*, p. 43.
37. M. Cheesewright, *Mirror to a mermaid: pictorial reminiscences of Mason College and the University of Birmingham, 1875–1975* (Birmingham, 1975), p. 33.
38. Tuke, p. 72.
39. R. D. Anderson, *Universities and elites in Britain since 1800* (London, 1992), pp. 22–3. More detailed figures can be found in the *University Grants Committee report for the period 1929–30 to 1934–5* (London, 1936). (See Appendix II)
40. L. Moore, *Bajanellas and semilinas: Aberdeen University and the education of women 1860–1920* (Aberdeen, 1991), pp. 43–4.
41. *Ibid.*, p. 44.
42. University Grants Committee, *Returns from universities and university colleges in receipt of Treasury grant, academic year 1937–8* (London, 1939), p. 6.
43. C. G. Robertson, "The provincial universities", *Sociological Review* 31, p. 253, 1939.
44. A. Gordon, "The after careers of university educated women", *The Nineteenth Century* 37, pp. 955–60, 1895; M. Sanderson, *The universities and British industry 1850–1970* (London, 1972), p. 315; J. W. Berman, *A sense of achievement: the significance of higher education for British women, 1890–1930*, PhD thesis (State University of New York at Buffalo, 1982), Chapter 5; K. Scobie, *Women at Glasgow University in the 1920s and 1930s*, MA dissertation (University of Glasgow, 1986); C. Logan, *Women at Glasgow University: determination or predetermination?* MA dissertation (University of Glasgow, 1986); T. Watt (ed.), *Roll of graduates of the University of Aberdeen, 1901–25* (Aberdeen, 1935).
45. Tuke, "Women students" p. 76.
46. E. Morley (ed.), *Women workers in seven professions* (London, 1914), p. 12.
47. Anderson, *Universities and elites*, p. 57.
48. *Ibid.*, p. 23; University Grants Committee Report, 1929–30, 1934–5, p. 4.
49. Hamilton, *Women and the Scottish universities*, pp. 98–9; Moore, *Bajanellas*, pp. 21–2.
50. Hamilton, pp. 108–9.
51. J. B. Thomas (ed.), *British universities and teacher education: a century of change* (Lewes: Falmer Press, 1990), p. 3.
52. R. W. Rich, *The training of teachers in England and Wales during the nineteenth century* (Cambridge, 1933, this edn Bath: Cedric Chivers, 1972), p. 274.
53. *Ibid.*, p. 274.
54. *Ibid.*, p. 263.
55. J. B. Thomas, "The day training college: a Victorian innovation in teacher training", *British Journal of Teacher Education* 4(3), 1978, pp. 249–61.

56. Rich, p. 227; J. B. Thomas, "Victorian beginnings", in *British universities and teacher education*, p. 14.
57. W. H. G. Armytage, *Civic universities, aspects of a British tradition* (London, 1955), p. 255; Thomas, "Day training college to Department of Education", in *British universities and teacher education*, p. 26.
58. P. Gosden & A. Taylor, *Studies in the history of a university 1874–1974* (Leeds, 1975), p. 50.
59. Armytage, p. 256.
60. Thomas, "Day training college to Department of Education", p. 28.
61. Gosden, in Gosden & Taylor, p. 50.
62. *Ibid.*, p. 57.
63. Thomas, "Victorian beginnings", p. 28.
64. Tylecote, *The education of women*, p. 47.
65. *Ibid.*, pp. 53–4.
66. Thomas, "Day training college to Department of Education", p. 26.
67. Hird, *Doves and dons, c.* p. 10.
68. C. W. Gibby, "Academic Durham in 1926" *Durham University Journal* LXXIX(2), p. 5, December 1986.
69. Minute books, St Hild's College University Students' Society, 1920 and 1929, MS 378.42811–15 F 20 (archives, Durham University).
70. M. Pease, "Some reminiscences of University College, Bristol", unpublished MS (archives, University of Bristol, 1942), p. 12.
71. D. W. Humphreys, "The education and training of teachers: the first fifty years", in *University and community: essays to mark the centenary of the founding of University College Bristol*, J. Macqueen & S. Taylor (eds) (Bristol, 1976), p. 47.
72. Sheavyn, *Higher education for women*, p. 6.
73. Tuke, "Women students", pp. 76–7.
74. *Ibid.*, p. 76.
75. J. Howarth & M. Curthoys, "The political economy of women's higher education in late nineteenth and early twentieth century Britain", *Historical Research* 60(142), pp. 208–231, 1987.
76. Tylecote, *The education of women*, p. 27.
77. Hamilton, *Women and the Scottish universities*, p. 390.
78. Sheavyn, *Higher education for women*, p. 19.
79. J. Gwynn Williams, *The University College of North Wales: foundations, 1884–1927* (Cardiff, 1985), plate 50.
80. W. Peck, *A little learning, or a Victorian childhood* (London, 1952), p. 166.
81. Hird, *Doves and dons, c.* p. 36.
82. B. Lees, "A family at Reading", unpublished MS in possession of author.
83. J. Hubback, *Wives who went to college* (London, 1957), p. 25.
84. Moore, *Bajanellas*, p. 122.
85. Anderson, *Universities and elites*, p. 54, pp. 56–7. An early historian of Nottingham claimed that according to Treasury inspectors in 1901–2, "Nottingham University College stood at the head of all English university

colleges in the number of students who entered from elementary schools and that the opportunities offered to young working men of promise were very considerable" E. Beckett, *The University College of Nottingham* (Nottingham, 1928), p. 54.

86. R. D. Anderson, *Education and opportunity in Victorian Scotland: schools and universities* (Oxford, 1983), p. 318.

87. Anderson, *Universities and elites*, p. 57.

88. W. Alexander, *First ladies of medicine* (Glasgow, 1987), p. 14.

89. *Ibid.*, p. 18.

90. F. Musgrove, "Middle-class education and employment in the nineteenth century", *Economic History Review* 23, pp. 99–111, 1959–60, cited by and discussed in Alexander, p. 19.

91. E. Bryson, *Look back in wonder* (1st edition 1966; Dundee, 1980).

92. *Ibid.*, p. 130.

93. *Ibid.*, p. 131.

94. Morley, *Women workers*, pp. 82–136.

95. Sheavyn, *Higher education for women*, p. 20.

96. C. Blake, *The charge of the parasols: women's entry to the medical profession* (London, 1990), p. 114ff.

97. Hamilton, *Women and the Scottish universities*, p. 35.

98. E. Fiddes, "Introduction" in Tylecote, *The education of women*, pp. 13–14.

99. Tylecote, p. 45.

100. Hird, *Doves and dons, c.* p. 3.

101. E. Boog Watson, *Edinburgh Association for the University Education of Women, 1867–1967* (Edinburgh, n.d.), pp. 14–15.

102. M. J. Shaen, *Memorials of two sisters: Susanna and Catherine Winkworth* (London, 1908), pp. 260–1, 330. See also minute book relating to Catherine Winkworth Scholarships Fund (archives, Bristol University).

103. Note on Taylour Thomson Bequest (November 1883), University of St Andrews, *Minutes of Senate* 20, p. 426.

104. Brochure advertising University House, 1909 (University House archives, special collections, Birmingham University).

105. Professor H. G. Fiedler to Charles Harding, 5 October 1903 (special collections, FH 79, Birmingham University).

106. Lord Shuttleworth, "The Gilchrist Educational Trust: pioneering work in education", an address delivered before the Bolton Education Society, Cambridge, 1930; "A sketch of the life of Doctor Gilchrist, with particulars of the educational trust founded by him", (archives of the Gilchrist Educational Trust, London, 1881).

107. See minutes of the Gilchrist Educational Trust, 1874 to present.

108. Lord Shuttleworth, p. 9, and list of trustees in appendix.

109. Lord Haldane, "Foreword" in G. S. M. Ellis, *The poor student and the university* (London, 1925), p. vi.

110. Ellis, p. 11.

111. *Ibid.*, p. 10.

112. Board of Education, *Interim report of the Consultative Committee on scholarships for higher education*, (London, 1916), Cd. 8291, vol. VIII, p. 65 para. 119.

113. Ellis, *The poor student*, p. 32.

114. *Ibid.*, p. 9.

115. Lord Haldane, Foreword to Ellis, p. vi.

116. Tylecote, *The education of women*, pp. 115–16.

117. Board of Education files on state scholarships, ED 54, nos 34, 35 and 37 (Public Record Office).

118. PRO, ED 54, No. 37: letter from Assistant Mistresses Association dated 20 May 1930 and comments, memorandum relating to interview with head-mistresses, 18 January 1932, and headmasters, 9 May 1933.

119. Board of Education, *Interim report of the Consultative Committee on scholarships*, 1916, p. 65, para 120.

120. Tuke, "Women students" p. 76.

121. Report from the Senior Tutor to Women Students in Birmingham (n.d., c.1935? University collection, Heslop Room, Birmingham University Library), 3 vii 1–2, 3 vi 7–8, 1926–47; Marjorie Rackstraw's typescript notes on Barbara M. Paterson, a first year arts student in Masson Hall, Edinburgh, in the 1930s, in (uncatalogued) box of papers relating to Masson Hall (archives, Edinburgh University); J. Lee, *This great journey* (New York, 1942), p. 56ff.

122. Central Employment Bureau for Women and Student Careers Association, *Report*, April 1924, p. 5.

123. Harte, *Admission of women*, p. 18.

124. M. Adamson, "University College and women science students, 1884–1885", unpublished manuscript (archives, University College London, UCL MEM 1B/18).

125. *Ibid.*

126. Tylecote, *The education of women*, pp. 24, 32.

127. *Ibid.*, p. 35.

128. *Ibid.*, p. 51.

129. Dr C. Chisholme to Mabel Tylecote, June 1934, cited in Tylecote, *The education of women*, p. 51.

130. H. Wilkie, "Steps which led to the appointment of a Woman Superintendent of Studies" *University of Edinburgh Journal*, 1971–2, pp. 136–8.

131. Moore, *Bajanellas*, p. 71.

132. *Ibid.*, p. 73.

133. E. Rideout, unpublished MSs reminiscences (archives, Liverpool University, D 255/3/3).

134. S. Jameson, "The University of Leeds in 1909–12", unpublished MS (archives, Leeds University), p. 15.

135. Tylecote, *The education of women*, p. 43.

136. *Ibid.*, p. 60.

137. Hamilton, *Women and the Scottish universities*, p. 165.

138. *Ibid.*, p. 158.
139. T. Kelly, *For advancement of learning: the University of Liverpool 1881–1981* (Liverpool, 1981), pp. 116–17.
140. *University of Southampton students handbook 1904–5* (special collection, Southampton University), p. 61.
141. "The women's reading room", *The Magnet* (21 June 1900), pp. 161–2 (archives, Bristol University).
142. V. Woolf, *A room of one's own* (Penguin, 1973), pp. 21–5.
143. J. G. Fitch, "Women and the universities", *Contemporary Review* 58, pp. 250–1, 1890.
144. C. S. Bremner, *Education of girls and women in Great Britain* (London, 1897), pp. 122–5.
145. Jones, *The origins of civic universities*, p. 95.
146. W. D. Rubinstein, *Men of property: the very wealthy in Britain since the Industrial Revolution* (London, 1981), p. 250.
147. J. Simmons, *Leicester and its university* (Leicester, 1963), p. 33.
148. M. Tuke, *A history of Bedford College for Women, 1849–1937* (Oxford, 1939), Chapters 1, 2 and Appendix I.
149. C. Bingham, *The history of Royal Holloway College, 1886–1986* (London, 1987), pp. 120–2.
150. E. Fiddes, "Introduction" in Tylecote, *The education of women*, pp. 1–2.
151. M. Shafe, *University education in Dundee, 1881–1981: a pictorial history* (Dundee, 1982), pp. 11–12.
152. *Ibid.*, p. 15.
153. Whiting, *The University of Durham*, p. 148.
154. *Ibid.*, p. 153.
155. Hird, *Doves and dons, c.* p. 5.
156. *Ibid., c.* p. 7.
157. *Ibid., c.* p. 9.
158. M. Rossiter, *Women scientists in America: struggles and strategies to 1940* (Baltimore, 1982), pp. 46–7.
159. S. D. Slater & D. A. Dow, *The Victoria Infirmary of Glasgow 1890–1990: a centenary history* (Glasgow, 1990), pp. 179–80.
160. Report of committee on negotiations with Muirhead trustees, March 1895, Appendix, Glasgow University Court minute book, no. 4 (archives, Glasgow University, GUA 50569).
161. *Ibid.*, p. 3.
162. Slater & Dow, p. 180; M. Gilchrist, "Some early recollections of the Queen Margaret Medical School", *Surgo* (March 1948).
163. Correspondence between Mrs Elder and Principal Caird, 11–17 October 1892 (GUA 62398).
164. *Ibid.*; Mrs Elder to Principal Storey, 15 April 1899, (DC 21/290–2).
165. A. J. and A. Graham to Principal Caird, 9 November 1895 (GUA 62401).
166. Correspondence between R. Lodge and Alan Clapperton, Secretary to the University Court, Glasgow, 27 January 1896, (GUA 62415).

167. "Memorial for the Queen Margaret College Committee of the University Court of Glasgow" Court minute book, no. 5, 1896 (GUA 50570).
168. F. Melville, "Queen Margaret College", *Pass It On* (special edition, 1935), p. 5.
169. Mrs Elder to Principal Storey, 2 April and 5 April 1899 (archives, Glasgow University, DC 21/290–2).
170. M. Gilchrist, *Surgo* (March 1948).
171. S. Delamont, "The contradictions in ladies' education", in *The nineteenth-century woman: her cultural and physical world*, S. Delamont & L. Duffin (eds) (London, 1978), p. 154.
172. Bingham, *History of Royal Holloway College*, pp. 91–2.
173. *Ibid.*, p. 90.
174. C. Dyhouse, *Girls growing up in late Victorian and Edwardian England* (London, 1981), p. 162ff.
175. N. Marsh, *The history of Queen Elizabeth College* (London, 1986), Chapters 1–3. Much of the following information is taken from this source.
176. Dyhouse, pp. 168–9.
177. H. D. Oakeley, "King's College for Women", in F. J. C. Hearnshaw, *The centenary history of King's College London, 1828–1928* (London, 1929) pp. 489–509; Oakeley, "Education in home science" in *History and progress* (London, 1923), pp. 220–29; and Oakeley, *My adventures in education* (London, 1939), p. 138ff, and her outcorrespondence file relating to the establishment of the home science course (archives, King's College London, KWA/GPF 11).
178. Marsh, *History of Queen Elizabeth College*, pp. 39–40.
179. *Ibid.*, pp. 43–6.
180. Hearnshaw, *The centenary history of King's College*, p. 508.
181. Oakeley, *My adventures in education*, pp. 146, 149.
182. *Ibid.*, pp. 149, 152.
183. *Ibid.*, p. 135.
184. *Ibid.*, p. 156.
185. Draft advertisement for administrative officer of King's College for Women, 3 July 1917 (archives, King's College London, KWA/GPF 20).

Chapter Two

৺

Patterns of supervision: lady superintendents and tutors to women students

Chaperonage and control: professors' wives and "lady tutors"

College statutes in medieval Oxford exemplified an almost obsessive concern with minimizing the contact between undergraduates and local women. The college laundry, for instance, could only be undertaken by washerwomen "of such age and appearance" (*talis aetatis talisque conditionis*) as to eliminate any danger of their seducing, or being seduced by, young men.[1] Even in the mid-nineteenth century we find the University of Cambridge in possession of a charter originally granted by Queen Elizabeth I, which enabled the Proctors to "make search after common women" and to imprison them pending the hearing and adjudication of the Vice-Chancellor.[2] That the Proctors might still show zeal for discharging this particular duty became evident in 1860, when a group of undergraduates invited some local girls to a party in Great Shelford village. The festivities were interrupted by a Pro-Proctor who gave orders for the girls to be locked up in the Spinning House, which was the university's prison. The girls protested that they were "virtuous dressmakers" to no avail; the Vice-Chancellor opined them to be prostitutes, "though not of the lowest class".[3] Hardly surprisingly, the action provoked outrage and controversy, but it certainly allows an insight into the privileges and patriarchal traditions of this near-monastic university community in its relations with women.

A few years after this incident, the gradual removal of the regulations requiring celibacy of Oxford and Cambridge dons inaugurated an important period of social change.[4] But the position of women, including wives, in these communities remained difficult and fraught with conflict for many decades.[5] Unlike the wives of Heads of House, Fellows and their wives generally lived outside college, and the tensions between domestic life and collegiality were notoriously hard to resolve. The social activities of the wives of dons were governed by the prescriptive codes and mores of the upper-middle class, even where standards, if there were no private sources of wealth or income with which to supplement academic salaries, were necessarily more frugal. The arrival of wives on the college scene coincided, of course, with the late nineteenth-century movement for the higher education of women, and with the establishment of the first women's colleges. Relations between wives and the women teachers in these new colleges were not always easy.[6] Clearly the independent, scholarly lifestyle of the latter group could be interpreted as an implicit challenge to that of the respectable, middle-class, conventionally married woman. There might also be important shades of class distinction between "Oxford and Cambridge ladies" and the "women students".

Nuances of rivalry and challenge could often be discerned in the tendency for wives to take on what they saw as the social obligations of chaperonage or of supervising the behaviour and demeanour of women students. Mary Paley Marshall recalled of her early student years that "some of the Cambridge Ladies did not approve of women students, and kept an eye on our dress".[7] But the categories of wife and woman scholar were never wholly distinct. There were many wives who were prominent in the movement to advance women's education, and many of the early women scholars, like Mary Paley herself, married dons.

The role played by professors' wives was important in all university communities in late nineteenth-century England. These women saw their responsibilities in terms of supporting their husbands' careers, acting as hostesses at university functions, and as contributing generally to the maintenance of a civilized standard of social life. There was often a direct line of influence from Oxford and Cambridge to the newer universities, for if in earlier years Oxbridge had populated the country with clerics, after around 1870 it became an important supplier of academics to the newer foundations. Men whose minds had been formed by Oxford or Cambridge took their ideals about the proper functioning of a university community, and often too, their wives, to the provincial universities, and set about reproducing the ideals and forms they valued.[8] Their wives were very likely to take an interest in the female students, and in the development of the special facilities – hostels, halls of residence, common rooms, and separate societies – which were becoming available to them.

In part this interest of professors' wives in the social arrangements for women students can be seen as deriving from traditional patterns of ladylike philanthropy and the social obligations of the bourgeoisie. Mrs Barrell, who accompanied her husband to Bristol in 1890 when he was appointed lecturer in charge of the mathematical department of the new University College (he became professor in 1893), described the kind of activities expected of the "Ladies of the College" in those years.[9] There were as yet no halls of residence for the women students, and many of the staff found room for them in their own houses:

> The fact of having students living under one's roof kept us very much in touch with their college life and constant musical evenings, games and whist parties were arranged for their entertainment in our houses. Book teas and quotation parties were always popular.[10]

Mrs Barrell frequented the Women's Reading Room at the college, and supported the activities of the Women's Literary Society, along with the Principal's wife, Mrs Lloyd Morgan, who acted as the society's president, giving papers of her own occasionally.[11] The wives joined in college expeditions and dances, acting as chaperons, decorating the hall, and arranging for the provision of refreshments.

Wives who were scholars in their own right might take an even more active role in university affairs. This was the case with Mary Paley Marshall, who accompanied her husband from Cambridge to Bristol in 1877. Marion Pease described the impact of the Marshalls' arrival in the community: among the women, excitement at having one of the pioneers of women's higher education in their midst overshadowed the interest in the appointment of a new Principal:

> The arrival of the Marshalls made the session of 1877–8 full of interest. Mrs Marshall's graceful charm attracted everybody, and to us she represented Newnham and the cause of the higher education of women. ... In this struggle Mrs Marshall had taken her part and we felt indeed honoured to have her among us. Very early on she started a women's debating society which

was so lively that on one occasion at least the debate had to be adjourned.[12]

Mrs Marshall's work in Bristol went far beyond the functions of hostessing and chaperonage. Alfred Marshall was often tired and unwell, and she supported him by taking over a good deal of his teaching for the college to free him for research.[13] Appointments were often fluid enough to permit this kind of arrangement at the time. Some sources name Mary Marshall as the first Tutor to Women Students in Bristol, although she never held a formal appointment with this title; the first Tutor to Women Students was Miss Rosamond Earle.[14]

The first women to hold formal appointments in universities were usually referred to as "Lady Tutors", and they were vested with responsibility for supervising the women students. Their duties were primarily pastoral rather than academic, although some of the women appointed to these posts were graduates and might undertake some teaching. University authorities were *in loco parentis*, and felt that women needed special protection and chaperonage that could only be discharged by a woman. The 1880s and 1890s were, after all, decades in which controversy still raged over the potentially deleterious effects of intellectual exertion on women's minds and physiology.[15] And if higher education could be seen as endangering femininity, the presence of an unattached contingent of young females was certainly perceived as a dangerous element in the university. A community such as Durham shared something of the monastic tradition inherited by Oxford and Cambridge, which was remarked on at the beginning of this chapter. Abbey House, the hostel for women students established in Durham in 1900, was popularly known as the "Dovecot" (or "prison" or "convent"), the women themselves were referred to as "the doves". Speculating on the origin of such designations led an undergraduate wit to muse on whether this might have been because "some think (the women) harmless?" This must have been quite incorrect, he concluded, "for they are kept under many strict regulations".[16] Careful supervision and chaperonage of the female students was an ever-present feature of life in the early years of the co-educational universities: the need for propriety, and the fear of scandal, were much in evidence.

Delicate issues and dangerous women:
Annie Besant and University College London

This can be illustrated from the career of one of the earliest women to be appointed "Lady Superintendent" of women students at University College London. When "friends of the higher education of women" decided to establish a hostel for women students in the college in the 1880s, they invited Eleanor Grove and her close friend Rosa Morison, both of whom had earlier been associated with developments in Queen's College, Harley Street, to act as Lady Resident and Assistant Lady Resident of the new hostel.[17] From 1883 it was decided that Rosa Morison should also act as Lady Superintendent of Women Students in the college. One of the duties of the Lady Superintendent was to preside over "passing in", a ritual whereby women who wished to enrol for classes were required to "present themselves" to Miss Morison, with testimonials, prior to registration as students. In May 1883, Annie Besant and Alice Bradlaugh applied for admission to the classes in practical botany in the college. They presented themselves to Miss Morison, who declined to enter their names. Pressed for an explanation of her refusal, she said "that there was a prejudice against them". Aggrieved by this reaction, the women felt even more insulted a few days later when they learned that the college Council had endorsed their rejection.[18]

A major controversy ensued. Annie Besant cannot have been wholly surprised by her reception. She had already gained a distinction for her studies in botany, but her earlier application for permission to study in the Botanical Gardens in Regents' Park had similarly resulted in a furore. The curator argued that his daughters often used the garden and he dared not let them be exposed to such a potentially corrupting presence.[19] The controversy over Besant's involvement, with Charles Bradlaugh, in the contentious debates over birth control following their publication of Charles Knowlton's pamphlet on the *Fruits of philosophy* in the 1870s, and Besant's own neo-Malthusian tract on the *Law of population* in 1877, was still rife.[20] The celebrated botanist Sir J. D. Hooker responded to what he considered an act of bigotry by sending her a ticket of admission to Kew – but even this had been accompanied by the cautious provision that she must use the gardens before the visiting hours arranged for the general public.[21] Academics were even more guarded. Besant's name was omitted from the list of successful students who had studied electricity at the Birkbeck Institute: on inquiry she was told that a committee seeking funding for new building feared that subscriptions would fall off were her name to be associated with the Institute's activities.[22]

University College's reputation for free thinking, however, added a slightly different gloss. So did its rejection of Alice Bradlaugh, who had taken no part in the public controversies that surrounded her father's activities. The minutes of an extraordinary general meeting convened at UCL to discuss the question in July 1883 survive and show the confusion and bitterness that characterized the whole affair.[23] The Earl of Kimberley presided: the case for the ladies, and particularly the innocence of Alice Bradlaugh, was argued by Dr Edward Aveling. Aveling's association with Annie Besant was well known, and he was unable to resist the temptation to pour scorn on what he saw as the bigotry of the medical profession towards women's education generally. His witty jibes against medical men can scarcely have eased the situation. But college principles, he maintained, stipulated the absence of exclusion on grounds of race or creed. Since all that might conceivably be held against Miss Bradlaugh were her atheism on the one hand, and her paternity on the other, it followed that these issues of race and creed were in fact the only grounds for her exclusion.[24] As for Mrs Besant, she was presumably being excluded on account of her involvement in "the burning questions of the day". Did this mean that the children of prominent politicians, of Mr Gladstone for instance, or Mr Chamberlain, would similarly be denied admission to UCL?[25] Aveling was supported by Mr Alfred Tyler who volunteered his opinion that Mrs Besant was "activated by the purest motives for the amelioration of her sex". His own wife had urged him to attend this particular meeting because of her concern for women whose lives were cut short by excessive childbearing. Mrs Besant faced "a very difficult task in attempting to draw attention to a very difficult branch of social science". He thought the social reception she was meeting with not unlike the burning of witches in previous centuries.[26]

These somewhat emotive arguments were cut short by Mr Justice Denman, who protested that no discourtesy had been intended, but that the Council had to proceed with extreme caution in the delicate business of co-education. Rosa Morison's actions were defended on the grounds that the Lady Superintendent had been instructed to seek "satisfactory evidence of respectability" before admitting any woman student to the college. The question then arose about whether "a higher standard of morality" was being required of potential women students than it was of men. The President managed to side-step this particularly touchy issue with a piece of rhetoric, the gist of which was that he hoped that in future an equally principled stance would be taken in the case of male applicants, and that men of "notorious and evil character" would be turned away.[27] Aveling's outraged protest that this phrase implied a slur on the characters of the women whose case was under discussion evoked soothing demurrals. The meeting was brought to an uneasy conclusion with support for the resolution that "in a matter concerning the admission of Ladies to this College, which involves some very delicate and difficult questions", the Council "must, in exercising their discretion, invariably refuse to give reasons".[28]

Tutors to women students: the politics of appointment, status and role

Rosa Morison continued as Lady Superintendent at University College until her death in 1912. In spite of the controversy of 1883, she appears to have established herself as an important guide and counsellor to the women students, many of whom spoke of her with affection and respect. Margaret Murray, the Egyptologist, remembered her as "a well-known educationalist and a charming, sensible woman":

> Though she did not make herself conspicuous, she saved the women students from the wrecking of the establishment of their various societies, which were often opposed seriously or threatened with extinction by male ridicule. She was liked and respected by the senior members of the staff who would bow to her opinion even if they did not really agree.[29]

It was Miss Morison who called the first meeting of the University College Women's Union Society in 1897.[30] She was also a key figure in establishing the Women Students' Debating Society, which came into existence earlier, in 1878, functioning as secretary of this society between 1885 and 1889.[31] As Margaret Murray indicated, the establishment of these early societies of women students had not always been easy. The minutes of the debating society, preserved in the college archives, show that in one particularly stormy meeting, chaired by Mrs Fawcett, as President in 1879, the committee was much disturbed by complaints that their habits were unbusinesslike, that many of the professors in the college disapproved of their activities, and that a plethora of internal disagreements were damaging the society's reputation.[32] With Miss Morison's support the storms were weathered and the society's activities resumed on a regular basis, although matters could still prove contentious: in the early years of the present century Miss Morison was somewhat alarmed by a plan, backed by Marie Stopes, the then President, to encourage joint debates with the men's debating society in University College Hall. According to an early account of the history of the women's society,

> Miss Stopes shewed then as she has not ceased to shew since that she is nothing if not daring and original in her ideas. The subject for the first debate was that women should smoke.[33]

The same writer tells us that when, a few years later, Dr Stopes was invited to return to UCL to address the women students she refused, on account of

> her indignation at the laxity of the Women's Union Debating Society in allowing the men to call their Union "*the* Union Society", instead of the "Men's Union" as they had done when she was here.[34]

Miss Morison was much supported in her work by her close friend Eleanor Grove. Together they presided over the very mixed group of women students who took up residence in College Hall, in Byng Place. Both were generous supporters of the college, not only through their work, but more materially in terms of frequent gifts of furniture and donations to college funds. In 1902 for instance, Miss Morison established a "Women's Fund", "to commemorate the noble efforts made by the pioneers of the education of women in London". The original idea was to endow a Chair of History in the college, and supporters included a number of prominent women teachers as well as former students.[35] In 1904, the money raised was transferred to the college Council, and the interest from the fund was used for the purchase of history books for the library.[36] In her will Rosa Morison left over £5,000 to the University of London, much of this sum being earmarked for scholarships for women students and the endowment of College Hall.[37] In spite of what students perceived as their "quaintly old-fashioned personalities", both Rosa Morison and Eleanor Grove supported women's suffrage and both were committed feminists, although always of a very discreet kind.[38]

It is unlikely that anything more than the most discreet form of feminism would have recommended itself to the university authorities responsible for appointing these early supervisors of women students. Edith Wilson, who embarked on her duties as Tutor to Women Students in the University of Manchester in the early 1880s, later confided to Mabel Tylecote that it had been indicated to her, at the time of her appointment, that her role should be

> to aid in whatever arrangements were in force for the good of women students, and not to agitate for any abstract theoretical rights.[39]

Her role was to be largely one of chaperonage: as the sister of an archdeacon she was considered well fitted for these duties, and she was not expected to take up any teaching in the department.[40] Miss Wilson appears to have been quite a self-effacing character, ever cautious in her dealings with authority. From 1892 she acquired an ally in the person of Catherine Isabella Dodd, who was appointed Mistress of Method in the new day training department for women. Dodd was a much more forceful character.[41] Wilson had been apprehensive at the time of her appointment:

> the appointment for the first time of a woman on the teaching staff of the College was a critical event for me. How would she and her Queen's scholars fit in with all the intricate arrangements which it was my office to explain and facilitate? Nor were vulgarities extinct: a member of the Council expressed to me his view that she should not be too good-looking, as in that case she might marry soon.[42]

Wilson approved of Dodd's appointment, even though at the interview she thought the latter's "boots too thin for Manchester". Forty years later she was reminded of a remark she no longer recalled making. Evidently someone asked Miss Wilson whether she thought Dodd a lady, and Wilson had rejoined that she did not know, "but that at any rate, she was a gentleman".[43] The two women became friends and shared lodgings together from 1895. Dodd was an ardent educational innovator and an enthusiast who threw herself into a range of social activities and societies for women students. She was far less discreet in her feminism than Edith Wilson, arguing that co-education could certainly work to the disadvantage of women, and generally involved their exclusion from senior and responsible posts.[44] Relationships between the two were often strained as a result of disagreement over these issues, but they were thrown together by their shared position of marginality in the university community. In 1902, for instance, a question arose over whether women should attend the university's jubilee celebrations, at which the Prince and Princess of Wales were to open Whitworth Hall. Wilson records that both she and Catherine Dodd found the question of dress a deterrent to their presence

> Neither of us had academic robes, and we should have appeared
> as a couple of sparrows following peacocks while the staff
> blazed in hoods of half a dozen universities.[45]

Some universities adopted a different policy and tried to ensure that the women they appointed as tutors or superintendents of female students had some academic status. In Bristol, "a Committee of Ladies interested in Women's Education" encouraged the college Council to appoint a "Lady Tutor". This committee drafted a scheme of duties for potential applicants that was "considered amended and adopted" by the Faculties of Arts and Science in 1899.[46] In addition to her pastoral and advisory functions the Lady Tutor was to undertake tutorial work and to be "competent to lecture in at least one subject". Preference was to be given to candidates who had "obtained honours at Oxford or Cambridge". The Lady Tutor was also to be entrusted with keeping a register of lodgings approved as suitable for those women students who could not find accommodation with friends or relatives.[47] Miss Burns, Miss Cocks and Miss Marian Pease (the Mistress of Method in the day training department) were to join Albert Fry, Mr Arrowsmith, the Bishop of Bristol and the Principal in forming a selection committee. This committee reported in May, 1899 that 50 applications for the post had been received.[48] Three ladies were invited for interview and in October, Miss Rosamond Earle was appointed Lady Tutor, with a salary of £200 p.a. Miss Earle was the daughter of a professor of Anglo-Saxon at Oxford; she herself had been a student, then Assistant Lecturer at Newnham College, Cambridge.[49] Between 1899 and 1904 she combined her tutorship of the women students in Bristol with teaching in modern history and English. When in 1904 she resigned from her post, she was succeeded by Margaret Tuke, also from Newnham, who was appointed as Tutor to Women Students and Lecturer in French.[50]

In Birmingham similarly, there was a concern to ensure the academic status of any tutor to women students, but here the business of making such an appointment appears to have been more controversial. The demand for a "Lady Tutor" seems to have emanated from "some of the Lady Governors", who indicated their willingness to contribute to the salary costs of such an appointment. Letters to Oliver Lodge, the Principal, indicate that Elsie Cadbury, Rachel Albright-King, and Edith Creak (Headmistress of King Edward's Girls' High School) were keen advocates of the proposal.[51] There were others who were less sympathetic. J. C. Frankland protested that separate provision for women students was unnecessary, and argued that "it would be insulting to presume the women students were feebler than the men". She herself

> had had no tutor to assist me at Bedford or University College, and surely, when a woman goes to College one important thing she has a chance of learning is to become responsible to herself, instead of, as she has been all her life previously, to others. This is one of the points which, to my mind, distinguishes the school from the college, and is one of the important lessons to be learnt there.[52]

The Lodge correspondence contains a detailed typescript list of duties suggested for any woman tutor, which was drawn up around 1901–2. This is in essentials similar to the scheme proposed in Bristol, although in the Birmingham plan, the woman tutor was apparently to combine pastoral, social, tutorial and lecturing obligations with remedial teaching and careers advisory work.[53] However, Senate was clearly divided over the advisability of making such an appointment. When eventually, Helen Wodehouse was appointed as Assistant Lecturer in Philosophy and Tutor to Women Students there was more contention. As an ex-student of Girton with developing interests in philosophy, Miss Wodehouse had academic credibility, but the ladies in Birmingham had envisaged an older and more experienced woman in the post of Tutor to Women Students. Rachel Albright-King wrote to Lodge to explain that one of the lady governors had decided to withdraw her previous offer of contributing to the salary of the Lady Tutor because she thought Miss Wodehouse "quite too young" for the job.[54] Others were prepared to give her a chance, and Mrs Albright-King thought that she could guarantee a subscription of about £152 p.a. in support of Miss Wodehouse's salary for the first three years.

She thought it important that the Principal should convey to Miss Wodehouse that although she was officially an Assistant Lecturer, "her appointment is entirely due to the hope that she will care for the welfare of the women students".[55] It seems likely, however, that Miss Wodehouse took her duties in philosophy at least as seriously as any pastoral work with female students. It is interesting that Birmingham University calendars make no mention of any separate formal arrangements for women students until much later in the 1920s, when Jane Johnston Milne assumed the title of Senior Tutor to Women Students in addition to her work as a lecturer in French. This appointment in 1926 was heralded as "a new venture".[56]

Protecting women's interests?
The question of the need for separate provision

Sometimes the pressure to appoint a Lady Superintendent in the universities came from local headmistresses. In March 1911, Liverpool University's Council received a memorial that was signed by 31 headmistresses of girls' secondary schools in the northwest of England, arguing that they felt it crucial that the university should consider the interests of its female students by appointing a woman official who could be relied upon to consider the "health, comfort and discipline" of these students.[57] They contended that:

> The question affects us closely. On the one hand, many of us know by experience that the presence of a Warden would be an inducement to parents of our pupils to send their daughters to this University. On the other hand, many of the University students will become teachers in our schools, and as Headmistresses we feel very strongly that those who will be responsible for the training of our girls should themselves, during their University career, have been under the influence of a wise and experienced woman.[58]

In addition they thought it most important that any woman who should be appointed Supervisor or Warden should possess high academic qualifications and ideally hold a teaching position in the university. This petition added fuel to the arguments of Miss Emma Holt, a generous benefactor of Liverpool University, who was one of the few women to hold a position on Council. Minutes of Council meetings show that Miss Holt had already succeeded, one year previously, in persuading Council to appoint a committee "to consider and report upon the advisability of increasing the proportion of women on the university staff, with power to call for such evidence as they may think desirable".[59] The memorial from local headmistresses was referred to this committee, which reported back to Council in November 1911.

This report makes interesting reading.[60] The committee were in agreement that the appointment of a woman to act as chaperon to the women students in Liverpool would be an unpopular innovation and would be neither desirable nor expedient. Most of the committee felt disinclined to support the demands of the headmistresses in this respect. However, they were united in their recommendation that more women should be appointed to the university staff, and that,

> in the case of subjects taught to a large number of students of both sexes, and where there are several teachers, at least one of the lecturers should be a woman provided always that a woman candidate of sufficient competence were available.[61]

The committee indicated their concern that women students had few role models available to them:

> at present the incentive to women to prepare for the work of university teaching was materially weakened owing to the fact that women were so rarely appointed to university posts and more particularly to the higher posts. The view was generally expressed that women have not had an equal chance with men of securing appointments on the teaching staffs of modern universities.[62]

And there was a feeling that the increased representation of women on university staffs might incline authorities to pay more attention to their "special intellectual needs", or at least to the development of branches of learning other than those "mainly profitable to the men". This might indeed be considered to have been a far-sighted report. Council "approved it in principle", in 1911, but it appears to have had little effect in practice.[63]

The stance taken by the headmistresses in 1911–12 precipitated a good deal of controversy elsewhere. In 1911 the Executive Committee of the Headmistresses' Association submitted a statement to the Haldane Commission on the University of London recommending

> that in every University and University College there should be a woman university official responsible for the health, control

and discipline of the women students.[64]

In questioning Sara Burstall and Sophie Bryant further about this resolution, Sir Robert Romer wondered whether it was not "rather a large order?" He was told that the Association of Headmistresses was presently conducting "an elaborate inquiry" into the subject.[65] The headmistresses had indeed recently appointed a sub-committee, chaired by Lilian Faithfull, to investigate arrangements for the supervision of girl students in the University of London. This committee reported in 1912.[66] The inquiries of the Haldane commissioners in 1911 met with a significantly mixed response. Some of the commissioners, like Robert Romer, were clearly sceptical about the headmistresses' demands. Mrs Creighton asked Sophie Bryant whether it was wise to call for separate provision for women?

> It seems to me the whole question rather touches on the status of the university women, as opposed to the schoolgirl, and the different treatment that she should receive, and I could not help feeling a little as if you were thinking of her still as a slightly older schoolgirl, and treating her in the same way as a schoolgirl?[67]

This was clearly a sensitive area, and headmistresses like Burstall and Lilian Faithfull were cornered into making some questionable claims, such as the suggestion that women students in lodgings were more likely to neglect meals and nutritional needs than were men.[68] This kind of argument about feminine vulnerability, and the need for special protection for young girls, was strongly dismissed by some of the other witnesses, including women in academic posts. Helen Gwynne Vaughan of Birkbeck College, for instance, insisted unequivocally that

> The graduates whom I represent would have preferred to leave untouched the question of the position of women in the University, since they are of opinion that the wisest course is to impose no special regulations, but to deal with women, as with men simply in their capacity as students, graduates or teachers.[69]

The British Federation of University Women were also anxious to distance themselves from the headmistresses' position.[70] If the universities were to appoint women tutors, they urged that these should be women with impeccable academic qualifications. Their disciplinary functions should be regarded as of far less importance than their advisory work, and they vehemently opposed any idea of separate disciplinary arrangements for women.[71]

The headmistresses, then, seem to have found themselves in something of an isolated position in the debate, although their claim was always that they represented the views of the majority of girls' parents at the time. They themselves were not wholly consistent. When the Haldane commissioners asked Lilian Faithfull directly whether she considered that girls should have "exceptional treatment" in the universities, her answer was "not in the least".[72] There was ambivalence, similarly, in Mrs Bryant's position. She tried to steer clear of any contention that girls needed tighter disciplinary arrangements than boys, arguing instead that women tutors were needed because female students might be understandably reluctant to submit personal problems to men for guidance. She felt that things would become easier when there were women professors in the universities, but that this was decidedly not the case at present.[73] Lilian Faithfull was similarly concerned, pointing out that:

> We were astonished to find that in some of the colleges, both in London and the Provinces, there was no Lady Superintendent, no Censor of Women Students, no lady at all for the women students to appeal to, absolutely no woman with an official position in the university at all.[74]

The evidence suggests that this was the case in only a minority of institutions. In St Andrews for instance, Principal Stewart's suggestion (in 1895–6) that a "Committee of Ladies" should be appointed to aid the Senatus in defining supervisory arrangements for the lady students seems to have fallen on stony ground, and no separate official was appointed.[75] The gap was filled to some extent, by the Warden of University Hall, although Louisa Lumsden, the first incumbent of the post, had difficulty in extending her authority over the women who lived in local lodgings, many of whom saw no reason to submit to her ideas about the organization of their societies or social life.[76] This led to a series of conflicts in the university, which contributed to Lumsden's decision to resign from St Andrews in 1900.[77] Aberdeen was particularly unusual in that not only was there no permanent lady superintendent, but no warden either since Aberdeen, unlike anywhere else in Britain, failed to establish any hall of residence for women students in the period. This may have had democratic or egalitarian implications, but Lindy Moore, Aberdeen's historian has suggested that it meant that the University had no senior woman, either academic or administrative, who could represent the interests of the female students and act as a role model, nor any physical centre around which women could develop an alternative culture to that of the male university.[78]

It is interesting to compare the situation in Aberdeen with that in Edinburgh. During the war years the number of women students, particularly in faculties of arts, increased considerably in most universities, while the proportion of male students declined. The women students in Edinburgh became much more vocal in complaining about discrimination in these years. The Students' Representative Council complained to the University Court in 1918 that many classes of women students were at a disadvantage because their teachers had no voice in their examinations, which was not the case with the male students.[79] The women also expressed resentment of the "Official Advisers" in the university who, they claimed, were friendly and sympathetic to the men students while giving short shrift to the women.[80] They accordingly petitioned the Senatus to appoint a "Woman Supervisor of Studies", outlining a detailed job description for the post. They respectfully suggested that scholarly qualifications were less important than "sympathy with, and understanding of student life and women's work", and above all they pleaded that anyone appointed "should be young in disposition".[81] The Senatus passed on the students' request to the faculty who stated that in their opinion it was "unnecessary and undesirable" to appoint a Woman Supervisor of Studies, but that they felt it "eminently desirable that there should be a lady of academic training and high character who could act as superintendent of all women students, and to whom they would be able to appeal in any difficulty".[82] The distinction is interesting, and shows a clear intention to differentiate between academic and pastoral responsibilities. In 1918 the "Office of Lady Warden" was accordingly created, the first incumbent being Mrs Garden Blaikie, at a salary of £200 p.a. Helen Wilkie, one of the students who had taken the initiative in this series of events, argued that Mrs Blaikie's appointment greatly facilitated the representation of the women students' interests in Edinburgh.[83]

The early superintendents of women students were made responsible for a wide variety of duties and received varying amounts of support from the university authorities, professors' wives, and from the women students themselves. Their position was often difficult, not least because the impetus for their appointment, as we have seen, might derive from a number of different sources. The feminist concerns of women interested in furthering women's representation within the university might well be in conflict with the paternalism of university authorities primarily concerned with propriety and decorum, and most crucially, in the avoidance of anything which might scandalize parents or bring the institutions into disrepute. There were a number of such incidents, particularly in the years before 1900. In Southampton, for instance, allegations of impropriety at a party in a hostel for women students in 1899 cost both the first Lady Superintendent and the Principal of the college their jobs.[84] It is not possible to establish exactly what happened on this occasion because the university took pains to keep details out of official records. In the first edition of Temple Patterson's centenary history of the university, published in 1962, there is no mention of the affair. However, an amended edition, published in 1967, contains an additional, typescript paragraph:

> It was at the close of the 1899–1900 Session that the college was deprived of Dr Stewart's leadership by what seems to have been a piece of imprudence or a lapse into human weakness on his part. The lady who owned the two houses in Avenue Place, which had served as a temporary hostel for women students, and who appears to have taken amiss the termination of this arrangement at rather short notice complained to the Hartley Council that his visits to the Lady Superintendent, Miss Blaxley, had been unnecessarily frequent, and in particular accused them both of improper behaviour during a party there. The Council accepted their "emphatic denial" on the matter of this accusation, but expressed the opinion that his visits had been "extremely indiscreet", and recommended the acceptance of his resignation, asking at the same time for Miss Blaxley's.[85]

Stewart subsequently secured appointment as Principal of the Harris Institute in Preston. Eva Blaxley had previously combined her supervision of the women students in Southampton with a lectureship in English and history. Details of her career after 1900 are not known.

Lady superintendents often combined their work with the wardenship of hostels for women students. One of the most explosive public controversies in the history of women's university education before

1900 brought an end to the career of Miss Hughes, Lady Superintendent of the women's hostel in Bangor, North Wales, in 1892–4.[86] This episode will be discussed in Chapter 3. But where the responsibilities of wardenship were combined with pastoral work and even academic duties, the workload of these early women officials could prove oppressively heavy. There were many cases of nervous exhaustion, ill health and near breakdown. In Manchester even the energetic Phoebe Sheavyn found her triple workload of lecturing, acting as Senior Tutor to Women Students and serving as Warden of Ashburne Hall too onerous. After a period of illness, in 1917 she decided to resign the wardenship.[87] Lady superintendents and women tutors were responsible for enforcing the elaborate codes of rules and disciplinary arrangements that existed in most universities before the First World War, and that were particularly stringent in the Welsh university colleges and in Durham. This brought an undercurrent of tension into relationships with female students, and, increasingly, open conflict. Some of the women tutors were themselves beginning to find the disciplinary restrictions on female students irksome. Hilda Oakeley, Phoebe Sheavyn's predecessor in Manchester, recorded in her autobiography of 1939 that she had found

> the position of Tutor to Women Students in the form which it had at that time somewhat distasteful . . .

adding that

> The vague idea of chaperonage of women students at a co-educational university has now, I think, been eliminated from this position.[88]

At the same time she was quick to point out that what she thought the main rationale for the position of tutor retained its force:

> viz. that in a University at which the Principal will certainly be a man there should be a woman in a leading administrative position to represent the woman's side.[89]

Events at University College London in 1912 showed that the women students there shared Oakeley's perspective. Rosa Morison died in 1912 and there was a good deal of discussion over the question of finding a successor. The regulations showed the "passing in" rule still in force, stipulating that:

> No woman, unless she is the wife or daughter of the Provost, of a Professor, or of an Emeritus Professor, is admitted as a student of the College except upon the recommendation of the Lady Su-

perintendent, and upon producing a satisfactory reference or introduction.[90]

This rule was increasingly resented by the women, who called for its abolition and urged the appointment of a woman with academic status who could serve as "Vice-Provost" or "Sub-Dean" for women students.[91] The minutes of the Women's Union Society indicate that the women staff counselled against such demands, but the students remained convinced of the need for any woman official to have full status to represent them on the college committee.[92] Rosa Morison was replaced by Miss Winifred Smith, the title of Lady Superintendent being abandoned in favour of Tutor to Women Students in 1912.[93] When Winifred Smith died in the 1920s there was another eruption of conflict. Margaret Murray recalled that:

> The Selection Committee consisted of members of the College Committee who were all men, not a woman amongst them. Professor Oliver was very keen that one of his staff should be appointed, but as a body we were against that because the lady in question, although she was very charming and we were all fond of her, was not yet thirty . . . and she had no experience that would fit her for so important an administrative and advisory post.[94]

The women on the staff protested that they, and the female students, had a right to be consulted on the matter of the appointment, although there was some anxiety lest they should be seen to be interfering. Margaret Murray herself wrote a carefully phrased letter to the selection committee, the outcome being the choice of a candidate acceptable to everyone. Murray herself described the incident in some detail as an exemplary story, castigating "that type of woman" still "afraid to express an opinion which might offend the men". Since then, she observed with satisfaction, "women have always been put on committees in which there are problems connected with the women in the College".[95]

Status uncertainties and troubled careers: the experience of women tutors

The tendency for women to manifest greater self-confidence in deploring chaperonage and seeking more effective representation can be seen elsewhere. In Sheffield for instance, Mary Sorby had served as Tutor to Women Students between 1905 and 1921; not much is known about her work, which seems to have involved little more than a pastoral role.[96] In 1921 Mrs Lucy Storr-Best was appointed on a part-time basis to replace her, at a salary of £100 p.a.[97] Lucy Storr-Best was an energetic woman with strong academic interests who quickly found herself chafing against the restrictions of her post.[98] A letter that she wrote in 1924 to Mr Gibbons, the Registrar, in which she announced her decision to resign from the tutorship, provides ample illustration of her discontent and of the difficulties she had encountered in her work.[99] She had found "the matron or chaperon role" barely tolerable, and the supervision of lodgings for female students had involved "a good deal of disagreeable and anxious work". More importantly, she had found herself frustrated by the lack of any clear academic role. She had not been consulted, or even recognized, by the male academics in the university: "Curricula, timetables and conditions affecting the women are changed without my knowing anything about it". "You may remember", she reminded the Registrar,

> that my idea was that it would be well for the Tutor to have something like a watching brief for the women at Faculty meetings. In some other modern universities she is a member of Senate and Council as well, but you told me that nothing of the sort was possible here.

> If there is no development in the tutorship I think it would be a good thing to have the office blended with that of a Warden or Lecturer. You are not likely to find a woman with power enough to deal with really awkward cases when they arise – there have been several in my experience – for whom either the status or the honorarium attached at present to the post would be permanently satisfactory, if that were her only link with the University.[100]

Mrs Storr-Best resigned in 1926.

In universities where women tutors managed to secure more senior positions and status, conflict might be equally or even more marked. This was apparently the case in Manchester during the early 1920s, although the evidence is patchy and it is not possible to reconstruct any precise sequence of events. We know that Phoebe Sheavyn, again a woman of strong personality with impeccable academic qualifications, had secured a seat on Senate, as Senior Tutor to Women Students, in 1912.[101] However, when she retired in 1925 it was decided *not* to make a similar appointment at a senior level. Her successor, Miss Phyllis Crump, already on the university's pay-roll as a lecturer in French, was appointed to a part-time post as "Adviser" to women students instead.[102] Tylecote tells us that the 1920s were years of considerable tension between men and women students in Manchester, but she tactfully glosses over Dr Sheavyn's role in these events, merely noting that

> Miss Sheavyn was a woman of charm, strong convictions and great sense of dignity. During the years that she was in Manchester her personality made a strong impression and she was widely known. She was a formidable feminist and the character of her contribution to the position of women in the University is still a subject of controversy.[103]

A letter from Mary Tout to Mabel Tylecote, written in 1940, allows us to speculate further. Mrs Tout judged that:

> You handle the very delicate history of the position of Miss Sheavyn very wisely and tactfully. Had she had her way, she'd have got herself appointed a sort of female VC which would have been a reactionary move in a co-educational university, where the whole effort should be towards unifying the student body. (Mr Fiddes has a complete knowledge of those trying times that preceded her resignation.) She is such a fine woman: it seemed strange that she had a bee in her bonnet.[104]

But where the circumstances of Phoebe Sheavyn's resignation from Manchester remain shadowy, the archives in Leeds allow the historian to piece together an interesting narrative illustrating what seems to have been a rather similar story. The first Tutor to Women Students in Leeds was Hannah Robertson, who had combined this office with her earlier position as Mistress of Method in the university's day training department between 1912 and 1921. Her salary for this double responsibility was £400 p.a. Hannah Robertson appears to have been a tactful, intelligent woman who was much liked by students and colleagues. Formal tributes on the retirement of university employees were generally courteous and appreciative, but in Miss Robertson's case these notices were particularly warm in tone.[105] Michael Sadler, the university's Vice-Chancellor, emphasized that she had been "one of the makers of tradition on the woman's side of the University" and that her counsel had been indispensable on all matters affecting the relationships between men and women staff and students.[106] In a characteristically generous gesture he commissioned Mrs Amato, a London portrait painter, to undertake a sketch of Miss Robertson, which he hoped would capture the "striking elusive beauty of the spirit in her face".[107]

Sadler was a romantic, who cultivated strong friendships with women. In Leeds, he encouraged and supported the careers of a number of women such as Mrs Redman King, Warden of Weetwood Hall, and Lynda Grier, who was acting head of the Economics Department between 1915 and 1919. Grier later wrote a tribute to Sadler's "radiant and creative personality", emphasizing the egalitarianism he had fostered in the university community in Leeds. There, she remembered:

> Women for the first time found themselves on equal terms with men in the academic world. To many it was exhilarating to have their opinion sought and treated with deference on public matters. It was also exhilarating to be expected to do as much work as if they were of the opposite sex. For the most part, they rose to meet the demands which were made on them.[108]

When Miss Robertson retired, a committee charged with the matter of considering her replacement unanimously decided that the work involved in the double office of Mistress of Method and Tutor to Women Students had escalated and was too much for one person. It was decided to divide the responsibility, and Sadler's vision was to create a new, senior post for a woman who would become "Dean of Women Students" in the university. She would be "the chief woman officer on the university staff".[109] He felt that it would be undesirable to define her duties too closely, because "as in the case of the Vice-Chancellor" she might be expected to develop her own vision. But her work would be all pervasive:

> Much correspondence from other universities would pass through her hands. She would be the Chief Adviser of the Vice-Chancellor on matters affecting the discipline and interests of women students. The parents of non-collegiate women students would rely on her for individual care of their daughters. In social matters affecting the personal and corporate life of the women students, the Dean's wisdom and experience would be of the greatest value to the undergraduates and to the University, and be welcome to the Wardens of the Hostels whose full re-

sponsibility for the welfare of their societies is respected by the
University and should not be trenched upon.[110]

This was the kind of job description that would have appealed to
the Headmistresses' Association, but it is worth noting that nothing is
said at this point about academic status, and further, that the last sen-
tence reflects some anticipatory unease about overlapping spheres of
responsibility. The woman recommended by the committee for this
post was, in fact, a headmistress, and a member of the Executive
Committee of the Headmistresses' Association into the bargain,
namely Alice Silcox, Head of Thoresby High School. As a Headmistress, the committee assured Council that she had been "singularly
successful" and was "beloved and highly respected". She had studied
at the University of Liverpool, and at Newnham College, and was a
graduate, in science, of the University of London. If called upon, she
was prepared to undertake "some teaching work in the University".[111] The committee suggested, rather in the nature of an after-
thought, that it might heighten her authority among the undergraduates were she to be seen as competent in this respect. In keeping with
the seniority envisaged for the post, Miss Silcox was to receive £650
rising to £800 p.a.;[112] a salary very much higher than that usually associated with women tutors in the universities, and even within the
professorial range.

Difficulties seem to have flared up almost as soon as Alice Silcox arrived. There were controversies over her role in admissions, and over
her desire to follow up individual student preferences regarding
courses in discussion with professors and heads of department.[113]
Here she was seen as overstepping her responsibilities and interfering
in academic matters. In a confidential memorandum that Wheeler,
the Registrar, addressed to the Vice-Chancellor, he stated emphatically that he did not think the Dean should be allowed any opportunity of discussing students' preferences with heads of department,
because this was a matter in which the professors could best advise.[114]
Most contentious of all was Alice Silcox's idea of making use of her
contacts with local headmistresses to elicit information about potential female applicants to the university. Wheeler saw this as quite ir-
regular, protesting that:

> The undertaking by the Dean of Women Students of corre-
> spondence with Head Mistresses about applicants for admis-
> sion might lead to embarrassing misunderstandings, and in my

opinion is neither necessary nor desirable. I should be sorry if we adopted a plan of labelling a student on admission with her Head Mistress's opinion of her ability, disposition and health. It is for the Heads of Departments to form their own judgement (and advise the Vice-Chancellor when necessary) as to the ability of a student.[115]

Wheeler concluded by apologizing to the Vice-Chancellor for finding himself so entirely in opposition to all the schemes propounded by the Dean for Women Students, but re-emphasized his conviction that she was stepping "outside her province".

Matters cannot have been made easier by Sadler's departure from Leeds in 1923. His successor, James Baillie, appears to have been rather more sceptical about the need for any Dean of Women Students. The friction over Miss Silcox's area of responsibility seems to have died down, as she came to terms with a diminished vision of her role, but the events of 1923 undoubtedly left a bitter legacy. In 1931 she was involved in a motor accident, and in February of that year she resigned, and retired to Westmorland.[116] The question of a successor caused Baillie some anxiety:

It will be a difficult post to fill, and great care will have to be exercised if we are to avoid a repetition of the friction which occurred when Miss Silcox first came here.[117]

Correspondence preserved in Leeds University's central filing office indicates that Baillie took pains to investigate the kind of role allocated to women tutors elsewhere. He received a long, confidential letter of advice from Charles Grant Robertson, then Vice-Chancellor of Birmingham University, which provides a wealth of insight into contemporary attitudes and certainly amplifies our understanding of the difficulties involved in appointments of this kind.[118]

Robertson informed Baillie that Birmingham had decided to appoint a Tutor to Women Students five or six years previously, after eliciting a great deal of evidence from universities that had instituted such appointments. The impetus had come from "important Headmistresses and some of the ladies in Birmingham who are particularly interested in the Women's Department". There had been unanimous agreement that anyone appointed should have "as high academic qualifications as possible" in order to secure the intellectual respect of both Senate and the women students themselves:

Students are very sensitive here, and unless someone in this office is fit to be on the staff they would start with the idea that she was a kind of dragooning governess.[119]

Robertson added that they had been warned that "the right woman would be of very great value", but that

the wrong one would do much more harm than good, and we had confidentially some evidence from other universities where the wrong one had been appointed, with unfortunate results.[120]

Birmingham had appointed Miss J. J. Milne, who had a doctorate from the University of Paris, and was already established as a lecturer in the French Department. On her appointment as Senior Tutor to Women Students, her academic work was reduced to that of a half-time post, but her tutorial work had since then expanded, so that by 1931 she had only a nominal connection with the French Department.

Milne had begun her work "without any particular definition of where her duties (were) to begin or end". According to Robertson, the main concern had been "for her to win the confidence of the girls", a task in which he judged her to have succeeded, for "they readily consult her on almost everything, from the colour of their stockings to research". She was also charged with co-operating with the Registrar who ran the university's appointments bureau, taking particular responsibility for the women graduates who were looking for employment.

On the whole, Robertson confessed himself well satisfied with J. J. Milne's appointment. However, he admitted that there were still areas of friction: in particular, relationships between the Senior Tutor, the Warden of the women's hostel, and the head of the Women's Education Department could prove strained. There had been clashes of personality and temperament, and "I have had to drop oil from time to time on very heated bearings". "Our *men* have created no difficulties", he added: "You will draw the necessary inference".[121]

All this clearly had its impact on Baillie, who drew up lengthy notes on the question of a successor to Miss Silcox for the consideration of Council a few days later.[122] These notes show careful attention to each of the points raised by Robertson. Council should look for a tutor who would be "the guide and friend" of all the woman students "and in a manner . . . to 'mother' them". She should "see them socially", take an interest in their health and development, and assist them in finding posts after graduation. Anyone appointed should be possessed of a "delicate tact", lest "she impinge upon the spheres of other people in the University". It should be made clear to her that she should have *no* responsibility for admissions, for discipline "nor in any way for the direction of the work of the University".[123] Baillie emphasized his conviction that it had been "an administrative blunder" to appoint Miss Silcox to a post of such seniority. "Very serious embarrassments" had arisen as she had "cut across and interfered with the work of the Heads of Department and of the Administrative Office".[124] He had been inclined to think her replacement altogether unnecessary, but long consideration led him to advocate the appointment of an "Advisor" or "Tutor" – certainly *not* a "Dean" for women students – at a considerably lower salary than that which Miss Silcox had enjoyed. In sum, the three qualifications that should be sought were:

> that the occupant should be a woman who will command the respect of the academic staff, that she should be a woman of some personality and character, and that she should have the influence of a lady.[125]

A ladylike successor to Miss Silcox was found in the person of Miss D. M. Hibgame, Headmistress of Batley Girls' Grammar School. She remained in the post until her retirement in 1948, and her work does not appear to have attracted any particular controversy.[126] She was succeeded (briefly) by a Miss Knight, and then in 1949 by a real lady, Lady Mary Ogilvie, who held the position for the next four years.[127]

Some women appointed to posts of this kind succeeded in establishing themselves as respected, authoritative figures in the university community. Lady Ogilvie was one of them. Another was Marjorie Rackstraw, originally appointed as Warden of Masson Hall, in Edinburgh, who took on additional responsibilities as General Advisor to Women Students in the university in 1927. This was a popular and effective appointment, and Rackstraw's decision to resign, ten years later, on the grounds that "it was not a job to grow old in" was greeted with many regrets.[128] With characteristic efficiency, Rackstraw typed out detailed particulars of her current responsibilities to serve as a guide for her successor. She noted that:

> The chief duties of the Adviser of Women Students are to give advice on careers, on general matters, and, where necessary, on accommodation. She interviews personally all the women students except those resident in recognised hostels. She is con-

cerned with the social life of the students generally and is responsible for keeping a Register of Lodgings which is reviewed every year. She is a member of the Appointments Board and of the Athletic Committee. She has an office in the Old College and the assistance of a part-time secretary.[129]

There were 915 women students in the university in 1935–6, about 25 per cent of whom were living in halls or recognized hostels. The Adviser to Women Students carried responsibility for personally interviewing all of the rest. And these duties, it should be remembered, were supplementary to those of the wardenship of Masson Hall. Marjorie Rackstraw would not have had much time for personal research. There were 44 applications to succeed her, out of which the committee chose Joan Sargeant, who had graduated with first-class honours from St Hugh's College, Oxford, in 1925.[130] Her previous appointment had been as a lecturer in education in the University of Sheffield.

Another example of a woman who established an effective career as Tutor to Women Students in the 1930s was the aforementioned Jane Johnston Milne, in Birmingham. Some of Milne's papers relating to her work as Senior Tutor to Women Students between 1926 and 1947 have survived and are preserved in the university archives.[131] They provide a useful indication of the scope of her responsibilities during these years, as well as some fascinating insights into attitudes towards women students at the time. Milne's relationships with women students were not always as cosy or harmonious as the Vice-Chancellor had suggested in his correspondence with Baillie in Leeds. There was an uncomfortable episode in 1929, for instance, when some of the students voiced their objection to lectures that their senior tutor had arranged with the local Public Health Department and British Social Hygiene Council, which apparently focused upon issues of individual and social morality and "sexual hygiene".[132] The students found the "matter and manner" of the lectures, which were given by a Miss Hillsdon of the Birmingham branch of the council, offensive. Miss Milne responded abruptly to what she considered "a want of taste" in the students' protest. Relationships became somewhat strained, until the university's Registrar saw fit to intervene, suggesting in a letter to Miss Milne that even "quite senior married ladies" who had attended Miss Hillsdon's lectures had been embarrassed by their tone and felt them "likely to do harm". Little more is known about this incident, but it might induce a degree of scepticism about Robertson's claim that Miss Milne enjoyed an easy intimacy with the students, who consulted her freely about matters such as "the colour of their stockings".

As already noted, Milne's academic responsibilities as a lecturer in French were reduced to the level of a half-time post upon her assumption of special responsibility for the women students in Birmingham. By the 1930s, her pastoral and administrative work had expanded to a level justifying the appointment of an assistant, Miss Mary Bodkin, at a salary of £100 p.a. Milne's files attest to her involvement in a wide range of activity with an emphasis on student loans and accommodation, job finding, the writing of testimonials, and, rather less expectedly, the promotion of Girl Guiding on campus.[133]

Whether she would have identified herself as a feminist or not, it is clear that Miss Milne was a staunch advocate of women's interests in the university. She was well aware that the interests of women students in terms of common room provision and the like tended to be overlooked, and she fought many a battle on their behalf. In her formal reports to the Vice-Chancellor and Senate she warned that headmistresses in the Midlands were discouraging their pupils from applying to Birmingham on account of the meagre provision that it offered: London, Leeds and Manchester were preferred "because of the better conditions in which the women students work there".[134] Milne repeatedly urged the university authorities to recognize the difficulties faced by women graduates in the job market. She felt that there was too much complacency about equal opportunities in the academic sense, and even went so far as to suggest that the curriculum might be reconsidered to allow broader-based study, with an extension of arts subjects, for the benefit of girls who contemplated careers in civic administration or public service rather than teaching.[135]

Jane Johnston Milne possessed considerable personal authority. Elsie Duncan-Jones (née Phare) who lectured in English at Birmingham in the 1930s and '40s, remembered her as a dignified, accomplished woman whose status as a senior officer in the university was never in doubt: "She was up there, with the Professors".[136] Contemplating her retirement in 1946, Miss Milne approached Mrs Duncan-Jones to find out whether she would be interested in serving as her successor. Although the post would have carried a higher salary than that attached to her lectureship in English, Mrs Duncan-Jones was not tempted: the duties of Senior Tutor seemed to her ill-defined, and she was content with her academic work and the close tutorial relationships with students that she already enjoyed.[137]

It is difficult to escape the conclusion that the post was indeed ill-defined, and, like tutorships with special responsibility for women students elsewhere, its status was uncertain. Milne's authority, and her influence in the university generally, owed more to her personal attributes than to any institutional definition of her post. Shortly after Milne's retirement, Eric Vincent and Percival Hinton published their study of *The University of Birmingham: its history and significance*.[138] Its celebratory tone is well captured in the conclusion to the chapter on student life, in which the writers congratulate their colleagues on the fact that "we have nowhere had occasion to write with specific differentiation of women's position in the University of Birmingham".[139] Neither J. J. Milne, nor the Tutorship to Women Students, was even mentioned in the volume.

Posts carrying special responsibility for women students, then, were an important element in what amounted to a gender-segregated labour market in academic life before 1914. Some additional features of this divided labour market will be discussed in Chapters 3 and 4. In Britain, as in the United States and elsewhere, the university authorities' concern to provide supervision for female undergraduates in the community generally, or more specifically in halls of residence or hostels, ensured the appointment of a certain number of female tutors.[140] Many intellectually well-qualified or able women took advantage of these posts to try to establish themselves in academic life, but the combination of academic and pastoral duties could be onerous, leaving little time for scholarship or personal research. The career trajectory of a tutor to women students was often troubled or uncertain: as we have seen, many felt marginalized, and there were a number of casualties, particularly in the 1920s and 1930s.

Notes

1. J. Fletcher & C. Upton, "'Monastic enclave' or 'open society'? A consideration of the role of women in the life of an Oxford college community in the early Tudor period", *History of Education* 16(1), pp. 1–9, 1987.
2. D. A. Winstanley, *Early Victorian Cambridge* (Cambridge, 1940), p. 380.
3. *Ibid.*, pp. 381–2.
4. S. Rothblatt, *The revolution of the dons* (Cambridge, 1968), p. 242.

5. L. Sciama, "'Ambivalence and dedication'; academic wives in Cambridge University, 1870–1970", and S. Ardener, "Incorporation and exclusion: Oxford academics' wives", both in *The incorporated wife*, H. Callan & S. Ardener (eds) (London, 1984).

6. Sciama, pp. 52–4.

7. M. Paley Marshall, *What I remember* (Cambridge, 1947), p. 12.

8. R. Lowe, "Structural change in English higher education, 1870–1920", in *The rise of the modern educational system: structural change and social reproduction*, D. K. Muller, F. K. Ringer, B. Simon (eds), (Cambridge, 1987), pp. 173–4.

9. Mrs Barrell, "'Reminiscences' 1890–," manuscript, n.d. (special collections, Bristol University).

10. *Ibid.*

11. *Ibid.*; Minute book of the Women's Literary Society, May 1898–June 1905 (special collections, Bristol University).

12. M. Pease, "Some reminiscences of University College, Bristol", typescript, 1942 (special collections, Bristol University).

13. "Account of the Marshalls' years at Bristol 1877 to 1883 by Mary Paley Marshall (lost in post) . . . notes from memory by M. F. Pease", manuscript, 1943 (special collections, Bristol University).

14. Prof. Tyndall, "Sixty years of academic life in Bristol", unpublished paper, 10 March 1958, p. 5 (special collections, Bristol University).

15. J. Burstyn, *Victorian education and the ideal of womanhood* (Rutgers University, 1984); C. Dyhouse, *Girls growing up in late Victorian and Edwardian England* (London, 1981), pp. 152–9.

16. M. Hird (ed.), *Doves and dons: a history of St Mary's College, Durham* (Durham, 1982), n.p., *c.* 27.

17. A. Copping, *The story of College Hall* (London, 1974), p. 24ff.; "The late Miss Rosa Morison", *Union Magazine* (University College London), 5, pp. 289–91, 1911–12; "Miss Eleanor Grove and her work . . . by an old student of College Hall", *University College Gazette*, (February 1901), p. 1968; "Miss Grove", unpublished typescript reminiscences (archives, UCL MEM 1 B/19).

18. A. Nethercott, *The first five lives of Annie Besant* (London, 1961), pp. 191–2.

19. *Ibid.*, p. 189.

20. J. A. Banks & O. Banks, "The Bradlaugh–Besant trial and the English newspapers", *Population Studies* 8, p. 22ff, 1954–5. For controversies around birth control in the late nineteenth century, see A. McLaren, *Birth control in nineteenth-century England* (London, 1978).

21. Nethercott, p. 189.

22. *Ibid.*

23. "Proceedings of an extraordinary general meeting of members of University College London, convened by requisition on 18 July 1883 and held in

the Botanical Theatre, with the Earl of Kimberley, President of the College, in the Chair", transcript from shorthand notes made by Mr T. Hill (records office, University College London).

24. *Ibid.*, p. 13.

25. *Ibid.*, pp. 8–9.

26. *Ibid.*, p. 23.

27. *Ibid.*, p. 68.

28. *Ibid.*, p. 80.

29. M. Murray, *My first hundred years*, (London, 1963), p. 157.

30. The records that survive from University College Women's Union Society are in the college records office (minutes from 1903 onwards) and in the manuscripts room (UCL MEM III B/1). The first volume of the minutes held in the records office includes a typescript account of the formation of the society in 1897.

31. Minutes of University College Women's Union Debating Society, founded 1878, 2 vols, 1878–1888, and 1924–1928, in MS ADD, 123–5 (University College London); see also an account of the history of this society in UCL MEM III/C 4.

32. *Ibid.* See first volume of minutes (1878–1888) for account of meeting chaired by Mrs Fawcett on 29 April 1879.

33. See account of the history of the Women's Union Debating Society UCL MEM III/C 4 (University College London).

34. *Ibid.*

35. See the account of the origins of the Women's Fund in minutes of the general meeting of the Women's Union Society, University College London, held on 31 May 1902, in the college's records office. See also a printed leaflet detailing subscriptions to "The women's fund for the endowment of the department of history", 1902, UCL Hist IV A/8 (manuscript room, University College London).

36. *Abstracts of Council minutes*, 7 March 1904 (University College London), p. 112; *Annual report*, 1904, p. 24 (University College London).

37. "The will of the late Miss Rosa Morison", *Union Magazine* (University College London), 5, 1911–12.

38. A. Copping, *The story of College Hall*.

39. Edith Wilson letter to Mabel Tylecote, June 1934, quoted in M. Tylecote, *The education of women at Manchester University, 1883–1933* (Manchester, 1941), p. 34.

40. *Ibid.*, p. 26.

41. E. Wilson, *Catherine Isabella Dodd, 1860–1936: a memorial sketch* (London: Sidgwick & Jackson, 1936). For a more recent assessment of her work see A. Robertson, "Catherine I. Dodd and innovation in teacher training, 1892–1905", *Bulletin of the History of Education Society* (Spring 1991) 47, pp. 32–41.

42. Wilson, *Catherine Isabella Dodd*, p. 7.

43. *Ibid.*, p. 10.

44. *Ibid.*, pp. 34–5.
45. *Ibid.*, p. 36.
46. Minutes of Bristol University College Council, 15 February 1899 (archives, Bristol University).
47. *Ibid.*, "Lady Tutor: suggestions of Ladies' Committee", MS note bound in with College Council minutes, 1899.
48. *Ibid.*, report of special meeting, 31 May 1899, to interview candidates for post of Lady Tutor.
49. *Newnham College Register*, vol. I, pp. 95–6, 1871–1923.
50. *Ibid.*, p. 7.
51. See papers and correspondence on "Appointment of a female tutor", 1901–3 (Lodge collection, Birmingham University, OL 218–232).
52. *Ibid.*, J. C. Frankland to Oliver Lodge, 9 January 1901, OL 222.
53. *Ibid.*, OL 218.
54. *Ibid.*, R. Albright-King to Oliver Lodge, June 1902, OL 229.
55. *Ibid.*
56. *Calendar* (Birmingham University), p. 96, 1938–9.
57. Memorial from local headmistresses 1 March 1911, bound in with minutes of the University Council, vol. III, 1911 (archives, Liverpool University).
58. *Ibid.*
59. Minutes of the University Council, Liverpool, 17 May 1910, and 14 March 1911.
60. Report of committee on the proportion of women on the staff, 10 November 1911, bound in with reports of the Council of the University of Liverpool, vol. 3, 1911 (archives, Liverpool University).
61. *Ibid.*, p. 3, para. 8.
62. *Ibid.*, p. 2, para. 6.
63. University of Liverpool annual report of the Council to Senate, November 1911, p. 9 para X; T. Kelly, *For advancement of learning: the University of Liverpool, 1881–1951* (Liverpool University, 1981), p. 207.
64. F. Gadesden, Statement quoted in minutes of evidence, Appendix to Third Report, *Report of Royal Commission on university education in London* (Haldane Commission) (London,1911), vol. XX, p. 149.
65. *Ibid.*, para. 8060ff.
66. Association of Headmistresses, *Report on the supervision of university girl students*, 1912 (annual reports of Headmistresses' Association, Modern Records Centre, Warwick University, MSS 188 TBN 47).
67. Appendix to Third Report, Haldane Commission, para. 8082.
68. *Ibid.*, paras. 10, 374 80, 389, para. 8076.
69. Helen Gwynne Vaughan, evidence submitted to Haldane Commission (Final Report, London, 1913), vol. XL, para. 25.
70. British Federation of University Women, minutes of meeting held on 1 June 1912 (BFUW archives).
71. *Ibid.*
72. Haldane Commission, 1911, vol. XX, para. 10,389.

73. *Ibid.*, para. 8085.
74. *Ibid.*, para. 10,370.
75. Meeting 9 November 1895, *Minutes of Senate*, University of St Andrews, 1895, vol. 22. See also reports of meetings on 14 December 1895 and 8 February 1896 (St Andrews University).
76. *College Echoes* X(2), pp. 13, 18, 1898. See also Louisa Lumsden's letters to Principal Donaldson, 1 & 2 November 1898 (St Andrews University).
77. Lumsden refers somewhat cryptically to her "five stormy years" as Warden of University Hall, St Andrews, in *Yellow leaves: memories of a long life* (Edinburgh & London, 1933), p. 119.
78. L. Moore, *Bajanellas and semilinas; Aberdeen University and the education of women, 1860–1920* (Aberdeen, 1991), p. 135.
79. Minutes of the University Court, vol. XII, May–July 1920 (archives, Edinburgh University), p. 275.
80. H. Wilkie, "Steps which led to the appointment of a Woman Supervisor of Studies", *University of Edinburgh Journal,* 1971–2, pp. 136–7.
81. *Ibid.*, p. 139.
82. *Ibid.*, p. 137.
83. *Ibid.*, p. 140.
84. A. Temple Patterson, *The University of Southampton: a centenary history of the evolution and development of the university, 1862–1962* (Southampton, 1962). See 1967 edition, copy amended by author (Southampton University), p. 105.
85. *Ibid.*
86. J. Gwynn Williams, *The University College of North Wales: foundations, 1884–1927* (Cardiff, 1985), pp. 105–111; W. G. Evans, *Education and female emancipation: the Welsh experience, 1847–1914* (Cardiff, 1990), pp. 244–52.
87. Tylecote, *The education of women*, p. 108.
88. H. Oakeley, *My adventures in education* (London, 1939), p. 135.
89. *Ibid.*
90. Calendars before 1912, University College London.
91. Minutes of Women's Union Society (University College London), 1912.
92. *Ibid.*
93. M. Murray, *My first hundred years*, p. 157.
94. *Ibid.*, p. 160.
95. *Ibid.*, p. 162.
96. The minutes of the University Council record Miss Sorby's resignation in May 1921 (archives, Sheffield University, SUA/5/1/146).
97. Minutes of University Council, July 1921 (Council X 73), Sheffield University.
98. On Lucy Storr-Best (née Morris) see "A woman tutor: Mrs Storr-Best's work at the university", *Sheffield Telegraph*, 16 June 1926. There is also a brief entry in the *Newnham College Register*, vol. I, 1871–1923, p. 121.
99. Correspondence, Lucy Storr-Best to Mr. Gibbons, 8 July 1924 (Chapman

collection, item 146, Sheffield University).

100. *Ibid.*
101. Tylecote, *The education of women*, pp. 138–9.
102. *Ibid.*, p. 139.
103. *Ibid.*, p. 162.
104. Correspondence, Mary Tout to Mabel Tylecote, 14 April 1940 (Mabel Tylecote collection, Manchester University).
105. "Miss Robertson's retirement", *The Gryphon* (University of Leeds magazine, December 1921), p. 32. See also information in central filing office, Leeds University.
106. E. G. Arnold & M. E. Sadler, "Memorandum to members of Council on retirement of Miss Robertson", 14 July 1921 (central filing office, Leeds University).
107. Correspondence, M. E. Sadler to Mrs Amato, 21 December 1921 (Leeds University).
108. L. Grier, *Achievement in education; the work of Michael Ernest Sadler, 1885–1935* (London, 1952), pp. 186–7.
109. Arnold & Sadler, Memorandum to Council, 14 July 1921 (Leeds University).
110. *Ibid.*
111. *Ibid.*
112. Alice Silcox file (Leeds University).
113. Correspondence, Alice Silcox to Vice-Chancellor, 17 June 1922 (Leeds University).
114. Correspondence, A. E. Wheeler to Vice-Chancellor, 5 July 1922 (Leeds University).
115. *Ibid.*
116. Correspondence, Alice Silcox to Vice-Chancellor, 29 January 1931, and letter of resignation, 23 February 1931 (Leeds University).
117. Copy of letter from Vice-Chancellor (?) to Colonel Tetley, 18 May 1931 (Leeds University).
118. Correspondence from Charles Grant Robertson to James Baillie, 15 May 1931 (Leeds University).
119. *Ibid.*, pp. 1–2.
120. *Ibid.*, p. 2.
121. *Ibid.*, pp. 5–6.
122. J. Baillie, "Notes on the appointment of a successor to Miss Wilcox", 18 May 1931 (Leeds University).
123. *Ibid.*, pp. 1–2.
124. *Ibid.*, p. 3.
125. *Ibid.*, p. 6.
126. File on Dora Margaret Hibgame (Leeds University).
127. Obituary of Lady Mary Ogilvie, *The Times*, 19 November 1990.
128. *Masson Hall Newsletter*, No. 14, p. 15, 1937 (Edinburgh University). It seems likely that Marjorie Rackstraw had become increasingly disheart-

ened by the collapse of plans for the building of a new Masson Hall, when the University Court decided to relinquish the West Mains Road site in 1936. See Minutes of Masson Hall executive committee, 23 June 1936 (Edinburgh University).

129. Typescript particulars for applicants for the post of Adviser to Women Students, Minutes of Masson Hall executive committee, March 1937 (Edinburgh University).

130. *Ibid.*, March 1937.

131. University collection, 3/vi/1, 3/vii/2, 3/vi/7, 3/vi/8, 1926–47 (Birmingham University).

132. *Ibid.*, box 3/vii/1. Correspondence J. J. Milne with Mary Hillsdon, 9 December 1926, 1 November 1928; M. Rigsby, 13 May 1929, 15 May 1929; Lilian Seckler and Costain, May 1929.

133. *Ibid.*, box 32/vii/2. Milne was a member of the Central Council Committee for Guiding and was keen to develop a university link. With the approval of the Vice-Chancellor she set about co-opting female students into Cadet Ranger Companies and supported a University Guides Club.

134. *Ibid.*, box 3/vii/1, n.d. (1926?), p. 2.

135. *Ibid.*, Confidential report from the Senior Tutor to Women Students to members of Council and Senate, February 1929, p. 4.

136. Interview with E. E. Duncan-Jones, 17 May 1994.

137. *Ibid.*

138. E. W. Vincent & P. Hinton, *The University of Birmingham: its history and significance* (Birmingham: Cornish, 1947).

139. *Ibid.*, p. 203.

140. G. J. Clifford (ed.), *Lone voyagers: academic women in co-educational institutions, 1870–1937* (New York, 1989), p. 11ff.

Chapter Three

✍

Residence: halls and hostels for women students

The ideal of college life

Personal reminiscences and letters written home by the first generation of women to enjoy college life in Oxford and Cambridge often
sparkle with exhilaration at the prospect of enjoying personal space,
"a room of one's own" in which to read and study unfettered by the
obligations of domestic life.[1] The young Dilys Glynne Jones, for instance, arriving in Newnham in 1877, wrote joyfully to her parents
with a detailed description of the plan of her room in college, giving
details of décor and furnishing, and even enclosing a small drawing
reproducing the pattern of her carpet.[2] Women arriving in the new
halls of residence that were built in connection with the newer universities in the late nineteenth century might share similar experiences.
Olive Marsh for example, embarking upon a teacher training course
in Aberystwyth in 1898, wrote to the young man who was to become
her fiancé extolling the facilities in Alexandra Hall. She described her
cubicle with its chest of drawers, washstand and looking glass as
"quite lovely", reporting that the students were expected to make
their own beds, but that was all: everything was provided for their
convenience, indeed there were 20-odd servants waiting at the table
during dinner.[3]

Women educationalists were quick to extol the benefits of college
life, particularly for female students. In the 1890s Agnes Maitland argued that halls of residence provided unparalleled opportunities for
women to study: they allowed girls space in which to work without
disturbance and where regular hours and regular meals could be guaranteed.[4] She argued that a respite from "the frictions of home life"

was crucial if girls were to use their new educational opportunities to the full. Families were often selfishly inward looking in their attitudes and conduct, whereas a college or hall of residence afforded ample opportunities for the cultivation of public spirit and corporate life. She urged parents to recognize the advantages of the hall of residence over lodgings or home study for their daughters:

> Where it is possible for a girl to enter a hall of residence rather than live in lodgings alone, my own feeling is that there is scarcely any sacrifice I would not make personally, were it a daughter of my own.[5]

Writing a few years later in 1900, Lilian Faithfull expressed very similar convictions.[6] She contended that women students in non-residential colleges would find it very difficult to satisfy the conflicting demands of home and college: this "dual life" was all too often "difficult and wearing". "The possession of a castle of one's own" was perhaps "the first keen joy of college life". Colleges allowed scope for women to develop their own habits of study and self-discipline, and this acquisition of self government was what distinguished them from schoolgirls. On the social side,

> college life offers to women unique opportunities of life-long friendships. Such opportunities men have had for centuries, women only in the last twenty years; and no one who has enjoyed the comradeship and intimacy of College will deny that friendships made there are unlike all others. There is the freedom of choice in the first place. No consideration of social station, or of calling acquaintance between respective parents, have any weight. The woman is taken for herself, her character is the determining factor in her relations with others, and so the right principle is established.[7]

According to Faithfull, this was the kind of environment in which corporate virtues would flourish, and women would be able to absorb those values of *esprit de corps* and *noblesse oblige* that college education had traditionally inculcated in boys.

By the 1930s the University Grants Committee was strongly emphasizing the educational and social potential of properly conducted halls of residence, described as "a great humanising force" in British university life.[8] The committee regretted that by 1936 only 16 per cent of full-time students could find accommodation in such halls, and urged the universities to find ways of expanding provision. The extent of such accommodation varied considerably between individual universities. Reading was commended as having developed a system of halls and hostels that could accommodate 68 per cent of its student population. Bristol could accommodate 37 per cent. But in Glasgow only 3.5 per cent of the students lived in recognized hostels, and Aberdeen was alone among British universities in making no residential provision at all.[9]

The universities' tradition of organizing residence for students had roots in the collegiate systems of Oxford, Cambridge and Durham, but gained marked impetus in the later nineteenth century from the need to provide particularly for *women* students. This was recognized by the UGC in a report printed in 1957, which pointed out that:

> Most of the Halls established before the turn of the century were intended for women, an arrangement perhaps not uninfluenced by Victorian ideas of chaperonage. Aberdare Hall at Cardiff opened in 1885, Alexandra Hall at Aberystwyth in 1896, Ashburne Hall (in Manchester) in 1900, and Clifton Hill House in Bristol in 1909.[10]

The writers of this report emphasized that the older, civic universities had provided mainly for local students, who attended lectures on a daily basis while living at home. Some hostel provision had developed to accommodate students who came from further afield, but the universities had tended to regard these hostels "as accretions, not as central to the community".[11] The newer universities, such as Reading, differed in that they had set out to provide residence for a large proportion of students from the outset, seeing this as an important part of a college education.

Putting aside the variation among individual universities, and looking at the numbers of full-time students in the country as a whole, we find that by 1937–8, 42.6 per cent of women, and 41 per cent of men were attending their local university and living at home.[12] Where this was not the case, a much smaller proportion of women than of men lived in lodgings, (19 per cent women students, as compared with 37.5 per cent men), while a correspondingly higher proportion of women than of men students were living in hostels or halls of residence (38 per cent of women, compared with 21 per cent of men).[13] For over a third of the female student population in these years just before the Second World War, the experience of university education was bound up with the experience of living in a hostel or a hall of residence under the aegis of the university authorities.

The provision of residential halls or hostels for women students, like the appointment of lady superintendents, stemmed from a whole variety of motives, sometimes pragmatic, sometimes paternalist, and sometimes feminist in origin. The desire to protect impressionable young women from the perceived dangers of unsupervised lodgings was often important, and the "Victorian ideas of chaperonage" cited by the UGC were clearly evident. Agnes Maitland emphasized the reassurance parents would receive from knowing that their daughters were subject to "wise supervision" in matters of health and social life.[14] There was also the belief that life in a respectable hostel, run along the lines of a gracious or civilized household, would exert a refining influence on girls from less cultured homes. This was sometimes thought to be of particular importance for girls intending to teach, as they often came from modest homes. In Glasgow, for instance, an advocate of hostels argued in 1907 that residential provision would afford "opportunity of improvement in manner, accent and general cultivation" that would be of great importance to women looking for posts in schools.[15]

The feminist advocacy of residential provision drew upon the kind of arguments put forward by Agnes Maitland and Lilian Faithfull. Many – indeed most – of the early hostels and halls of residence came about through the voluntary efforts of professors' wives and the women who had been prominent in the work of the Ladies' Educational Associations earlier in the century. Women like Mrs Tout in Manchester, Lady Aberdare and Mrs Viriamu Jones in Cardiff, Emma Holt, Eva Melly and Mrs Herdman in Liverpool, or Miss Houldsworth and Sara Mair in Edinburgh, were all inspired by the idea of providing institutions on the model of the Oxbridge women's colleges in their own university towns. Masson Hall, in Edinburgh, could accommodate only 15 students when it first opened in 1897, but the ladies responsible for its foundation hoped that it would

> in time come to fill somewhat the same place in relation to university life in Edinburgh that is filled by such halls as Somerville, Lady Margaret and St Hugh's at Oxford.[16]

The establishment of a hall of residence in St Andrews was similarly inspired by the idea of creating "a Scottish Girton".[17] Helen Gladstone, when called upon to open the new hall of residence for women students in Bangor in 1897, expressed her welcome to this "younger sister of Newnham".[18] Mrs Sidgwick, the well-known Principal of Newnham College, was herself much in demand at the opening ceremonies of these newer women's hostels: she presided at the opening of Ashburne Hall in Manchester in 1900, as she had at Aberdare in Cardiff a few years earlier.[19]

The practicalities of provision

More pragmatically, the need to establish residential provision for women students was driven by the Board of Education's policies on teacher education and particularly by the development of the day training departments in civic universities after 1890. In Cardiff, the Ladies' Committee that had taken the initiative in offering a house for women students in Richmond Road in 1884, insisted that the expansion of Cardiff's role in teacher education made it imperative in 1891 to begin work on the building of a new hall of residence for women students. A site was purchased in Cathays Park and the new Aberdare Hall opened its doors in 1895.[20] Minutes of the day training college committee in Leeds between 1910 and 1913 show the committee regularly urging the university to think about hostel accommodation for women students. Private houses in Leeds were adapted and extended in a makeshift fashion during these years, but there was considerable anxiety that Board of Education requirements were not being met.[21] The Board's regulations from 1910 required those women students not residing with parents or guardians to live in recognized hostels. Margery Knight, who was Warden of Liverpool's hall of residence for women students, University Hall, from 1943, remembered the importance of the teacher training students in the early growth of the hall:

> The first modest quota of four students (in 1900) was the beginning of a swelling stream of students from the Day Training Department which eventually formed the bulk of students in residence in the Hostel. In fact, it later became a regulation in the Department, that all women students who could not travel daily from their homes must live in the Hostel. That involved the approval of the Hostel by the Board of Education, not by any means an unmixed blessing, as the Board had views about cubic space per student and insisted upon a surveyor's report

about the well-being of the "drains". Two committee meetings were taken up with the difficulties experienced by the surveyor in *finding* the "drains" of 163 Edge Lane, but eventually the Hostel was "approved".[22]

The number of women embarking on teacher training rose rapidly before 1914 and through the 1920s, declining again in the 1930s, and the business of providing adequate accommodation for them, of a standard that would meet the Board of Education's requirements, involved wardens and the staff of the day training departments in a good deal of work and negotiation. In Cardiff Kate Hurlbatt, Warden of Aberdare Hall, received a telegraph from the Board of Education in 1917 vetoing her suggestion that those students who could not be accommodated in hall might live in hostels provided by the Girls' Friendly Society or the Young Women's Christian Association. The Board agreed, however, to recognize overflow accommodation that had been provided in a house in Corbett Road.[23] In Birmingham, correspondence in the University House collection indicates that in 1921 the Board had relaxed its regulations sufficiently to allow some of the women students who could not find rooms in University House to live in lodgings, but that this was seen as a temporary expedient. Miss Monkhouse, from the Board of Education, wrote to Grant Robertson indicating reluctance to continue recognizing lodgings that were really deemed unsuitable for young women:

> This would, I fear, mean a reduction in the number of women students admitted to the university from outside the Birmingham area.
>
> The Board are of course very sympathetic with you in your difficulties and are anxious that arrangements should be as economical as possible. If, therefore, the University is unable to provide a new University Hostel of the accepted standard, they would consider any reasonable proposal for the temporary housing of women students which provided communal life in clean and healthy surroundings under the direction of an educated woman, or failing this, would probably extend the temporary recognition of lodgings if suitable ones become available.[24]

Even the Scottish universities, more comfortable with a tradition of students living in lodgings, and independent of the Board of Education in London, found themselves drawn into considering residential provision in response to the increasing numbers of teachers in training. The Edinburgh Association for the Provision of Hostels for Women Students came into being in 1910–11, bringing together the university, the Episcopal Training College and other training institutions in the town.[25] The association suggested that Scotland should follow England's lead in aiming to provide proper halls of residence for all women students not living at home.[26] In 1912 it sent a deputation to investigate arrangements in six halls of residence in England – two in Manchester, and one each in Liverpool, Birmingham, Nottingham and Leeds. A full report was published, estimates were drawn up and detailed discussions about administration and management followed. The association arranged a loan of £25,000 from the Carnegie trustees, and expected to rely on £63,650 from Treasury grants, grants from the Education (Scotland) Fund, and from the funds of the Edinburgh Provincial Committee for the Training of Teachers. A site was secured in Craigmillar Park and three hostels, each to accommodate 52 women students, were advertised as due for completion in 1916–17.[27]

These operations and the extent of their financial underpinning were unusual. The early growth of most residential provision in British universities came about in a piecemeal, hand-to-mouth way, financed by local benefactors and voluntary subscriptions. Many of the hostels were established through private subscriptions or by the establishment of limited liability companies that were formally independent of the universities at the outset. However, university principals, professors and their wives were prominent on their executive and management committees, and gradually, the hostels passed into university control. Masson Hall in Edinburgh, for instance, was incorporated as a non-profit-making company in 1894, absorbing assets from the Edinburgh Association for the University Education of Women and raising £5,835 through subscription.[28] The Principal of the university was Honorary President of the scheme, but its most energetic promoters were Miss Houldsworth, the President, Sara Mair, who served as Honorary Treasurer, and Louisa Stevenson, the Secretary. Louisa Stevenson headed the subscription list with a donation of £1,000, Miss Houldsworth contributed £731, £600 of which was to be put towards an endowment fund.[29] (When she died in 1909, Miss Houldsworth left a further £3,000 plus a gift of furniture to the hall.)[30] The subscription fund was supplemented by a further £2,000 obtained from the Pfeiffer trustees.[31] (Emily Pfeiffer, née Davis, was a poet and feminist who had died in 1890, leaving a substantial fund of money to be used for the promotion of the higher education of women. Her trustees allotted sums of £2,000 towards the foundation of three halls of residence for women in the 1890s: Masson Hall, Aberdare Hall in Cardiff, and University Hall in St Andrews.[32]) Masson Hall was thus enabled to open its doors free of debt in 1897. Although it was formally taken over by the university in 1919–20, continuity in management was ensured by many of the original executive committee retaining positions on the house committee responsible for the general administration of the hall.[33]

This was a fairly typical pattern. Sometimes the universities made some contribution towards the cost of the new halls. In Cardiff, for instance, the college Council agreed to guarantee the interest on any loan required to supplement public subscriptions raised by the Ladies' Hall Committee towards the cost of building a new hall of residence for women in 1891.[34] In St Andrews, it was agreed that the profits that the university had reaped through the operation of its separate examination scheme for women (the LLA) could be used to supplement the £2,000 from the Pfeiffer trustees and subscriptions raised for a new university hall for women.[35] In Aberystwyth, the college Council itself took responsibility for an appeal committee to raise funds for the building of Alexandra Hall. Here, the Pfeiffer grant and voluntary contributions had to be supplemented by a substantial bank loan, although Aberystwyth Town Council generously offered a free site for the new building.[36] In Birmingham, Neville Chamberlain chaired the building committee vested with responsibility for a new hall of residence for women and his wife chaired the appeals committee. Here, a series of complex negotiations with the Board of Education together with some creative accountancy allowed the university to secure a small grant from the government towards the building of University Hall, on condition that a proportion of the accommodation in the hall be reserved exclusively for teachers in training.[37]

The Board of Education was not normally prepared to make grants towards the building costs of halls or hostels associated with the universities.[38] There were many local variations in the pattern of financing these institutions, but reliance on local benefaction was a common theme. University Hall in Liverpool received constant injections of cash from Emma Holt, variously described as the hall's "fairy Godmother", "Patron Saint", and "ever constant friend".[39] The university paid tribute to her "princely" benevolence in awarding her an honorary degree in 1928.[40] Quite apart from a series of substantial gifts to the university itself, Emma Holt's endless subsidies to University Hall had made it possible for the hall committee to make a gift of the hall itself "representing an expenditure of well over £35,000 and capable of housing over 100 students" to the university in 1921, providing only that the Council took responsibility for its future maintenance.[41] As in the case of Masson Hall, the executive committee in Liverpool's University Hall stayed on, as a house committee. The university's hostels committee was thereafter responsible for finance, although

> Mrs Hugh Rathbone, with great understanding gave to Miss Holt as Chairman of the House Committee the sum of £1,000 which she said was to be kept for any special items, "which the Committee might not like to ask the men for".[42]

In Bristol, the acquisition of Clifton Hill House as a hall of residence for women students owed much to the initiative of May Staveley, the university's Tutor to Women Students. May Staveley was a friend of Margery Fry, the popular and successful Warden of Birmingham University's hall of residence for women. Inspired by Birmingham's success, a local committee was formed under the presidency of Lloyd Morgan, Bristol's Principal, and this committee began the usual appeal for funds.[43] In 1909 Clifton Hill House came onto the market, and undeterred by what might have looked like a daunting financial commitment, it was purchased by the committee. This act of "almost reckless initiative" was made possible by two anonymous donors "keenly interested in women's education".[44] The university Council contributed £2,000 on condition that the independent hall committee should furnish and maintain the hall for the next two years, when it was to hand the property over in its entirety to the university.[45] The principal benefactor of Clifton Hill House retained her anonymity, whereas elsewhere in the country halls might be named after their benefactors. This was the case in Nottingham, for instance, where the generosity of Lady Trent, wife of the chemist Jesse Boot, was commemorated in Florence Boot Hall, a purpose-built hall of residence for women students constructed in 1928.[46] While it is not, of course, possible to construct a detailed catalogue of the many hundreds of smaller bequests and donations that went into financing women's halls and hostels in university communities across the country, it is important to recognize the commitment made by the first generation of university women themselves. Not only did many of the wardens of these early hostels work unremunerated or for very low salaries indeed, but many of them subsidized these ventures further through personal gifts, or by willing property to them when they died. Both Isabel Bruce and Isabel Don, the first two Principals of Aberdare Hall in Cardiff, worked without salary.[47] Margery Fry, as Warden of University House in Birmingham in 1904, was paid £60 p.a.[48] On inheriting a substantial estate from her uncle in 1913 she relaid the lawn at University House:

> I feel that Uncle Joseph's money *is* after all . . . being spent on the turf, but not quite in the way he feared – it is the kind of interpretation to please a Greek oracle out of Herodotus, isn't it?[49]

We have seen in a previous chapter how both Rosa Morison and Eleanor Grove in College Hall, London, worked initially without salary, and how Rosa Morison's will entailed bequests of over £7,000 to the hall.[50] This pattern of generosity continued throughout the period with which this book is concerned.

Lady superintendents, principals and wardens

When the Ladies' Hall Committee in Cardiff drew up estimates for a hostel in 1884 it suggested that they could disregard the question of salary for any lady superintendent:

> as we think it may be possible that some Lady interested in the work of Women's Education might be willing to undertake it, (i.e. the position of Resident Superintendent) at any rate for the first year or two, without a salary. Her Board *would* have to be provided, but that the surplus will amply cover . . .[51]

The first Lady Superintendent, the Hon. Isabel Bruce, was Lady Aberdare's daughter. Educated women of private means might be attracted by positions of this kind, which offered scope for social and educational work in a quasi-domestic setting. For widows or unmarried daughters, such work was consistent with respectable, middle-class notions of femininity. The emphasis on the home-like qualities of the early hostels was important here. In Sheffield for instance, the establishment of St Peter's, or the Mason-Fenn Memorial Home in

1887, seems to have come about through a blend of traditional, lady-like philanthropy, clerical paternalism, and a recognition of new needs. The object of St Peter's, founded by the "many friends of the late rector of Tankersley", was to provide "a comfortable and wisely conducted home" for "the protection of young women studying at the Firth College, the Sheffield High School, and the Sheffield School of Art".[52] Princess Helena agreed to be patroness, and "to receive purses" in aid of the venture in Westminster Abbey in 1887. In 1907 this establishment was taken over by the university, with Mrs Mason-Fenn remaining on the executive committee of the hostel.[53]

St Peter's had a "Lady Principal" who was responsible for the "tone of the house" in the 1890s, but the prospectuses do not give her name. In part because the supply of university educated women was limited, at least before 1900, the earliest superintendents of women's hostels included many women without much formal education. Such women were often appointed on the strength of their family connections, either for reasons of respectability (any clerical connections conferred particular suitability here) or because their background indicated what we might now refer to as cultural capital. If they had an interest in the developing field of women's education, then so much the better. Helen Stephen, the first Warden of Ashburne House in Manchester and afterwards Warden of Alexandra Hall in Aberystwyth, was considered a particularly suitable choice: she was the daughter of a judge and baronet, and her sister Katharine was Vice-Principal and later Principal of Newnham.[54] Miss Frances Hughes, Lady Principal of Bangor's first hall of residence for women (which opened in 1886) was the sister of a prominent Wesleyan minister. At the time of her appointment it was accounted "something in her favour" that she was also the sister of Miss E. P. Hughes of the Cambridge Training College for Women.[55]

Hardly surprisingly, the hostel superintendents of the 1880s and 1890s were much occupied with social propriety and the whole business of defining what would be appropriate in the way of relationships between the sexes in the co-educational environment of the new universities. There is plenty of evidence of what Sara Delamont has termed "double conformity", that is, the need to reassure authorities and parents that women students could be ladies as well as scholars.[56]

Miss Carpenter, as first Lady Principal of the women's hostel in Aberystwyth, watched her young charges with unremitting vigilance.

A student in the 1880s remembered that:
> wherever we went after hours, except to church or chapel, the
> Lady Principal accompanied us: the wall of her sitting room was
> adorned with a careful synopsis of our classes . . . and on return
> from evening classes every student reported to the dragon in her
> den.[57]

On retiring from Alexandra Hall in 1905, Miss Carpenter suc-
cinctly explained the precept (*Festina Lente*) that had guided her
strategy as Lady Principal for 18 years:
> I can, of course, see many points where, had the wisdom of to-
> day been my guide, other action and other measures would have
> been adopted; but throughout those eighteen years I can hon-
> estly say that I have had but one purpose, to strengthen the posi-
> tion of our women in their efforts after the higher education and
> personal freedom that were denied to all women in my young
> days. And if, at times, I have seemed obstructive, it has only been
> because it was evident to me that too early an advance would
> lose them the whole field.[58]

The archives of Aberdare Hall in Cardiff in the 1880s show the
Warden and Ladies' Hall Committee, keen supporters of women's
education, much concerned with the prospect of women students going on "mixed pic-nics" or joining with the young men in producing
"theatrical entertainments". Lady Aberdare was prevailed upon to explain to the young women
> that these questions are considered by the Committee not as
> questions of student rights, but of what is right and expedient
> for the students.[59]

The vogue for picnicking caused consternation elsewhere in Wales,
since the energies of lady chaperons were rarely sufficient to match
the more exuberant activities of the young. Olive Marsh penned a
lively description of such an occasion to her fiancé in 1899:
> We started at 9 o'clock in most awful weather, but in about an
> hour it left off raining and gradually the weather improved so
> that on the whole we really had quite a fine day. The men waited
> for our brake about 1½ miles out, aren't they imps? But that is
> not the worst. About 8 miles out a little exchange went on and
> we did the rest of the journey men and women mixed. Isn't it
> daring after all that was said? I was afraid of my life that Miss C.
> [Miss Carpenter] would ask if we changed brakes but she hasn't

so far. We came back in the same way till within three miles of
Aber: I had no idea they would go to such lengths as that. . . . We
arrived home at 10 mins. to eleven. We have to be very guarded
in our descriptions of the affair. We had our photos taken 3
times altogether, once in the brake and twice out. One of the
couples got "lost in the woods" and were left out of the photo;
that will look suspicious won't it?[60]

"Sweet girl graduates" and the serpent: the Bangor controversy of 1892

The Welsh university colleges, sensitive as they were to the need for
respectability, received a hard lesson in the cost of allegations of impropriety from a scandal that erupted in Bangor in 1892. This affair,
which arose out of comments made about a student by the Lady Principal of the women's hostel, escalated out of all proportion to its origins, leading to a full inquiry by Senate, expressions of concern in
parliament, and a complex and expensive libel case in which Miss
Hughes was found innocent of charges that she had acted in a "base"
and "dishonourable" fashion.[61]

Frances Hughes, it will be recalled, was the sister of Miss E. P.
Hughes of the Cambridge Training College, and had been appointed
Lady Principal of the women's hall of residence in Bangor in 1886.
The hall was independent of, but recognized by, the University College. Frances Hughes appears to have been a rather inflexible person
of a narrowly respectable outlook who had already fallen foul of the
college registrar and forfeited the confidence of some of the well-
known women educationalists (Frances Buss, Sophie Bryant and
Dilys Davies) who had originally been associated with the hall.[62] The
scandal erupted in 1892, when Violet Osborn, a graduate student
who had formerly lived in the hall, learned that Miss Hughes had intimated to the mother of a younger student and friend of hers that Miss
Osborn was an unfit companion for her daughter. The allegations
were that Miss Osborn was "a woman of the world", possessed of "a
corrupt and impure mind", that she was untruthful, and that she had
shown "an indecorous behaviour towards men". Violet Osborn immediately complained to the college Senate, which held a thorough
inquiry into the matter in November 1892.

A limited number of copies of the 89 page report of the Senate inquiry, marked "private and confidential", were issued to carefully selected individuals.[63] Fifteen persons gave evidence, although Miss Hughes herself refused to attend any of the ten meetings that were held. The inquiry was extraordinarily detailed, involving scrutiny of Violet Osborn's encounters with men both in college (notably in connection with an incident involving the Professor of Philosophy, who was alleged to have "brushed her face" with some papers in a manner suggesting familiarity) and while staying with a friend during the vacation. Miss Hughes' suggestion that Violet had shown "indelicacy" in confiding "unpleasant family secrets", touching on the question of whether her deceased father had been unfaithful to her mother, or whether such allegations were the product of nervous "delusions" on the part of her mentally unstable mother, were also considered. Clearly many of the witnesses found this all very unsavoury, and a tone of chivalry is evident in the protestations of Violet's supporters. Dr Griffith Evans, for instance, protested that Violet's distress had earlier led her to confide something of her family troubles to Miss Hughes, and that this "would have elicited tender sympathy from any true woman", whereas Miss Hughes had abused the confidence with malicious intent.[64] The unanimous verdict was that "the charges were utterly without foundation", and that Miss Osborn's "conduct and character had been those of a refined and honourable woman".[65]

This may have satisfied Miss Osborn, but events did not stop there. The college Council's decision to withdraw the licence that it had previously granted to the hall of residence for women caused outrage among some of the directors. The controversy made headlines in the local and the national press, and following one article in which Miss Hughes was described as having acted in a "base" and "dishonourable" fashion, she brought a libel action against the newspaper's proprietors. The four-day trial at Chester Assizes in July 1893 brought acute embarrassment to the University College. Miss Hughes had strong supporters, who were inclined to see her as the victim of sectarian and political prejudice.[66] Six members of the college Council, including its chairman, resigned before the hearing. During the hearing, Reichel, the college Principal, was censured by the judge for having conducted an inquiry in which the college had in effect acted as accusers, judge and jury, "without the slightest attention to the ordinary form of judicial proceedings".[67] Miss Hughes was awarded £300 compensation.

All parties were hurt in the affair: Reichel subsequently recalled it as having "threatened to wreck the women's side in the University College of North Wales altogether".[68] Violet Osborn and Frances Hughes felt that they had experienced loss of character. Both of them, apparently, sought solace in marriage: Miss Osborn to E. V. Arnold, Professor of Classics and one of her staunchest academic defenders at the time of the inquiry; Miss Hughes to an Anglican prebendary.[69] Keri Evans, the Professor of Philosophy, faced censure by Senate for not having acted "with that due discretion and reserve which ought to characterize the conduct of a Professor in his relation to women students", and felt obliged to resign shortly afterwards.[70] Events had been so acrimonious that at one point the professors were on the verge of leaving *en bloc*. J. Gwynn Williams, Bangor's historian, suggests that Reichel, as college Principal, was deeply scarred by the episode: "Thereafter, he tended to become rigid in disciplinary matters, particularly when they involved relations between the sexes".[71] Many observers saw the incident as underlining the need for universities to assume more direct control over halls of residence and their wardens and principals. When Bangor's new hall of residence was opened in 1897, its "Lady Principal", Miss Mary Maude, was carefully chosen: she was the niece of a local vicar, an ex-student of the college, and very well known in the area. As Warden of Women Students, moreover, she was an employee of the University College.[72] According to Reichel, "she did for Bangor much what Miss Clough did for Newnham", and when she died in 1926, he expressed his gratitude to her for having "built up the women's side of the College anew".[73]

Lady wardens: trials and tribulations

Undoubtedly many of those responsible for women students in the new hostels were nonplussed by the demands of their charges, and with few role-models and precedents to guide them, they were often uncertain how best to respond. Louisa Lumsden, appointed Warden of the new hall of residence for women students in St Andrews, had had experience of college life as one of the pioneer students of Girton, Cambridge, and she had also been headmistress of a girls' school.[74]

Even these experiences failed to protect her from antagonizing some of the older women students in St Andrews, with whom she quickly came into conflict.[75] Her vision of a ladylike, academic community does not seem to have recommended itself to those women students who enjoyed a less supervised lifestyle in the lodgings available in the town. The conflict also had a class dimension: it was comparatively expensive to live in hall, and students in the town were reluctant to subsidize the cost of those facilities that Lumsden envisaged as integral to college life.[76] There were similar conflicts in Glasgow, where the executive committee of Queen Margaret Hall met with opposition from women students who wanted to take responsibility for formulating their own rules. Here, an early tussle erupted in 1902 over what was to prove one of the perennial sources of conflict in women's halls of residence through the period: the question of rules relating to the entertaining of male visitors.[77] Mrs Riddoch, the secretary of the house committee in Queen Margaret College, wrote anxiously to other wardens inquiring about their practice in this respect. Both Frances Melville (who had replaced Louisa Lumsden in St Andrews), and Frances Simson in Masson Hall, Edinburgh, were quick to reassure her that only fathers and brothers were allowed in private rooms: other gentlemen visitors automatically confined their visits to the public sitting rooms.[78] Miss Simson insisted that:

> If any resident here were not content with the permission to entertain her friends in one of the public rooms, I should think she was rather too "emancipated" a young woman to be a desirable inmate of a Hall, and should welcome her departure.[79]

This practice of writing round to other wardens for information and reassurance continued throughout the period. Many such examples survive in archives around the country, particularly up until the Second World War.[80] After 1942 the foundation of an Association of Principals, Wardens and Advisers of University Women Students provided a more regular forum for communication and the pooling of experience.[81]

In 1902 Queen Margaret Hall was little more than an extended household in Bute Gardens.[82] As hostels increased in size they changed in character, and any model of a cultured bourgeois household became less appropriate to their functioning. Some of the early lady principals found it difficult to cope with the transition. Helen Stephen, for instance, suffered greatly after leaving Ashburne House in Manchester for Alexandra Hall in Aberystwyth. Even in Manchester, some of the students had found her rather aloof. Alison Uttley recalled a lack of sympathy towards students from poorer homes for whom stringent economies were necessary.[83] Ashburne House had originally accommodated nine students, although numbers were to grow rapidly. Alexandra Hall, originally designed to accommodate 110 students, and after the completion of the North Wing in 1898 able to accommodate 200, was obviously on an entirely different scale.[84] Miss Stephen had been appointed as successor to Miss Carpenter in Aberystwyth because she was seen as "a highly educated and widely cultured woman" of distinguished family connection who, it was felt, would "raise the tone" of Alexandra Hall. But her upper-middle-class Englishness did not go down at all well with the Welsh girls, and relationships in the hall steadily deteriorated.[85] The students were led in their resistance to Miss Stephen by Olive Wheeler, described as "a spirited young woman of marked ability",[86] who in later life went on to become Professor of Education in University College, Cardiff, and a Dame of the British Empire. In 1907, simmering dissatisfaction boiled up in a full-scale student revolt, the students submitting a long catalogue of complaints about food and service in hall to Senate and the college Council, together with the assertion that the Warden was demonstrably out of sympathy with their concerns. Miss Stephen suffered a breakdown in health shortly afterward, and the following year, on medical advice, she resigned.[87]

The task of running these new halls of residence was indeed becoming ever more complex, requiring a wide variety of social and practical skills. The work of furnishing, employing domestic servants, and physical maintenance alone could prove formidable, as surviving accounts of expenditure and purchases demonstrate.[88] Housekeepers and bursars were increasingly likely to be appointed in the larger halls, to relieve wardens of some of their duties, but this was not always the case, and many principals struggled with a daunting array of responsibilities. Reflecting on the qualities that Mrs Fewings, successor to Miss Stephen in Alexandra Hall, might be expected to bring to her work as warden, one writer mused:

> A merely academic mind, a practical domestic one, an uncompromising feminist – however valuable each might be in relation to certain needs – each is too limited for the many-sided activity

the post demands. Yet something of each, those who know her best know to be blended in our new warden. Love of learning, capacity for facing hygienic, domestic, administrative, financial problems, keen interest in movements for women's improvement – and consequent responsibility and enfranchisement – are all characteristic of her; and a happy sense of humour and love of participation in kindly fun promise pleasant days for the future of Alexandra Hall.[89]

In the same year (1908–9), Frances Melville, who was vacating the wardenship of University Hall, St Andrews, to be Mistress of Queen Margaret College in Glasgow, compiled a memorandum "On the Duties of the Warden of University Hall" for the University Court in St Andrews. Intended as a guide for those appointing a new Warden, the memorandum (only slightly tongue-in-cheek) details an extraordinary catalogue of responsibilities for her successor.[90] (See Appendix.)

Some women rose to the challenge. After 1900, many of the new generation of university educated women saw the wardenship of university hostels and halls of residence as a valuable career opening, offering scope for their talents, qualifications and experience. Frances Melville was one such woman.[91] Several of the women who had studied at Somerville College Oxford in the 1880s and 1890s went on to become wardens. Ethel Hurlbatt, Hilda Oakeley, Phoebe Sheavyn, May Staveley and Margery Fry were all ex-Somervillians. As the highly successful and popular Warden of University House, Birmingham, between 1904 and 1914, Fry's work demands special scrutiny: she acted as an inspiration for women involved in similar work elsewhere. Through this work in Birmingham, her later position on the University Grants Committee, and her principalship of Somerville, she exerted considerable influence over the shape of provision for women in universities across the country before 1939.

A sense of community: Margery Fry in Birmingham

Fry accepted the wardenship of what was originally an unprepossessing house, 215, Hagley Road, Birmingham, in 1904, at what she admitted was a "*very* meagre" salary of £60 p.a. Her first impressions were bleak:

very depressing it looked, with its crumbling plaster and rank little back garden. . . . The dining room was a mixture of gory wallpaper and embossed chocolate dado and the hall resplendent in sky blue and cream set off with stained glass.[92]

She wryly recalled the warning received from one of her male cousins, who had evidently suggested that "to housekeep over a hencoop in a provincial suburban villa" was "just like a Fry with a swelled conscience".[93] The contrast with Somerville was poignant:

We seemed a very haphazard set of people when at last we actually gathered at the beginning of term, and to me, used to the College life at Oxford, it seemed sometimes at first almost hopeless to look for the growth of that community feeling which was so conspicuous by its absence.[94]

A sense of community nonetheless began to emerge:

I think the first thing we really all, or several of us, did together was on a bitter Saturday afternoon when we "made" Sir Oliver Lodge in snow in the back garden.[95]

Helen Wodehouse, as lecturer in philosophy, and Rose Sidgwick, who was appointed lecturer in history, came to live in the hostel. Sir Oliver Lodge (in the flesh) was a frequent visitor, who came to read plays to the residents. Fry encouraged a variety of dramatic productions, ranging from *Andromache* and *Scenes from Jane Austen* through to *Alice In Wonderland* and a short play entitled *The Quacks*, written by Miss Sidgwick, Miss Wodehouse and Miss Fry. Helen Wodehouse, who improvised her part, starred as Apollo, and the story featured four nymphs who were turned into ducks for daring to advise the god. There was also a suffragette play, produced by the staff.[96] Fry's talents as a producer so impressed the Principal and Birmingham's professors that she was persuaded to co-produce the university play for a number of years.[97] She also made use of drama to foster camaraderie among the domestic staff: one vacation, when the students had left University House, she

kept the servants from moping by getting out the old costumes and scenery and producing *The rose and the ring*, performed by the students a year earlier. Miss Fry herself took part, and the show was put on at a Settlement social.[98]

Fry's talent for social leadership was matched by her enthusiasm for the practical work involved in financing, planning and supervising the building of a new hall of residence for women in Birmingham. She set about this work thoroughly, learning what she could of similar ventures in Liverpool and Manchester, and discussing the aesthetics of décor and architectural details with her brother, Roger Fry. The new University House, designed to accommodate 50 women, opened in Edgbaston in 1908:

> On the last Sunday evening at Hagley Road the whole company carried a picnic supper to the new hostel. They drank a toast to the new home in chipped cups. Then with shouts of triumph they smashed these symbols of penury against the new walls.[99]

Fry's vision was a generous one. Her biographer emphasizes her belief that women should be taught "not to 'pinch' (a word which in the Fry vocabulary meant the practice of frugality, not theft)".[100] She had insisted on large windows and on spacious, well proportioned rooms.

This same generosity of vision underlay Fry's remarkable success in relating to both students and domestic staff. Her regime was a liberal one: as few rules as possible, together with the expectation that girls would show the same consideration and courtesy towards the staff that they would show towards their parents. She was never patronizing, always reasonable, and many of her practices, such as that of allowing the girls to invite men friends to dances in hall, were considered rather advanced at the time.[101] Unlike her contemporary Helen Stephen, Fry showed considerable sensitivity to the needs of girls from poorer homes, many of them burdened by heavy work and responsibility. She believed it "more useful to evoke youthful high spirits than to suppress them", an attitude reflected in a number of anecdotes that survive from these years, such as the time when

> she threw everyone into confusion by appearing as a Spanish parent, veiled in black lace, and demanding to see the Warden, turning back, while a distinguished scholar waited in her room, to finish a set of tennis, convinced when the maid summoned her to meet "Dr Fraud" that someone had arranged a retaliatory leg-pull.[102]

Fry's success as a warden stemmed in part from qualities of temperament and personal charisma, and her influence as a role-model was directly acknowledged by contemporaries such as Marjorie Rackstraw, one of her deputies in University House who went on, as we have seen, to a highly successful career as Warden of Masson Hall, Edinburgh, and Tutor to Women Students in the university as a whole. May Staveley, a close friend of Fry's in Somerville, was also inspired by her example, as was Mrs Redman King, Warden of Leeds University's Weetwood Hall. Brenda Carey, in her obituary of Mrs King, acknowledged the link:

> Mrs King, in sympathy with the pioneer work of Margery Fry on behalf of residence, treated her students as adults: she gave them as much freedom as was possible but in return she expected them to behave in a responsible manner.[103]

But important as these personal qualities undoubtedly were, Fry's example went further by suggesting a vision of community life, and an important ideal of what universities might strive to provide in the way of facilities for their women students in the first instance, but ultimately for the student population as a whole.

Families, boarding houses or colleges? Models of community life

It has been suggested that the earliest hostels, accommodating only a handful of students, were often run on domestic or quasi-familial lines. The idea of providing a substitute home for girls whose studies necessitated their leaving their own homes and families strongly influenced the shape of much of the early provision. M. W. Hughes, compiling a history of Ashburne Hall in Manchester, tells us that Mrs Worthington, the hall's benefactor,

> from the first set the tradition, which has always been followed, that Ashburne should be a home, not a college, and that the instruction of students should be entirely centred in the University.[104]

Numbers increased, but efforts to preserve a family atmosphere were sustained: partly formally, through the institution of separate sub-hostels and wings, and partly informally, through the encouragement of family groups among the residents. Ashburne continued to represent its former students as one big, extended family, referring to the "daughters" of the hall.[105]

Some of these tendencies – particularly the grouping of students into families within the hall – were common elsewhere, but the scale of expansion in most places necessitated new models. Another aspect of the vision of some of the early benefactors, that of establishing provincial equivalents to the Oxbridge women's colleges, has already been considered. However, the obstacles in the way of achieving this collegiate vision were many. In the first place, although the Oxbridge women's colleges were undoubtedly poor relative to their male equivalents, their resources still exceeded those generally available to wardens in the civic universities. Secondly, as the above quotation relating to Ashburne Hall reminds us, the provincial halls of residence *were* in the main simply residential: they did not provide teaching. St Mary's College in Durham, and Queen Margaret College in Glasgow, were exceptions, but in Glasgow, the college, as distinct from the associated venture, Queen Margaret Hall, did not provide residence. Fry's appointment in Birmingham specified her functions as the superintendence of housekeeping and the maintenance of discipline, and this

> separation of discipline from academic responsibility had seemed to set the regime of the Hostel far below the true collegiate life she had known at Somerville.[106]

But the influence of Somerville remained strong, and even in the domestic setting of Hagley Road, Fry's rejection of the family model – "shelter from their own families is often what they need most of all" – was unequivocal.[107]

Conditions more favourable to the development of a collegiate atmosphere developed where female members of the academic staff took up residence in hall alongside students. This was an important factor in Birmingham, Manchester and elsewhere. Sometimes, particularly in the early years when women academics were thin on the ground, women teaching in local schools or working as independent researchers would come to live in the halls associated with universities. Daisy McAlpine (née Scott), a very early student resident of University Hall, Liverpool, remembered a number of what she had then perceived as elderly ladies as co-residents:

> They were beings from the older universities come to use Liverpool's wonderful new laboratories to engage in scientific research, such as Harriet Chick; or mistresses in local schools seeking a congenial home, as Anne Loveday, or people with astonishing titles, as Caroline Graveson, Mistress of Method.[108]

In Manchester, Phoebe Sheavyn persuaded the authorities to allow university lecturers to live in Ashburne Hall

> so that the students might have the benefit of daily contact with minds of distinction in various departments of scholarship not necessarily their own.[109]

The presence of Senior Residents, together with their involvement in social activities, was a crucial source of support to wardens in these years, many of whom worked energetically to foster intellectual discourse and cultural activities among the students. "High Table" conversation could not be sustained without a supporting cast.

Efforts made by wardens in this respect were not always welcomed by students. Accounts of the tribulations endured by those singled out to converse with the warden at dinner are legion.[110] But equally, the cultural stimulus provided by wardens such as Fry, Mrs Hope Hogg in Manchester (who kept a cabinet of reproductions for picture showings to students on Sunday afternoons), or Miss Buller and Miss Chapman in Liverpool, were remembered by many with great affection.[111] E. L. Ellis, compiling a history of Alexandra Hall, Aberystwyth, attributed the student revolt of 1907 to the existence of two different concepts of residential provision:

> The so-called Alexandra Hall "revolt" of 1907 has an interest that goes beyond questions of the number and quality of eggs provided for breakfast. The fact is that two different conceptions of the Hall were at issue. Miss Stephen had been imported to make it a collegiate hall where academic values were given considerably greater prominence than hitherto. The students seemed to prefer to have a Warden, as Rendel said, who was "little more than a lodging house-keeper".[112]

However, it seems more than likely that Miss Stephen's personality, together with what the students perceived as her patronizing middle-class manner towards them, was the real bone of contention. Wardens like Fry, Hope-Hogg and Buller achieved considerable success in fostering a more academic and collegiate ethos, not least because they avoided talking down to students and treated them as adults.

Relationships between students and the hall authorities were particularly likely to deteriorate where the former felt that they were being treated like schoolchildren, and where the atmosphere in hall was reminiscent of a boarding school. Some of the early wardens and women tutors had previously worked as mistresses or headmistresses in girls' schools, and the situation was not uncommon. Muriel Hood (née Dodds), a Durham University lecturer who lived for a few years in St Mary's College, Durham, before the Second World War, recorded that:

> What impressed me most when I came to St Mary's College was

that the atmosphere was that of a boarding school rather than that of a University College . . . any breach of discipline, personal untidiness, noisiness or bad manners, meant a summons to the Principal's study, from which the delinquent frequently emerged in tears. A German student, here for a year, was gated for a week after having been seen cycling in the College wearing a gown and smoking a cigarette. . . .

Yes . . . quite a strict boarding school, which probably did a lot for the girls' manners, savoir-faire, and possibly, characters. But I could have wished for more intellectual adventure.[113]

This is interesting because St Mary's, originally the women's hostel in Durham, had been granted full college status in 1920.[114] Miss Donaldson, as Principal, held a university lectureship in classics. A domestic bursar shouldered the burden of household administration, leaving Miss Donaldson and a senior tutor to concentrate on their responsibilities of supervising the students' academic work.

If students were wary of arrangements less suggestive of a college than of a boarding school, then the parallel fear in the minds of many wardens and principals was that the failure to sustain any collegiate vision would reduce their establishments to the level of the boarding house, with their own role degenerating to the level of the lodging-house keeper. This was the vision deprecated by Rendel in Aberystwyth in 1907, and it haunted those authorities most aware of their duties *in loco parentis*, particularly against a background of student demands for more autonomy, and less interference in their personal lives, in the 1920s and 1930s.

Students or schoolgirls?

The archives that survive from halls of residence in this period bear witness to some troubled times. In Masson Hall, Edinburgh, for instance, student complaints about food, and discontent over regulations relating to staying out late at night, brought confrontation in 1920 between the students' house committee and Miss Bell, the Warden.[115] The authorities took peremptory action. Two students who had stayed out late without permission were asked to leave, and it was judged that since "it was evident that the House Committee did not understand its duties", it should be dissolved forthwith.[116] Agnes Bell, whose previous work had included managing a Women's Army Auxiliary Corps hostel, together with an officer's mess, followed by a spell as housekeeper in a boarding school, forfeited the confidence of many of the Masson Hall residents who submitted a petition to the house committee calling upon them to ask the Warden to resign.[117] This produced consternation. In the committee's view it "showed an entire absence of all sense of discipline" and it was suggested that all those who had signed the petition should be asked to leave the hall. It was conceded that some of the culprits "might not be fully conscious of the gravity of their actions", and the committee indicated their preparedness to reconsider the expulsion edict if the residents promised to observe the rules. A letter to this effect was sent to all those involved; copies of the letter were also mailed to the students' parents and guardians.[118]

The Masson Hall committee minutes for November 1920 report the illness of Miss Bell, and we learn that shortly after these events "by Doctor's orders, she left the Hall without terminating her engagement".[119] A temporary warden was found in the person of a Miss Wilson, but doctor's orders similarly prescribed Miss Wilson's resignation in March 1921.[120] In June, Miss Bailey was appointed Warden, chosen by the committee out of 19 applicants for the post. Disaster soon struck. It is difficult to know exactly what happened since several pages have been excised from the minutes at this point (13 March to 8 May 1922).[121] A rewritten account refers to a "regrettable incident" in which two residents, returning to hall at 2.30 am, allegedly found that their pass key failed to operate; a young man accompanying them had climbed into hall through a lavatory window and opened the door from the inside. This potentially scandalous incident unnerved the authorities and may well have influenced Sara Mair's decision to resign from the house committee in April 1922: Mair had been a founder member and important figure in the life of the hall.

Flora Masson, Mair's friend and associate on the committee, expressed some unease over the Warden's ability to handle students, but Miss Bailey stayed in post until yet another scandal erupted, in 1924.[122] The minutes of a special meeting held on 2 June 1924 indicate an air of urgency, in part, because of the presence of the university secretary, who "attended to advise". It had emerged that Miss Addison, one of the residents of Masson Hall, who had been granted leave of absence ostensibly in order to visit her sick father in Forfar, had actually spent the night in an hotel in St Andrews. Miss Addison was asked to leave, and the committee was clearly relieved to accept the Warden's resignation at the same time. The post was advertised yet again,[123] but this time the committee appointed someone who would prove particularly successful in the work. Marjorie Rackstraw, who had worked alongside Fry in Birmingham, was a highly intelligent woman whose new, professional attitude to the work of warden may perhaps be seen in her insistence on an adequate salary, together with membership of the universities' superannuation scheme (FSSU).[124] She was sensitive to the needs of students and possessed the requisite social skills. A new era of harmony was inaugurated in the internal relationships of Masson Hall, which flourished as a community throughout Rackstraw's term of wardenship (1925–37).

Harmony was less in evidence in some of the halls associated with the Welsh university colleges in the 1920s and 1930s. In Aberystwyth, Mrs Guthkelch, Warden of Alexandra Hall, engaged in constant wrangles with student residents over questions of discipline, sometimes of a particularly petty kind. Mrs Guthkelch was a stickler for dress codes, and her line on hats scarcely seems calculated to have capitalized on any nascent sense of community responsibility among the girls. Without any sense of absurdity Mrs Guthkelch confided to her fellow warden Miss Macgregor that:

> After much painful thought I decided that the best treatment of the hat question was to appeal to the loyalty of the whole Hall. I thanked those who had been faithful to the agreement – and emphasized that they must try to give as well as to take, if living in this community meant anything to them. I also, with complete and foolhardy rashness, told them of my hatred of punishment.[125]

Mrs Guthkelch issued a formal proclamation about dress codes in April 1926. No student was to wear a gym tunic outside without a mackintosh; heads should be covered at (almost) all times. "I have ruled that . . . students may go without a hat only (a) on the front and (b) between College and Galloway's shop by way of King Street", she declared magisterially.[126]

Relationships between Mrs Guthkelch and the residents of Alexandra Hall deteriorated in the early 1930s. A decline in the numbers of students in residence brought hall finances to the edge of deficit and there were attempts to economize on food, which merely exacerbated student dissatisfaction. In February 1933, all 134 students in residence signed a petition to Senate complaining about inadequate food, excessive fees, and the alleged high-handed and arbitrary administration of Mrs Guthkelch, who was accused of ignoring student opinion on all of these issues. But student opinion seems to have gone on being ignored: Mrs Guthkelch recorded with some relish that the dissidents received "crushing snubs" from the authorities on this occasion.[127]

The embattled Mrs Guthkelch found a sympathetic ear in North Wales: she poured out her troubles to Muriel Orlidge Davis, Warden of the women's hall of residence in Bangor, who herself confessed to having experienced "a good deal of bother with the Bolshie Element" in hall.[128] Miss Davis blistered with resentment over the activities of Bangor's female Vice-President of the Student Representative Committee, whom she dismissed as "a very stupid and disgruntled woman", who "made it her business to stir up trouble" and for whom "any attempt at culture or refinement" in hall life was tantamount to a "waste of time":

> Her idea is that the Hostels are to be run as cheap hotels – and I do not think that she has an idea of what a woman's college can be, or should be.[129]

Miss Davis confessed that she had refused to allow this student a room in the main block of buildings in the hall. One passage in the correspondence shows her close to exploding with resentment:

> I think the tendency of the female undergraduate of today is to grumble very loudly at what she is getting at the public expense. The modern provincial university young woman wants a latch-key, a continuous supply of hot water, and hot meals at any hour of the day, plus the pleasure of making a butt of her female supervisors (but with the expectation of their ready help if she gets into money or social difficulties) and all this "free, gratis and for nothing!"
>
> Of course one wants to see them all happy and comfortable; and the original aim of Hostels was to free them from domestic cares and anxieties in order that they might work; and also that by maintaining a decent standard of home life, they might be prevented from sinking into that squalor and apathy which so easily besets literary and scholastic females; i.e. the results of no

baths and tinned salmon. Your aim is to turn out healthy, pre-
sentable young women, of blameless reputation; and if you have
any who wish to be anything else, the sooner you get rid of them
the better![130]

As will have become abundantly clear from the discussion so far, it
is by no means easy to generalize about student experiences of hall life
either across the country, or throughout the period with which this
book is concerned. There is certainly no shortage of evidence. University archives contain richly relevant material. Many students have left
detailed accounts of their experiences of residence; in letters home, in
journals and autobiographies, in student publications and in the
newsletters and many anniversary histories produced under the auspices of ex-student and old-girl associations of the halls themselves.
Social experiences varied widely. Louisa Martindale's recollections of
life in College Hall under Miss Grove and Miss Morison in turn-of-
the-century London highlight a colourful social milieu in which
women from very varied social backgrounds were brought together
by little more than the common experience of studying for various examinations in London. Martindale herself was studying medicine. She
recalled that:

In addition to the medical students there were many art students
and even a law student, whose sister, Nina, afterwards became
the Duchess of Hamilton; as a result we did not talk much shop.
There was a very fat Russian countess whom we called Bobs, a
near relation of the Czar. She owned huge estates in Russia and
wanted to qualify so that she could doctor her peasants. In the
meantime she had a terrible habit of walking along to the school
with her anatomy bones sticking out of her pockets. There was
the little Dutch baroness (Baroness de Constant Rebecque),
whom we called "Bones", whose sister was maid of honour to
the Queen of Holland; she was studying art but could paint
nothing but horses. There were several missionary students and
then there was dear Rukhmabai. She was a very charming In-
dian who had been married at the age of twelve but, aided and
abetted by her father, who held advanced views, had refused to
live with her husband. Professor Max Müller and Mrs Eva
Maclaren had befriended her and brought her to England.
Many years later, when I visited her in India, she had just done
her first operation, for which she had received four annas. Then

there was Miss Aldrich Blake who had returned to College Hall to take her M. S. degree – she was the first woman to get it – and her friend, an art student, who one day astonished us all by coming back from being presented at court looking perfectly lovely in her feathers and train.[131]

The cosmopolitan and social mix were unusual. Martindale's experiences were a world apart from those of Olive Marsh, for instance, in Alexandra Hall in Aberystwyth around the same time. As we have seen, Marsh's letters to her fiancé are packed with details of disciplinary regulations and suggest a boarding-school regime. Her recounting of one incident, on 20 October 1898 conveys the ethos well:

You will remember I told you about that girl who was encored at the concert and sang for an encore, "I want yer my honey, yes I do". Well, I was told that Miss Carpenter got to hear of it, and told her she was not fit to sing at the concert again until she had more sense. Last Thursday the Principal of the college, Mr.Roberts, caught her talking after hours to some fellows on the back stairs and on Friday she was caught talking to a fellow out of one of the windows of our Hall. Well, on Saturday her mother was sent for and she was expelled. She is a clergyman's daughter, and well-off; isn't it dreadful? All our girls are full of it.[132]

"Calling out of windows" was a heinous crime for women students in Alexandra Hall, a regulation that provoked a good deal of derision from the men. A poet in the student magazine *The Dragon* in 1911 mused accordingly:

Three women stus. in the Prom
A hostel window high
A whistle from the Prom
The window up doth fly.
Another whistle shrill
A fair hand on the sill
One whistle more they gave
A handkerchief doth wave
High! High! o'erhead it flutters
How! How! each man then utters
O, lady stu. how brave!
O, Breach of Rules how grave![133]

There was a tendency towards more social homogeneity in halls of

119

residence as numbers increased, and as the route through higher education became more established for girls in their late teens from middle and lower-middle class homes. Fees for residence became increasingly standardized: a common practice in the early years had been to offer various grades of accommodation, ranging from comparatively expensive and spacious single rooms down to cheaper cubicles surrounded by curtains in dormitories. These latter were rarely popular and many halls ceased providing them. The custom of offering the better rooms to students in their third year, or to those who had spent longest in residence, tended to replace the earlier system of differential fees in most places. The newer purpose-built halls of residence, in any case, tended to offer more uniform accommodation. The individual study-bedroom became standard form in this period, although Florence Boot Hall, newly constructed in Nottingham, offered rather more de luxe accommodation with additional dressing rooms.

Subtle class distinctions remained in some systems of residence. Elspeth Huxley, studying in Reading in the 1920s, recalled a social pecking order among students that was reflected in the residential provision:

> to be an "agri" was all right, and so was a "horti"; pure scientists, historians and classicists occupied a middle range, and at the bottom, I regret to say, came the future teachers.... "Edu's" tended to cluster together looking earnest, pallid (probably from malnutrition) and even more drearily dressed than the rest of us; to dodge coffees in the Buttery because twopence was beyond their means, and, if girls, to live at a remote hall called St George's that no-one else ever visited. The smart hall was St Andrews, just as among the men it was Wantage, with St Patrick's in second place.[134]

But as Huxley herself recognized, this was in the years when education students followed the old two-year diploma course, rather than taking the full degree. Cintra Lodge, originally a hostel for these teachers-in-training in Reading, had just been incorporated into St George's, and this had affected its reputation.[135] Once the newer, consecutive pattern of teacher training became established, these older distinctions and prejudices faded.

A woman's space? Students, domestic staff and the privileges of hall life

Martha Vicinus, exploring the history of the separate women's colleges in Oxford, Cambridge and London between 1850 and 1920, has emphasized the importance of these institutions in providing "a special women's space", in which "duty to self and community took precedence over all outside obligations".[136] Intellectual adventure, in the context of unusual freedom from domestic and family ties, rendered college "a glorious interlude" in many women's lives.[137] This assessment would certainly substantiate the claims made by those advocates of residential college life for women whose views were discussed at the beginning of this chapter. But to what extent can the residential hostels provided in the civic universities be said to have matched the achievement of the Oxbridge women's colleges, or of Bedford, Royal Holloway and Westfield? We have seen that these halls of residence were primarily residential institutions, and that unlike academic colleges in the full sense, their connections with teaching were somewhat tangential. Nonetheless, they undoubtedly offered freedom from the domestic obligations that would normally accrue to women.

The larger halls were well supplied with domestic staff. Accommodation in Ashburne Hall by 1932 included a whole wing of rooms for maids.[138] An ex-resident of Liverpool's University Hall remembered "the pink or blue ginghamed figures of innumerable maids" in the 1920s.[139] Alexandra Hall in Aberystwyth boasted one maid to every two students around 1900, and we may recall Olive Marsh's image of 20 waitresses standing by the table at dinner.[140] The history of these servants, their relationships with the women students and the hall authorities, together with their conditions of service, has yet to be written. Anne McCullough, head parlourmaid at Liverpool's University Hall, retired in 1939 after more than 25 years of service and such stories of long periods of unbroken employment were very common.[141] As early as 1898 Miss Carpenter inaugurated a "Blue-Ribbon Day" for servants in Alexandra Hall. On this occasion maids who had completed ten years of service were presented with "prettily carved wardrobes in walnut", together with keys hanging from "the blue ribbons of their profession".[142] A detail enshrined in the history of Liverpool's Hall is the memory of Margaret, one of the parlourmaids who "bor-

121

rowed and read learned books" from the students.[143] Maids were not just attentive to students' needs; they might also serve a supervisory function. There are stories of those who would adopt a severe attitude towards students who were still in bed when the maid knocked with hot water for the morning's ablutions.[144] Mrs Guthkelch's "Rules for Maids" in the 1930s makes this quasi-disciplinary potential quite clear. When visitors called for students, it was incumbent on the hall room maid to have the visitors' book signed first by the Warden or her deputy, *before* contacting the student, and once the front door had been locked, early in the evening, the maids were obliged to ensure that no unauthorized student slipped out.[145] Students were not always appreciative of such vigilance, and there could be undertones of class resentment. The first issue of *The Dolphin*, the magazine of University House, Birmingham, which appeared in 1914, featured doggerel about servants' intrusiveness:

I'm Mrs Briggs, charwoman, wot cleans the 'ostel floors,

An' I always know the latest noos, by listening at the doors.[146]

In a speech following the opening of Alexandra Hall in 1896, Mr Edward Davies had expressed delight in the new opportunities for women: he hoped that the hostel would constitute a breath of "intellectual ozone" for girls "to correspond with the ozone of the sea".[147] It is hard to associate Mrs Guthkelch's regime with any heady whiff of "intellectual ozone". There were aspects of hall life in many universities well into the 1930s, which retained the imprint of the boarding school. This was not always attributable to wardens: as we have seen, some of the most successful wardens sought to operate with a minimum of rules and regulations in order to foster independence and social responsibility among the students. But the minute books of student committees themselves, recording the elections of "Senior Students", "Complaints Monitors" and "Silence Prefects", with their litanies of protest against the "bagging of seats" at table, and deprecations of "marmalade stodge", can be strongly suggestive of school life.[148] The evolution of a feminine variant of student culture, with cocoa parties, "starvers", and ritualized raidings and rumplings of other students' rooms, is apparent in this period.[149]

An aversion to the more regimented aspects of hostel existence, disdain for the more juvenile forms of social activity it sometimes fostered, or simply the question of finance, might lead some women to seek accommodation outside the halls.[150] However, it is important to note that this was not always an option. All women students not living with their families in Aberystwyth, Liverpool or Cardiff were, at various times, *required* to live in hall. This undoubtedly caused resentment. In Cardiff, for instance, a group of women medical students protested in 1919 to the college Senate that they did not want to live in Aberdare Hall. Senate appointed a committee to consider their case.[151] The women on this committee, including Kate Hurlbatt, Warden of Aberdare Hall, were not unsympathetic to the students' viewpoint. They conceded that lodgings were cheaper than accommodation in hall and could appreciate the medical women's demand to be allowed the same freedom in their choice of accommodation as the men. "As old college students" themselves, they suggested:

> We understand and sympathise with the desire that there should be no unfavourable distinction between men and women, but we think that the right way to view this particular differentiation is that the women in this College are favoured beyond the men in having the opportunity of a Hostel life, an opportunity which should be extended to men students.[152]

It was probable, they nevertheless conceded,

> that after several years of residence, most students have learned nearly all that is to be learned by Hostel life, and that some may even profit by a life of greater independence.[153]

The committee recommended that women over the age of 21 should be allowed the option of approved lodgings, as an alternative to compulsory residence in Aberdare Hall.

Notwithstanding all of the foregoing reservations, it is apparent that the halls of residence for female students did constitute an important "women's space" in universities, and that at their best they nourished a vigorous social and community life. The regular reports of hall activities in student magazines across the country provide evidence of this. Several of the halls produced their own magazines, the early editions of which were sometimes handwritten and lovingly decorated and coloured. The earliest issues of Ashburne Hall's *Yggdrasill* and of University Hall Liverpool's *The Phoenix* were hand-produced in this way.[154] Photograph albums commemorate year groups and "families" of students, theatrical productions, outings and anniversary dinners. Further evidence of the extent to which hall communities nurtured lifelong friendships exists in the newsletters and records of the ex-student and old-girl networks. Most halls held annual reunions, increasingly under the auspices of formally constituted old student associations. These associations were frequently active in fundraising for hall extensions and improvements, or in attempts to provide bursaries for students in need. The committee minutes of Clifton Hill House, Bristol, record a number of anonymous individual gifts from old students,

> such as the £10 sent during the hard times of 1931–2 "to help any student in need, since I want others to have the help that I had at CHH"; or the cheque sent as "a very small token of appreciation for all that the Hall – in a very comprehensive sense – meant for me".[155]

Evidence of a desire to acknowledge and somehow to repay the privilege of having been a student in hall is common. Alison Uttley, whose experiences of Ashburne Hall improved markedly once Helen Stephen had been replaced as Warden by Hilda Oakeley in 1905, experienced a lasting affection and gratitude.[156] She bequeathed a third of the future income from her literary property, after her son's death, to Ashburne Hall, for students in need. An Alison Uttley Bursary was established at Ashburne in 1984.[157] Affectionate memories abound, and for many women in the civic universities, life in the hall of residence was precisely what made the memory of their college years a happy one. Mary Mitchell, writing in 1952 about her student life in Liverpool 20 years earlier, remarked that

> When I look back . . . to my university days, I find myself thinking not of lectures, nor of professors, not of long silent sessions in the Tate Library, nor even of the suspense and horror of Finals, but of life in University Hall.[158]

Nancy Anderson (née Nixon), who had been an arts student in Liverpool around ten years earlier, echoed Mary Mitchell's sentiments. She recorded that when questioned by her son about "What did you do at the university, Mother?" the happy memories of life in hall came thick and fast:

> At the University, my son, I had occasional lectures; yes, I frequently visited the University. But it was at Hall that I really lived.[159]

Notes

1. P. Williams, "Pioneer women students at Cambridge, 1869–1881", in *Lessons for life: the schooling of girls and women, 1850–1950*, F. Hunt (ed.) (Oxford, 1987), p. 181.
2. D. Glynne Jones (née Lloyd Davies), *Letters from Newnham College, Cambridge, 1877–78*, introduced by Jean Pace (bound typescript volume presented to department of Welsh history, University College of North Wales, Bangor), pp. 2–4. (Currently held by Professor Gwynn Williams. The original correspondence is held by Mrs Gaynor Andrew and will eventually be lodged in the archives of the University College of North Wales.)
3. "Life at Aberystwyth and Alexandra Hall at the end of the nineteenth century . . . being extracts from the letters of Lady Stamp (née Olive Marsh), 1898–1900" (archives, University College of Wales, Aberystwyth), pp. 1–2.
4. A. Maitland, "The student life of women in halls of residence", proof copy of paper submitted to Conference of National Union of Women Workers in Nottingham, 1894 (archives, Glasgow University, DC 233, 2/24/11).
5. *Ibid.*, p. 52.
6. L. Faithfull, "College education for women", *King's College Magazine* (Lent term 1900), pp. 6–10, and (Easter term 1900), pp. 5–9 (archives, King's College London, K SER 17/10, 17/11).
7. *Ibid.*, K SER 17/11, p. 8.
8. University Grants Committee, *Report for the period 1929–30 to 1934–35* (London, 1936), p. 17.
9. *Ibid.*
10. University Grants Committee, *Report of subcommittee on halls of residence* (London, 1957), p. 4.
11. *Ibid.*, p. 5.
12. See appendices. The figures are extracted from those published by the University Grants Committee, *Returns from universities and university colleges in receipt of Treasury grant for the academic year 1937–38* (London, 1939), table 1.
13. *Ibid.* (the percentages have been calculated from these figures).
14. Maitland, "The student life of women", p. 52.
15. "Notes on hostels for women students", typescript memorandum 23 March 1907 (archives, Glasgow University, DC 233 2/13/18/1).
16. *Education and graduation of women at Edinburgh University: the Masson Hall of Residence for women students*, Masson Hall papers (Edinburgh University, n.d., c.1900), p. 15.
17. L. I. Lumsden, *Yellow leaves: memories of a long life* (Edinburgh & London, 1933), p. 118.
18. "Report of proceedings at the formal opening of the County School for Girls, Bangor, and the University Hall for women students on 9 October 1897", *North Wales Chronicle* (October 1897), p. 5 (archives, University

College of North Wales).

19. M. W. Hughes, *Ashburne Hall: the first fifty years, 1899–1949* (Manchester, 1949), p. 5; *Aberdare Hall, 1885–1935* (Cardiff, 1936), p. 9.

20. Minutes of Ladies' Hall Committee (archives, Aberdare Hall, Cardiff). The report of the annual meeting of the governors of Aberdare Hall in February 1891 records the resolution proposed by Lady Aberdare, seconded by Principal Jones: "That in view of the probable large increase in the number of women students coming from a distance to the University College the governors are of the opinion that it is necessary forthwith to make adequate provision for their accommodation". See also J. N. Harding (ed.), *Aberdare Hall, 1885–1985* (Cardiff, 1986), pp. 4–13.

21. University of Leeds, committee books, reports of day training college committee, October 1910, December 1910 (archives, Leeds University).

22. M. Knight, "A seed which grew and the tree into which it developed", in *University Hall Association, fiftieth anniversary bulletin* (Liverpool, 1952), p. 18.

23. Correspondence between Kate Hurlbatt and the Board of Education, 1917 (archives, uncatalogued, Aberdare Hall, University College of Wales, Aberystwyth).

24. Correspondence, Miss R. L. Monkhouse at the Board of Education to Charles Grant Robertson, 29 October 1921 (University House collection, 1/62, archives, Birmingham University).

25. "Memorandum on proposed scheme of residential halls for students in Edinburgh", in *Minute books of Edinburgh Association for the Provision of Hostels for Women Students*, vol I, 15 January 1913–16 December 1915, pp. 7–20 (special collections, Edinburgh University).

26. *Ibid.*, p. 17.

27. *Ibid.*, see also *Minutes of meeting of the Board of Management of the Edinburgh Association*, 12 February 1913 (Edinburgh University), pp. 33–42.

28. *Masson Hall, incorporated, 1894: residence and union for university women students* (subscription lists), 1901, 1904 (Masson Hall collection, Edinburgh University).

29. *Ibid.*

30. Minutes of executive committee, 1894–1937, Masson Hall (Edinburgh University). Annual balance sheets and reports are incorporated with these minutes; for details of Miss Houldsworth's bequest see report for 1910.

31. Correspondence relating to Pfeiffer bequest, 11 April 1894 (Masson Hall Papers, DA 64 MAS 35, Edinburgh University). See also typescript notes on Pfeiffer bequest (special collections, Edinburgh University).

32. B. Herbertson, *The Pfeiffer bequest and the education of women: a centenary review* (Cambridge: Hughes Hall, printed for private circulation, 1993).

33. Report of meeting of new house committee, minutes of executive committee, Masson Hall, 5 November 1920 (Edinburgh University, DA 64 MAS 3).

34. *Aberdare Hall*, p. 7.

35. R. N. Smart, "Literate ladies – a fifty year experiment", *Alumnus Chronicle* (St Andrews, June 1968), pp. 25–6; W. Knight, *A history of the LLA examination and diploma for women and of the University Hall for women students at the University of St Andrews* (Dundee, 1896).

36. E. L. Ellis, "Alexandra Hall, 1896–1986", in *Alexandra Hall, 1896–1986*, E. L. Ellis (ed.) (Aberystwyth, 1986), pp. 3–4.

37. See correspondence between Neville Chamberlain and the Right Hon. R. McKenna, 11 December 1907, in the Public Record Office, ED 87/20. The file also contains information about a deputation (comprising Sir Oliver Lodge, Professor Hughes, Miss Fry and Neville Chamberlain) received by the Board in relation to the proposed building scheme in Birmingham, together with details of the financial arrangements that followed.

38. See Margery Fry's correspondence with the Board of Education, 26 August 1907 (University House collection, 1/23, Birmingham University).

39. Knight, "A seed which grew", p. 19.

40. D. Chapman, "University Hall, 1911–1931", *University Hall Association, fiftieth anniversary bulletin*, p. 32.

41. H. T. Graham, "The first twenty-one years", *University Hall Association, fiftieth anniversary bulletin*, pp. 14–15, 21.

42. Knight, "A seed which grew" p. 21.

43. E. E. Butcher, *Clifton Hill House: the first phase, 1909–1959* (Bristol, n.d.), pp. 54–7.

44. *Ibid.*, p. 6.

45. *Ibid.*

46. A. C. Wood, *A history of the University College Nottingham, 1881–1948* (Oxford, 1953), pp. 93–8.

47. Minutes of Ladies' Hall Committee, Aberdare Hall, November 1884–November 1893 (Aberdare Hall, Cardiff). Following Isabel Bruce's resignation in 1887 it was suggested that a salary of £100 p.a. should be offered to the new Warden, (see report of meeting held on 21 February 1887 in the minutes). However, on 27 May 1887, it was resolved to ask Miss Bruce's successor, Miss Don, "to take the Principalship without salary for the first year".

48. E. Huws-Jones, *Margery Fry, the essential amateur* (London, 1966), p. 66.

49. *Ibid.*, p. 91.

50. A. M. Copping, *The story of College Hall* (London, 1974), p. 16; "The will of the late Rosa Morison" in *Union Magazine* (University College London, no. 5, 1911–12), pp. 289–91.

51. Minutes of Ladies' Hall Committee, Aberdare Hall: see note relating to estimates of initial expenditure in 1884.

52. "St Peter's Hall: the Mason Fenn Memorial at Sheffield", *The Churchwoman*, 18 November 1898, pp. 114–5; see also correspondence and press cuttings relating to foundation, together with prospectus (n.d.), report, and list of subscriptions (Krebs Room, SUA/5/1/85, Sheffield University).

53. *Ibid.*

54. Ellis, "Alexandra Hall", p. 9.
55. Correspondence, William Cadwaladr Davies to Dilys Glynne Jones, 25 July 1856 (University College of North Wales, Bangor).
56. S. Delamont, "The contradictions in ladies' education", in *The nineteenth-century woman: her cultural and physical world*, S. Delamont & L. Duffin (eds) (London, 1978), pp. 134–63, esp. p. 140.
57. "Hall reminiscences", *University College of Wales Magazine* XVIII, p. 196, cited in Ellis, "Alexandra Hall", p. 4.
58. E. A. Carpenter, "Parting words", *The Dragon* (May, 1905), p. 220.
59. Minutes of Ladies' Hall Committee, 13 December 1887, Aberdare Hall. See also report of meeting on 18 June 1887.
60. Letter, 23 May 1899, "Life at Aberystwyth and Alexandra Hall . . . extracts from the letters of Lady Stamp" (University College of Wales, Aberystwyth), p. 136.
61. The controversy of 1892 is well documented. There are accounts in J. Gwynn Williams, *The University College of North Wales: foundations, 1884–1927* (Cardiff, 1985), pp. 105–111, and W. Gareth Evans, *Education and female emancipation: the Welsh experience, 1847–1914* (Cardiff, 1990), pp. 244–252. Gareth Evans' interpretation has been criticized by Sara Delamont in "Distant dangers and forgotten standards: pollution control strategies in the British girls' school, 1860–1920", *Women's History Review*, 2, pp. 233–51, 1993. An extensive collection of press cuttings relating to the dispute and to the subsequent libel action, including a transcript of court proceedings printed in the *Liverpool Mercury*, 26–31 July, 1893, is held in University College of North Wales, Bangor. The library also holds a copy of the printed minutes of the Senate enquiry held in autumn 1892, and laid before Council on 2 December 1892. Other sources include H. R. Reichel, "The Bangor controversy, a statement of facts", *Educational Review Reprints* (V), 1893; Frances E. Hughes "The Bangor controversy: a reply to Professor Reichel", October 1893, and Thomas Richards, *Atgofion Cardi*, 1960.
62. Correspondence, W. Cadwaladr Davies to Dilys Glynne Jones, 10 and 14 March 1887 (University College of North Wales).
63. Minutes of Senate enquiry (University College of North Wales).
64. *Ibid.*, statement by Dr Griffith Evans, p. 45.
65. *Ibid.*, pp. 11–12.
66. Gwynn Williams, *The University College of North Wales*, p. 108.
67. *Ibid.*, p. 109.
68. *North Wales Chronicle*, 12 February 1916, quoted in Gareth Evans, *Education and female emancipation*, p. 248.
69. Gwynn Williams, *The University College of North Wales*, p. 109.
70. *Ibid.*, p. 110.
71. *Ibid.*, p. 111.
72. *Report of the meeting of the Court of Governors*, 25 October 1893, reprinted from *North Wales Chronicle*, 28 October 1893 (University College

of North Wales), pp. 5–6. See also Reichel's obituary of Mary Maude, *North Wales Chronicle*, 12 February 1926 (University College of North Wales).

73. Reichel, "Miss Mary Maude", obituary in *North Wales Chronicle*, 12 February 1926.

74. Experiences documented rather thinly in her autobiography, *Yellow leaves*. Lumsden's career and her friendships with other women are discussed by Martha Vicinus, *Independent women: work and community for single women, 1850–1920* (London, 1985).

75. In *Yellow leaves*, p. 119, Lumsden speaks of her "five stormy years" as Warden in St Andrews, commenting briefly that: "Residence for a few students while a much larger number lived in lodgings naturally brought about friction of all sorts, jealousy, discontent and opposition."

76. Further information on the nature of the dispute comes from *College Echoes* X(2), pp. 13–14, 1898; see also "The college gate dispute" in the same vol. p. 18; and correspondence, Louisa Lumsden to Principal Donaldson, 1 November 1898 and 2 November 1898 (University of St Andrews). On the relationships between town students and hall see Elizabeth Bryson, *Look back in wonder* (Dundee, 1980), pp. 107–9.

77. See regulations and discussions about discipline in Queen Margaret Hall, DC 233/2/13/10/4, and DC 233/2/13/10/9 (Glasgow University).

78. *Ibid.*, letters Mrs Riddoch from Frances Melville, 16 February 1902, Miss Galloway, 8 March 1902 and Frances Simson, 13 and 19 February 1902, DC 233/2/13/10/9.

79. *Ibid.*

80. See correspondence over hostel arrangements elsewhere in Britain: KWA/ GPF/22 (King's College London); University House collection, 2/315, 2/ 316 and 2/318 (Birmingham University); correspondence between Mrs Guthkelch and M. O. Davies in Alexandra Hall papers (University College of Wales, Aberystwyth).

81. On the origins of this association and the location of its records, A. Allan, *University bodies: a survey of inter and supra university bodies and their records* (Liverpool University, Archives Unit, Chippenham, 1990), pp. 31–2.

82. *Prospectus*, 1893–4, Queen Margaret Hall, and "House rules" (n.d.), DC 233/2/13/10/3 and 4 (Glasgow University).

83. D. Judd, *Alison Uttley, the life of a country child, 1884–1976* (London, 1986), p. 54.

84. *Facts relating to the University of Wales, the University College of Wales, Aberystwyth; and the Alexandra Hall for women students, Aberystwyth*, June 1896 (University College of Wales, Aberystwyth); "The new hall of residence", *University College of Wales Magazine* XVII, pp. 85–92, 1894; and Gareth Evans, *Education and female emancipation*, p. 222.

85. Ellis, "Alexandra Hall", pp. 9–10.

86. *Ibid.*, p. 11.

87. *Ibid.*
88. A full and particularly detailed set of accounts relating to expenditure on furniture and maintenance survives for University Hall (St Andrews University).
89. "The new warden", *The Dragon* XXX, pp. 23–5, 1908–9.
90. University Court of St Andrews, *Memorandum with regard to the duties of the Warden of University Hall*, August 1909 (reproduced in Appendix IV).
91. Frances Melville graduated from Edinburgh with a first class honours degree in philosophy in 1897. She was appointed Warden of University Hall in St Andrews in 1909 and managed to combine the duties of the post with part-time study for a second degree in divinity. She was awarded her BD in 1910.
92. Margery Fry, "Recollections of early years as warden of University House, Birmingham", MS 1911, University House collection 1/11 (Birmingham University).
93. Huws-Jones, *Margery Fry*, p. 67.
94. Fry, "Recollections . . . of University House".
95. *Ibid.*
96. *Ibid.*, see also Huws-Jones, *Margery Fry*, p. 71.
97. Huws-Jones, *Margery Fry*, p. 79.
98. *Ibid.*, p. 71.
99. *Ibid.*, pp. 81–2.
100. *Ibid.*, p. 80.
101. *Ibid.*, p. 82 ff.
102. *Ibid.*, pp. 82–3.
103. B. Carey, "Mrs A. Redman King", *University of Leeds Review* XI(1), p. 72, 1968.
104. M. W. Hughes, *Ashburne Hall: the first fifty years 1899–1944* (Manchester, 1949), p. 4.
105. *Ibid.*, p. 1. A slightly different interpretation has been put forward in Deborah Woodgate, *Ashburne Hall, Manchester, 1899–1925. The first 25 years: the construction of a history of student life in a university women's hall of residence*, BA dissertation (University of Manchester, 1994). Woodgate suggests that a "collegiate" rather than a "familial" ethos prevailed quite early in the history of the hall.
106. Huws-Jones, *Margery Fry*, p. 70.
107. *Ibid.*, p. 80.
108. D. McAlpine, "Very early days in university hall", *University Hall, fiftieth anniversary bulletin*, p. 47.
109. Hughes, *Ashburne Hall*, p. 8.
110. P. Porritt, "Recollections of University Hall, 1916–1921" *University Hall, fiftieth anniversary bulletin*, p. 53. "Dining was a word full of meaning. Many students will remember the scramble to dress for dinner at 6.55 after Mary or Anne had knocked gently on the door, and given, by a look, the invitation to dine with Miss Chapman at her table for four. This was an ordeal

for a nervous student, but Miss Chapman was skilled in conversational openings and all sorts of interests were drawn out and our social graces developed".

111. On Mrs Hope Hogg see Hughes, *Ashburne Hall*, pp. 10–11, and *Mary Hope Hogg, 1863–1936* (Manchester, 1936). Eleanor Rathbone considered Mrs Hope Hogg to have represented "the perfect Head of a Women's hall", *ibid.*, p. 12. For Miss Buller and Miss Chapman, see *University Hall Association, fiftieth anniversary bulletin*, pp. 22–4, pp. 49, 53 and *passim*.

112. Ellis, "Alexandra Hall, 1896–1986", p. 11.

113. Quoted in M. Hird (ed.), *Doves and dons: a history of St Mary's College, Durham* (Durham, 1982), n.p., *c.* p. 40.

114. *Ibid., c.* p. 34.

115. Minutes of executive committee, Masson Hall, reports of meetings on 9 February and 14 June 1920 (Edinburgh University).

116. *Ibid.*

117. *Ibid.*, report of meeting held on 14 June 1920.

118. *Ibid.*

119. *Ibid.*, report of meeting held on 8 November 1920.

120. *Ibid.*, report of meeting held on 28 March 1920.

121. *Ibid.*, reports of house committee meetings, 11 April 1921, 13 March 1922, 8 May 1922.

122. *Ibid.*, report of house committee meeting, 26 June 1922.

123. *Ibid.*, reports of house committee meeting on 7 May 1924, and special meetings on 14 May 1924 and 2 June 1924. See also report of house committee meeting on 4 June 1924.

124. *Ibid.*

125. Ellis, "Alexandra Hall, 1896–1986", p. 17.

126. Correspondence, Mrs Guthkelch to Miss Macgregor, 27 April 1926 (University College of Wales, Aberystwyth).

127. Ellis, "Alexandra Hall, 1896–1986", p. 18.

128. Correspondence, M. O. Davies to K. Guthkelch, 22 February 1933 (University College of Wales, Aberystwyth).

129. *Ibid.*

130. *Ibid.*, Davies to Guthkelch, 2 March 1933.

131. L. Martindale, *A woman surgeon* (London, 1951), pp. 33–34.

132. "Life at Aberystwyth and Alexandra Hall . . . Extracts from the letters of Lady Stamp", 24 October 1898.

133. Quoted by T. Moore, "Those were the days my friend . . .", *The Courier* (October 1972), p. 10.

134. E. Huxley, *Love among the daughters* (London, 1968), p. 49.

135. J. C. Holt, *The University of Reading: the first fifty years* (Reading, 1977), footnote on p. 74.

136. M. Vicinus, *Independent women*, p. 124.

137. *Ibid.*

138. Hughes, *Ashburne Hall*, pp. 16–17.

139. Edith Greenwood (née Walsh), "The dancing twenties", *University Hall, fiftieth anniversary bulletin*, p. 57.
140. "Life at Aberystwyth and Alexandra Hall ... Extracts from the letters of Lady Stamp"; Ellis, "Alexandra Hall, 1896–1986", p. 20; "Save Alex", in *The Courier* (May, 1984), p. 2.
141. Knight, "A seed which grew", p. 24.
142. *College Notes* (November 1898), p. 91 (University College of Wales, Aberystwyth).
143. D. McAlpine, "Very early days in University Hall", p. 48.
144. *Ibid.*, p. 47.
145. Mrs Guthkelch, "Rules for hall room maids", Alexandra Hall papers, n.d., 1930s (University College of Wales, Aberystwyth).
146. *The Dolphin*, Issue 1, 1914, University House collection, 2/321 (Birmingham University).
147. Quoted in *Bye-Gones* (1 July 1896), p. 393 (University College of Wales, Aberystwyth).
148. See, *inter alia*, Aberdare Hall, students' minute book, 28 October 1931, and *passim*, Aberdare Hall archives, Cardiff; Liverpool University House students' house committee minute books, 1927–1931 (Liverpool University). Complaints about food in University House, Liverpool, elicited some interesting responses from the authorities; see for instance the comment following complaints of the house committee on 22 January 1931: "The eggs are guaranteed; if a student finds an egg which is not fresh, she should return it to the hatch: on one occasion only has the meat been high".
149. Cocoa parties were ubiquitous. For "starvers" see Violet Watson, "Hostel Life", in *The college by the sea*, I. Morgan (ed.) (Aberystwyth, 1928), pp. 199–200: "mention must be made of the time honoured institution of starvers – another means of strengthening the bond between members of the same table. For the purpose of observing the rites of a starver the members of a given table forgather in the 'head of tables' room – if it be large enough – as soon after 10 pm as possible. They proceed to regale themselves with a miscellaneous menu, usually containing cream buns and chips, and then spend the next two or three hours in gossip and games. These orgies take place during the second week of term, and for that period peace does not reign in the establishment until the small hours of the morning".

   Further insights into the nature of the feminine student subculture that flourished in women's halls of residence in the 1930s may be gleaned from CHS, "*Plus ça change, plus c'est la même chose*", unpublished typescript notes, n.d. (Florence Boot Hall, Nottingham). This short piece was compiled from the series of "Hall Notes", which originally appeared in Nottingham's student magazine, *The Gong*, between 1929 and 1939.
150. E. Huxley, *Love among the daughters*, (London, 1968)p. 47. On the advantages of living in lodgings see Storm Jameson, "The University of Leeds in 1909–12", unpublished typescript (Leeds University), pp. 1–2.
151. University College of Wales, Cardiff, "Memorandum submitted to Senate

by committee appointed to report on the application of women medical students for permission to reside outside hall", 1919 (Aberdare Hall).

152. *Ibid.*
153. *Ibid.*
154. Manuscript editions of *Yggdrasill* 1901–9 (Ashburne Hall); of *The Phoenix*, 1912–16 (Liverpool University).
155. Cited in Butcher, *Clifton Hill House*, p. 14.
156. Judd, *Alison Uttley*, p. 55.
157. *Ibid.*
158. G. Mary Mitchell, "Hall choir", *University Hall Liverpool, fiftieth anniversary bulletin*, p. 65.
159. N. Anderson (née Nixon), "Happy families, 1923", *University Hall Liverpool, fiftieth anniversary bulletin*, p. 61.

Chapter Four

❧

Women academics

The first appointments

Teaching in higher education was an occupation riven – indeed structured – by sexual divisions. The influx of women students into British universities was not matched by any commensurate increase in the appointment of women teachers in these institutions. Fewer women than men went on to research. Janet Sondheimer, reflecting on the 1900s, commented tartly that:

> Those who aspired to further academic honours, even if they had the private means to allow them to pursue the necessary research for advancement, found the way blocked; faculty and university boards were solidly male, professorial chairs, apparently, were designed to accommodate only the masculine frame.[1]

In 1888 Jane Harrison, the celebrated classicist, was a runner-up for the Chair of Archaeology at University College London. The selection committee suggested that she should act as an "occasional lecturer" during the absence of the professor. The recommendation was opposed by the Professor of History, E. S. Beesly, who deemed it "undesirable that any teaching in University College should be conducted by a woman".[2]

Court minutes from the University of Edinburgh in 1894 record a query from Mary Bentinck Smith of Girton, about whether women might be considered eligible for lectureships in French and German, which had recently been advertised by the university.[3] The Secretary was instructed to reply that the court "did not contemplate the appointment of women to these posts".[4] Miss Bentinck Smith went on to build her career in the women's colleges instead. After two years in the Victoria College, Belfast, she took up a post in Royal Holloway, returning to Girton in 1899.[5]

The Scottish universities were slower than elsewhere to appoint women. There were some teaching assistants, but women with formal teaching appointments are conspicuous mainly through their absence in the Scottish university calendars, at least before 1918. Although women scholars like Ethelwyn Bruce Lemon undertook coaching, and played an important part in the activities of the women students, Edinburgh does not seem to have appointed women to lectureships before the First World War.[6] After the war, a shortage of applicants for posts, together with the passing of the Sex Disqualification (Removal) Act in 1919, may have facilitated such appointments. Alice Bruce Lennox and Mary Burns were appointed to lectureships in geography and French respectively in Edinburgh in 1919.[7] Aberdeen appointed women as university assistants with the status of lecturer somewhat earlier, but even by the beginning of the Second World War, Aberdeen only had one full-status woman lecturer in post.[8]

In England and Wales there were earlier appointments, although as Edith Morley observed in 1914, much depended upon the "personal idiosyncrasy" of heads of department, the importance of the post, and the salary offered.[9] In Manchester, the appointment of Alice Cooke as Assistant Lecturer in History in Owens College in 1893, owed much to the fact that Professor Tout, "a medievalist in his studies but most modern in his views" was a stalwart proponent of women's claims to higher education.[10] Although she was initially appointed as a historian, Alice Cooke became Assistant Tutor to Women Students in 1897, adding the responsibilities of acting as Honorary Secretary of Ashburne House two years later.[11] As we have seen in earlier chapters, this pattern was common in reverse. Women might gain their entry into university employment through being appointed as tutor to women students, or as warden of a women's hostel, and then seek to supplement this with more academic work. Helen Wodehouse seems to have shown less interest in her semi-official position as Tutor to Women Students in Birmingham after 1903 than in her academic work in philosophy.[12] Margery Fry taught mathematics to a matriculation class in Birmingham, tutoring male students, with some trepidation, for the first time.[13]

Another route of entry into university teaching for women came with the advent of the day training departments after 1890. In several universities the "Mistress of Method", or "Normal Mistress" in charge of women training to be teachers constituted the first female appointment. The careers of Marian Pease in Bristol, Hannah Robertson in Leeds, and Catherine Dodd in Manchester have already been mentioned.[14] There are many other examples. The status of these appointments was often rather ambiguous, particularly in the early years, when the diploma students tended to be somewhat isolated from the rest of the student body. Teacher training carried uncertain status. Certain aspects of it, such as the need to provide instruction in needlework and hygiene, appeared particularly lowly. The records of the day training committee in Bangor in the 1890s, show that these aspects of the work might well be shunned by the Mistress of Method, particularly if she had graduate status. In 1898 the Registrar reported that in accordance with the instructions of the committee,

> candidates for the post of Assistant Lecturer had *not* been required to possess a knowledge of needlework, and that separate arrangements would have to be made for the teaching of the subject.[15]

As the committee hoped to attract a woman from Girton, Somerville or Royal Holloway to the assistant lectureship in education, they thought it expedient to farm out the needlework (a Board of Education requirement in the training of women teachers) to a part-time instructress, at the rate of £30 p.a.[16]

The standing of the staff associated with the day training departments improved somewhat as these institutions became more fully integrated with the universities, and as more of their students came to undertake a full degree course. Masters and Mistresses of Method might find their job titles reformulated as Lecturers or Assistant Lecturers in a university department of education. Marian Pease was appointed Mistress of Method in Bristol's day training college in 1892. She is described in a 1906 calendar as "Reader" in education.[17] Bristol received its charter in 1909 and Marian Pease wrote of her "honour and satisfaction" at becoming a member of the staff of the university before she retired.[18] There seems to have been some fluidity and an absence of standardization around job titles in training departments in these years. In the day training department associated with University College Cardiff for instance, we learn that both the Master of Method, Mr Raymont, and the Normal Mistress, Mrs Mackenzie, were promoted to professorial status in 1904.[19] Mrs Mackenzie may have been the first woman to be addressed as Professor in Britain, although formally her rank was that of Associate Professor until 1910, when she became a "full" Professor of Education.[20] There were more women teaching in education and day training departments during this period than in any other departments of the universities, but the highly equivocal status of many of these jobs can give a false impression; in estimating the proportion of women in academic lectureships it can be difficult to judge whether they count or not.

The numbers of women teachers

Halsey and Trow have estimated that there were around 2,000 university teachers in Britain by 1900, although regular statistics were not available until the University Grants Committee began to publish data relating to numbers of staff and their grades from 1923 onwards.[21] The UGC figures suggest that Britain had 3,501 teachers in university and university colleges by 1903: 2,541 in England, and 960 in Scotland and Wales.[22] These figures were not disaggregated by sex. There are various ways in which the historian can seek to determine the proportion of women in these totals. The *Commonwealth Universities Yearbook*, (earlier the *Yearbook of the Universities of the Empire and the Commonwealth*) which was published annually from 1914, gives more detailed information, as do the published calendars of the individual universities and university colleges themselves.[23] These sources can be supplemented by handbooks and directories such as *The directory of women teachers*, which was published in 1913, 1914, 1925 and 1927, and *Hutchinson's woman's Who's Who*, published in 1934.[24] This latter volume contained a 14-page list of the names, qualifications and addresses of women on the teaching staff of universities and colleges; although not comprehensive, it can be useful in conjunction with other sources.[25] Another source of data comes from a survey of the numbers and grades of women employed in university teaching in Britain which was collected by the British Federation of University Women (BFUW) in 1931. The BFUW sent detailed questionnaires to all universities and university colleges, eliciting some interesting returns which are preserved in the Federation's archive.[26]

According to Margherita Rendel, who attempted to measure the proportions of women engaged in university teaching through the period 1912–76 using the statistics in the *Commonwealth Universities Yearbook*, the proportion of women on the staff of all British universities excluding Oxbridge was about 10.7 per cent in 1931.[27] Breaking this down further she estimated that in the same year the proportion of women teaching in the London colleges was 11.7 per cent; in the older civic universities, 10.2 per cent; in the university colleges and younger civics, 19.4 per cent; in Wales, 12 per cent, and in Scotland, 7.2 per cent.[28] In a more recent investigation, and using data from university calendars, Fernanda Perrone has contended that Rendel's estimates are too low.[29] Perrone has noted, for instance, that Rendel's figures for London represent only those women teachers who were formally recognized by the university; they exclude those tutors in the women's colleges who had not received this recognition. According to Perrone's estimates, women represented about 21 per cent of university tutors in London, and about 14 per cent of the total in universities and university colleges in England as a whole, not including Scotland and Wales.[30] However, the figures that Perrone has derived from calendars are in some instances markedly higher than those submitted by those completing returns for the BFUW survey in 1931, and they undoubtedly include a number of part-time assistants and demonstrators, as well as teachers of non-academic subjects such as domestic science, physical education and handicrafts, often associated with diploma work in the day training departments. The BFUW's estimates lay somewhere between Rendel's and Perrone's figures. In 1931 the Federation claimed that there were 13 women professors in England and Wales, as compared with 829 men; and 585 women lecturers and demonstrators, as compared with 3,103 men.[31] According to these figures, women represented 13 per cent of the total. As Rendel pointed out, this means that effectively, the proportion of women teaching in British universities remained fairly constant between the 1920s and the 1970s.[32]

Rendel also showed that the proportion of women academics holding senior posts in the 1970s was virtually the same as it had been in the 1930s, emphasizing that in the earlier period, the existence of the single-sex women's colleges guaranteed more opportunities for women to secure senior positions.[33] Contemporaries certainly recognized that women's opportunities for promotion were fewer in the mixed-sex institutions. Edith Morley commented in 1914 that although:

> At almost all the new universities men and women are nominally alike eligible for every teaching post, in practice, women are rarely if ever selected for the higher positions.[34]

And a few years later Phoebe Sheavyn similarly observed that,

> the present position of women upon the staffs of the universities and colleges is one of comparative subordination. Very few occupy senior posts of importance and prestige. Except in the Women's Colleges, the higher direction of the teaching and the general administration are still almost wholly in the hands of men; and this is the case even where, as in Wales, the number of men and women students is fairly equal.[35]

Sheavyn and Morley had both experienced difficult careers in mixed-sex institutions. Sheavyn's difficulties, as Senior Tutor to Women Students in Manchester, have been discussed in Chapter 2, and some of the problems that marred Edith Morley's career in Reading will be explored below. Morley was keen to encourage individual women to pursue careers and advancement in the newer universities, but she spoke with feeling when she warned that:

> Women who are unwilling or unable to assert themselves when necessary are not in place at a co-educational university.[36]

There is no shortage of evidence in support of Margherita Rendel's suggestion that "men and women constituted two different populations for promotion" in universities at this time.[37] Morley and Sheavyn clearly recognized this, both in directing more ambitious women scholars towards single-sex institutions, and in their awareness of the fact that the few realistically obtainable senior positions for women in co-educational universities were specifically women's jobs, that is, the handful of posts designated for senior tutors to women students and the like.[38] Both were equally well aware that the status and duties attached to such positions could be far from desirable: there was rarely any time left over for research. In Morley's analysis of the openings for women in higher education there is a clear recognition of the existence of a dual market. At the junior level certain posts, particularly in education, were available to women, although these posts were often underpaid, insecure, and carried heavy teaching responsibilities:

> If a lecturer be known to teach between twenty and thirty hours

a week, it is tolerably, though not entirely, safe to assume that it is a woman who is so foolish.[39]

The majority of women in professorial posts or full staff lectureships were to be found in the protected market of the women's colleges. Morley pointed out that comparatively few women professors or readers held their posts as a result of open competition against other women, let alone men.[40] At the time she was writing (1914) the University of London had two women professors. Caroline Spurgeon had been appointed to a new university Chair in English Literature, tenable at Bedford College in 1913, after open competition, whereas Margaret Benson's Chair in Botany, in 1912, had come about through internal promotion. There were also "one or two women professors at the newer universities", Morley observed,

> but these as a rule retain their positions by right of past service in a struggling institution, not as a result of open competition, when university status had been obtained and reasonable stipends were offered to newcomers.[41]

This was in effect Morley's own position: already in post, she had been granted the title of Professor of English Language at Reading in 1908. Interestingly, Morley was a strong advocate of open competition, even in the women's colleges:

> It is a sign of the times that in at least one Women's College in a mixed university, it has been recently necessary to rule that posts are open to men as well as to women, unless it is specially stated to the contrary. Thus, when the power is theirs, women also may be unwisely tempted to erect a new form of sex barrier. . . . The most suitable candidate for a post is the one who should be selected, irrespective of sex. It is this principle that women are endeavouring to establish. They must do so by scrupulous fairness when the power is theirs: by making themselves indisputably most fitted, when they are knocking at the closed door.[42]

This was a somewhat sensitive issue. In 1913 a controversy had erupted around the question of whether some form of positive discrimination should be exercised in appointing a Professor of Chemistry, tenable at Royal Holloway College.[43] Many would have preferred to see a woman in this Chair, although in the end a male candidate, George Barger, was appointed. Minutes of the British Federation of University Women indicate that a similar controversy flared up in 1915, when a man was appointed Reader in Chemistry in the Home

Science Department of King's College for Women. Several members expressed their unease over the fact that in a college concerned primarily with women and the "household arts", "all the head scientific posts" should be held by men.[44]

Obstacles: research and sponsorship

Those who were concerned to see more women teachers in universities pointed to a number of obstacles in their path. At the postgraduate level it was much harder for women to secure grants for research. This was a consideration emphasized by Morley, who drew up a detailed list of scholarships available to women, at both the undergraduate and postgraduate level, in the survey of women's work in the professions that she edited for the Fabian Women's Group in 1914.[45] It was a concern shared by most of those interested in women's higher education at that time, and one of the factors that brought about the foundation of the British Federation of University Women in 1907. The Federation originated in a meeting of 17 women in the library of Manchester High School for Girls in March of that year.[46] The impetus had come from Dr Ida Smedley, who had been appointed Assistant Lecturer in Chemistry at the University in Manchester one year previously. Dr Merry Smith, the first woman doctor to be employed by the Public Health Department in Manchester, was present at the meeting and vividly recalled Ida Smedley's account of "her difficulties about promotion in the University and funds for research because she was a woman".

> Miss Smedley, fair-haired and blue-eyed, held forth vigorously as we sat on the benches and she advocated the formation of a Federation of University Women with the objects of helping women to promotion on university or similar staffs and raising money for research.[47]

The BFUW moved its headquarters to London in 1909, and local branches were soon formed elsewhere. At the first recorded meeting in Russell Square, London in 1909, it was decided to begin "the collection of statistics with regard to Fellowships".[48] Miss Dobell undertook to collect information for Wales, Miss Cullis for London, and information as to the remainder of Britain would be collected as far as possible through secretaries of local associations.[49] The objects of the

BFUW were formulated broadly: the intention was to bring together all women who had enjoyed a university education to work for the removal of sex disabilities and promote women's involvement in municipal and public life. But the initial object of encouraging independent research and scholarship remained.[50] Women who held posts in the universities and colleges dominated the executive committee in the early years, and one of the Federation's first achievements was the setting up of an annual prize fellowship for women. In 1935 Ida Smedley congratulated the Federation, with some justification, on its choice of Fellows: of the five women who had been elected between 1912 and 1916 three, Caroline Spurgeon, May Whiteley, and Mary Williams, had been subsequently elevated to professorships.[51]

Members of the BFUW maintained a high level of activity in fundraising to support scholarships and fellowships throughout the inter-war years; local branches organized collections, and annual bazaars and Christmas sales were held in London, after 1926 in the dignified setting of the Federation's newly acquired premises in Crosby Hall.[52] But competition for research fellowships could be fierce, as the records of applications show.[53] A concern to widen opportunities for women to pursue research motivated a host of minor initiatives and benefactions during these years. The women's colleges in Oxford, Cambridge and London began to institute research fellowships but their funds were limited, leading to a constant struggle to attract money from elsewhere.[54] The Gilchrist Educational Trust was the recipient of many applications, and grants from this source enabled a long list of women, including Helen Wodehouse, Ada Levett, Marion Pick, E. M. Butler, Enid Starkie and Nora Jolliffe, to carry out research before 1925.[55] In a research environment that was relatively friendly towards women, at the London School of Economics (LSE), Charlotte Payne Townshend (Mrs George Bernard Shaw) endowed a series of research studentships after 1900, to the value of 100 guineas per year.[56] Marion Phillips was awarded a "Shaw studentship" in 1901, but five of these awards between 1906 and 1910 went to male applicants. In 1911 Mrs Shaw wrote to Miss McTaggart, the Secretary of the school, to inform her of her decision that the scholarship should henceforth be awarded to women only, and that she herself would choose the subject of the research that was to be carried out.[57] The next recipients of Shaw scholarships were Alice Clark, in 1911–12, and Eileen Power, in 1913–14. Charlotte Shaw had arrived at a clear sense of her objectives: as a committed feminist, and a member of the Fabian Society Women's Group, she was bent on sponsoring research that would reinterpret history from "a woman's point of view". She outlined this agenda to Miss McTaggart:

> What I want is a series of monographs on the position of women in England (or Britain) from early days to the present, which are to dovetail into one another finally.[58]

Alice Clark would take care of the seventeenth century, the middle ages should be kept for Eileen Power. This is a nice example of feminist intervention, serving both to open doors for women scholars and to influence the shape of the curriculum. Research opportunities for women at LSE benefited further by a gift of £2,000 from B. L. Hutchins in 1926.[59] An independent scholar, known for her work on the history of factory legislation (with Amy Harrison) and her study of *Women in modern industry* (published in 1915), Hutchins had long been associated with the LSE.[60] Her gift established "the Women's Studentship Trust, which made awards of £150 p.a. for two years to women keen to undertake research in economic history.[61]

Another important, if less tangible, consideration that affected women's decisions whether or not to embark on research in any university department was that of sponsorship. This covered a range of issues, such as the extent of encouragement received from established scholars to the availability of supervision when it came to registering for a higher degree. It is not easy to chart these processes from historical evidence, although individual autobiographies sometimes provide insights into the way in which women could be deflected from studying certain subjects, in many cases well before they arrived at university. Kathleen Lonsdale, who had the distinction of being one of the first women to be elected Fellow of the Royal Society in 1944, recalled the opposition she had met with from her headmistress at school when she had first announced her intention to specialize in physics:

> she wanted me to concentrate on mathematics and assured me that in physics there would be far more competition from men and that I would be a fool to think that, with my comparative lack of background of any practical skill and knowledge, I would be able to compete in "a man's field".[62]

The lack of encouragement for girls to study science was even more evident at the university level. In 1911 Lord Haldane questioned

Margaret Tuke about the extent of provision for graduate work in science available to students from Bedford College. He asked whether any of the students went to "distinguished outside teaching", "such as Professor Ramsay, for instance?" Tuke replied that:

> They do not go to Professor Ramsay. He does not encourage women to research with him particularly. I think I am not misstating the fact that he rather discourages women in his laboratory for research purposes.[63]

Haldane asked whether there was anyone else the women students might go to, who was "more encouraging to your sex?" "Not outside our own College, in Science", came Tuke's reply.[64]

We have seen in Chapter 2 how the committee appointed by Liverpool University's Council in 1911 to report on the proportion of women on the university's staff emphasized that

> the incentive to women to prepare for the work of university teaching was materially weakened owing to the fact that women were so rarely appointed to university posts and more particularly to the higher posts.[65]

Feminists on the committee, such as Emma Holt and Eleanor Rathbone, clearly recognized that what we would now call role-models were important. The interchange between Tuke and Haldane quoted above supplies insights into why the appointment of men to senior posts in science in the women's colleges was such a vexed issue.

There were some eminent male scientists who were more encouraging towards women, but the fact that their attitudes in this respect are so frequently remarked on, tends to suggest that this encouragement was unusual. J. D. Bernal and Sir William Bragg are usually cited as having been well known for their willingness to take on women research students, and it has been suggested that this may explain why there have been so many successful women crystallographers in Britain.[66] Kathleen Lonsdale records that although the Davy-Faraday Research Laboratories of the Royal Institution, founded in 1896, were formally open to both sexes:

> It was not . . . until Sir William Bragg, the eminent crystallographer, became director in 1923 that the laboratory personnel included any considerable number (20 per cent) of women. Some of us came with his research team from University College London; others came at his invitation or by their own application from other parts of Britain and from other countries.[67]

Gowland Hopkins and Rutherford have also been singled out as having been unusually well disposed towards women.[68] Rosaleen Love has drawn attention to Karl Pearson's encouragement of women researchers in the Biometric and Galton Eugenics Laboratories in University College London around the turn of the century.[69] She points out that economic considerations may well have come into play here: women were cheaper to employ than men.[70] There were limits to the "woman friendliness" of even this department. One of Pearson's protégées, Alice Lee, encountered problems in the examination of her doctoral thesis, which was concerned with the relationship between skull capacity, sex and intellectual distinction. This was dangerous territory, and not made any safer by the fact that Lee had unwittingly featured the skull dimensions of one of her examiners (the anatomist, Sir William Turner) among her data. (His skull was small, by the standards of his contemporaries.) Galton, called in to adjudicate, was less than sympathetic to Lee's contention that skull capacity and intellectual distinction were unrelated. However, Pearson, who could undoubtedly show ambivalence in his intellectual support for women, was on this occasion consistently supportive and Alice Lee obtained her doctorate from London University in 1901.[71]

The importance of encouragement from tutors sympathetic to women's scholarly ambitions emerges in all areas of higher education. Two interesting investigations into women's academic networks in the early twentieth century have highlighted the ways in which individual scholars, both men and women, were particularly encouraging towards women graduates, offering support and supervision, sometimes in connection with academic projects involving the investigation of women's lives and experience. Doreen Weston has focused on women academic historians, the extent to which they acted as rolemodels for their female students, and whether or not they were encouraging towards studies in women's history.[72] Her answers to these questions are rather guarded. She points out that many of these pioneer women, anxious to establish their credentials in a male-dominated university world, tended towards academic conservatism. There were nevertheless important networks of supervision and assistance among women historians that can be traced from the 1880s to the present.[73] Maxine Berg's investigations of the careers of the first women economic historians in Britain highlights the importance

145

of these networks still further.[74] In late nineteenth-century Cambridge, the economic historian W. Cunningham was particularly encouraging of women's scholarship. As chairman of Girton's College Council, he established a studentship and publications fund in the college, and collaborated fruitfully with Ellen McArthur, one of the earliest women tutors in economic history in Cambridge.[75] However, Alfred Marshall, Cunningham's contemporary, preferred male students and consistently opposed any attempts to strengthen women's position in the university. Marshall was known for his generosity in encouraging young scholars to undertake research, but as Berg points out, this did not include women.[76] When Ellen McArthur became the first female extension lecturer in Cambridge in 1893, Marshall approached the Vice-Chancellor in an attempt to prevent the appointment:

> With Marshall's ascendancy in the discipline and especially over
> Cunningham, this cannot but have had a devastating effect on
> the entry of women into economics. Women continued to study
> the subject, but with no career prospects in Cambridge.[77]

Thereafter the promising female economists and historians turned to the London School of Economics, where McArthur had already established a connection. Lilian Knowles, who had studied under Cunningham, held a scholarship at LSE for some years prior to her appointment there as Lecturer in 1904. She was promoted to a readership in 1908, and became Professor of Economic History in 1921. During her career Knowles supervised and guided a long list of female students of economic and social history: Alice Clark, Ivy Pinchbeck, Mabel Buer, Dorothy George, Julia de Lacy Mann, Alice Radice (née Murray) and Vera Anstey were just a few. Knowles was a conservative, a patriot and an imperialist, but nonetheless she had a radical impact on the study of economic history.[78]

So, too, did Eileen Power, appointed Lecturer at LSE in 1921, Reader in 1924, and Professor in 1931. Maxine Berg has emphasized Power's central importance in attracting women to the study of economic history in these years. This owed something to her personal attractiveness; her energy, charisma and the air of glamour that surrounded her as "a very public historian" and as "a part of literary London" between the wars.[79] Power's feminism informed her scholarship and shaped her attitude to academic life. Her work for the Economic History Society ensured a high level of women's involvement in the society's organization and activities between 1926 and 1940.[80] She was sensitive to the difficulties faced by women in academic life and well aware of the need to encourage their ambitions. Power claimed that she owed her own career to the support and intervention of Winifred Mercier, one of the tutors at Girton:

> She simply made my career. I hadn't the foggiest idea what it would be possible for me to do, but she said "You must get a scholarship and go to the "École des Chartes" (of which I had never heard) to train for historical research", and she organised everything so that I did.[81]

Power claimed Mercier as a role-model:

> She was a perfect revelation as a don in fact, and formed all my own subsequent notions about what a don ought to be like.[82]

Berg suggests that Power herself, intelligent, charming, with political integrity and social purpose, may have been one of the most attractive role-models of her generation.

Obstacles: femininity and "worldly knowledge"

Power succeeded in combining scholarship and femininity, qualities that were often seen as irreconcilable. Representations of the dowdy, sexless woman don abound in popular literature and particularly in novels based on university life between the 1920s and the 1950s.[83] It comes as no surprise to find that even in educated circles, certain forms of knowledge were deemed particularly inappropriate for women. Power reported that at the time of her interview for the Kahn Travelling Scholarship, Sir Cooper Perry had observed that he had "often been amused at women historians", because "so many of the springs of human action must be hidden from them".[84] To be in possession of worldly knowledge, as a woman, might impugn morality. We may recall how the characters of Annie Besant, or Violet Osborn, were brought into question by their being described as "women of the world".[85] Margaret Murray remembered being chided by Sidney Hartland at a meeting of the British Association in 1913, that anthropology was "not a subject for women" on the grounds of feminine modesty and because, he alleged, there were "many things a woman ought not to know":

> He was not the only anthropologist of the time who held those

opinions. When, encouraged by Seligman and Haddon, I began to write articles on what were then called unpleasant subjects as part of hitherto unrecognised conditions in Ancient Egypt, I had difficulty at first in finding a journal that would take them.[86]

Murray recorded that one of her articles, on a title in Ancient Egypt that could be held by both men and women, was rejected by her mentor, Petrie ("I think it was the only article of mine that he ever refused") and *The Journal of Egyptian Archaeology*:

It was not the refusal I minded so much as the fact that a few months later the *Journal* published a paper on the same subject by Professor Kurt Sethe putting forward the same anthropological and grammatical proofs that I had done. To me it showed that a man might write on such subjects and be praised for his knowledge and insight, but not a woman.[87]

It took time for such attitudes to change: Margaret Murray pointed to the liberating influence of Freud. But conventions about feminine modesty and propriety lingered on well into the inter-war period in medicine, where they obstructed women's access to the infirmaries. Even in the arts, there could be difficulties. Enid Starkie's biographer has suggested that Constable's rejection of Starkie's first book in 1933 may have been because they were "alarmed by its frank discussion of Baudelaire's sexual problems".[88] E. M. Butler, whose book on Pückler Muskau became a best-seller in the late 1920s, dealing as it did with the fascinating aberrations of the Prince's personal life, records the horror and vituperation this brought from her colleagues in Newnham: "I was treated like a pariah for the rest of the term".[89] Butler, who was decidedly more worldly in her outlook than the rest of the Newnham dons, admits that she contemplated abandoning academic life at this juncture.[90]

Obstacles: salaries and pensions

What were material conditions like for women teachers in universities outside Oxbridge before 1939? As contemporaries like Morley and subsequent commentators have observed, salaries could be low. Wardens and lady superintendents at the turn of the century might have expected around £150 p.a. – little more than the average salary of a graduate assistant mistress in a girls' secondary school.[91] Wardens, with board and lodging, might be paid much less: Marjorie Fry started in Birmingham in 1904 on £60 p.a. There were considerable variations in academic salaries across the country. In University College London, in the 1890s, professors in charge of the smaller departments who wanted help with teaching, appointed personal assistants, paying them out of their own pockets. Margaret Murray has described how she came to work as an (unqualified) assistant to Flinders Petrie in the 1890s. She received her wages rather erratically, as Petrie was unable to pay her until his own salary came in: "but fortunately, I was living at home and so the delay was not important to me".[92] Rosaleen Love notes that in Karl Pearson's laboratories a number of women worked as unpaid, voluntary assistants, eager to find some outlet for their education.[93] Pearson frankly acknowledged that qualified women were cheaper to employ than men, because women were more likely to continue to live at home with their families.[94] Alice Lee and Ethel Elderton, Pearson's research assistants in the 1900s, were paid around £90–£100 p.a.[95]

Using data from the reports of the University Grants Committee, Harold Perkin suggests that in 1923–4 an assistant lecturer might earn, on average, £307 p.a.; a lecturer, £444; a reader or assistant professor, about £582; and a professor, on average, £977 p.a.[96] By 1938–9 these figures had risen slightly to a professorial average of £1,115, with full lecturers around £477, and assistant lecturers around £313 p.a. But there were considerable variations. Southampton had the reputation of paying its staff less than elsewhere: male lecturers earned £300 p.a., but Southampton's contracts book from 1900 to 1929 shows that women lecturers were paid £50 less than their male counterparts, and only received £250 p.a.[97] The survey conducted by the BFUW in 1931 showed clearly that women were clustered in the lower grades of employment: very few of them were earning more than £300 p.a. Many of the questionnaires distributed by the Federation were altered by respondents who adjusted the lowest grade of salary suggested for "Division III: Assistants on Probation" from the Federation's estimate of £300 p.a. *downwards*, indicating that a substantial number of women were only receiving £250 p.a.[98]

Even the salaries of those women employed as full lecturers might compare rather badly with those of the headmistresses of girls' schools. In 1931 the Vice-Chancellor of Leeds University, bent on downgrading the position of Dean to Women Students following Miss Silcox's resignation, wrote to the Leeds Education Department inquiring about headmistresses' salaries in the city.[99] The maximum salaries quoted for headmistresses of secondary schools of up to 300, 400 and over 400 pupils were £600, £750 and £800, respectively.[100] The salary attached to this "senior" post of Tutor to Women Students in the university was reduced accordingly: Dora Hibgame, forty-eight years of age and previously Headmistress of Batley Girls' Grammar School, was given a starting salary of £500 p.a.[101] This was much less than her predecessor: ten years previously Miss Silcox had started at £650, rising to £800 p.a.[102] It was also considerably lower than the £700–900 p.a. that the BFUW had envisaged as appropriate for "Teachers, other than Professors, holding posts of Special Responsibility".[103] There were very few women earning this much, and only a handful of women professors across the country. The BFUW statistics list 16 women professors in 1931.[104]

The fact that women were clustered at the bottom of the salary range increased their problems when it came to retirement. The superannuation scheme (FSSU), which was introduced into all British universities in receipt of government grant in 1913, was compulsory only where individual staff were appointed on salaries of £300 p.a. or more. Those with starting salaries of between £200 and £300 had the option of joining FSSU, while those beginning between £160 and £200 could join only with the consent of the institution.[105] Those earning less than £160 per year were ineligible, which excluded large numbers of part-time female assistants and demonstrators. Stories of hardship among retired academic women are common. Love comments that during Alice Lee's retirement,

> she lived in reduced circumstances: she had worked for a woman's wage all her life, and the college pension scheme had started too late for her to join. However, in 1923 Pearson and Margaret Tuke were able to get her a civil list pension of £70 per annum.[106]

Alice Lee died in 1939. Retirement also brought hardship for another UCL employee, Margaret Murray, whose predicament was not eased by her longevity – Murray died after her one hundredth birthday in 1963. As a junior lecturer in 1898 she had been paid £40 p.a., and her pension in 1947 was only £115 p.a. It was raised in the 1950s to £290 p.a., but this was still inadequate, and in 1960 the college authorities secured a cheque for £100 from the Samuel Sharpe fund in an attempt to alleviate her difficulties.[107] This fund made provision for "grants to Professors of distinction who had been inadequately rewarded in their day". Murray had been an "Assistant Professor" when she retired in 1933, and her salary at that date had risen to £450 p.a. She treated the £100 from the Sharpe fund as a loan, and tried to repay it later.[108]

Of course, women were not the only university employees to suffer from low salaries and inadequate provision for retirement, especially before 1914. However, their position was singled out for special mention in the reports of the University Grants Committee in the 1920s. One can detect the influence of Margery Fry in the UGC report for 1923–4, which included the following passage:

> We would specially emphasise the importance of adequate status as well as emoluments for women teachers. The numbers, as well as the duties of women teachers are steadily increasing, and we believe this development is generally regarded as satisfactory and successful. It is clearly of the first importance that women of the highest ability should be attracted to this work and we think that a more ample recognition of their claim is due from certain of the Authorities.[109]

The report added that so long as women teachers continued to constitute a minority of the academic staff in universities, "there may be need to take special steps to ensure their representation" on university bodies, particularly in respect of discipline and accommodation.[110] However, the UGC's special concern with women staff seems to have faded in the context of the economic restraints of the 1930s.

Obstacles: working conditions

Women academics often had to make do with a working environment inferior to that of their male colleagues. They were not always admitted to the senior common rooms. Lindy Moore has observed that there was nowhere where women staff in the University of Aberdeen could meet before 1918, unless they arranged to have tea altogether once a week.[111] Margaret Murray has left a humorous account of the sexual politics attached to the provision of common rooms in University College London just after the 1914–18 war.[112] As their numbers increased, the women staff asked for a common room and were given "a long narrow strip of a room", which could only accommodate a few of their number at any one time. Requests for a larger space met repeated refusals, until the women devised their own ruse to demonstrate the room's inadequacies. They invited the Provost to coffee, together with all of their colleagues, who packed in after him. Literally trapped, he was brought to recognize the justice of their demands. The women were given an old chemistry laboratory, "its stink-cupboard fitted up . . . with a gas-ring and the apparatus for making coffee".[113] They furnished it themselves.

Murray confessed herself "opposed to the segregation of the sexes in social matters" and encouraged her colleagues to invite men into the women's room. Reciprocity was a different matter, and her brave acceptance of an invitation to coffee in the men's common room (carefully calculated to take place on a day when "very few of the old diehards" would be present) provoked outrage, and "such a sanacker-towzer of a row" that the attempt was not repeated.[114] Gwyn Jones, recalling his early career in Cardiff in the 1930s, observed that:

> Not everyone recognised the desirability of a mixed common room. We men had a splendid one; women staff had one less splendid; and when the experiment of a small one for both sexes was tried in a reasonably inaccessible corner no man to the best of my knowledge ever set foot in it.[115]

Mary Stocks remembered that when she accompanied her husband to Liverpool in the 1930s, "one measure of reform called aloud for immediate attention":

> It concerned the position of the women members of the university staff, for it appeared that outside academic discussions they had almost no day-to-day opportunities for social contacts with their male colleagues. There appeared to be no senior common-room life – indeed, as far as I can remember, no senior common-room. This was because members of the university staff achieved such contacts as members of an excellent club not far from the university, at which they mixed with leading civic and business personalities. Such mixing was of great value, both to the city and the university. But it was hard on the university women, because club membership was exclusively male. They could not even lunch with their academic colleagues, except possibly as occasional guests.[116]

As Liverpool's new Vice-Chancellor, and according to his wife "an excellent feminist", John Stocks hoped that the building of new senior common rooms for both sexes would remedy the situation.[117]

The nature of discrimination

Discrimination is a complex issue. It can be overt or covert, direct or indirect; it can operate subtly and the acknowledgement or even the perception of having experienced it can carry political implications. In the 1960s, Ingrid Sommerkorn, who studied women university teachers in England, commented perceptively on the many contradictions in the evidence.[118] She observed that Jessie Bernard, whose study of academic women in America was published in 1964, had played down the question of discrimination, stating that she herself had never experienced any professional handicap on account of her sex.[119] However, the two male academics, Ben Euwema and David Riesman, who contributed the foreword and the introduction to Bernard's book, both contended that their own experiences of academic life convinced them that discrimination against women was still rife.[120] Sommerkorn similarly found that in her own interviews with academics, men were likely to perceive discrimination as still existing, whereas women were somewhat ambivalent. A majority felt that it operated, but only a small minority admitted to having experienced it personally. Many were cautious about committing themselves, partly because they saw themselves as having been emancipated and believed in the existence of a meritocracy: they regarded themselves as having succeeded within the system. Sommerkorn drew on Goffman's insights into "stigmatised individuals" and "spoiled identities" to explain some of these apparent inconsistencies:

> Officially, all discrimination has been eliminated; if, nevertheless, difficulties or unfair treatment are encountered, it is very likely that this is attributed to personal deficiencies since – formally – other reasons are no longer valid. Because – consciously or unconsciously – women might fear such criticism, it is possible that they refrain from complaining about having experienced a sex-differentiated treatment in the academic world.[121]

This encourages us to look somewhat more judiciously at claims of women academics in the past who alleged that discrimination no

153

longer existed. Enid Starkie, for instance, in reviewing Vera Brittain's book *The women at Oxford* in 1960, contended that "women today, in learning and scholarship, are allowed to forget their sex".[122] But Starkie's attitude was ambivalent. Her claim was, in part, wish-fulfilment, as she presumably identified with "the Oxford women" she wrote of,

> whose gorge rises at the thought of the sordid and shaming beginnings of their intellectual emancipation, who ask for nothing better than to be allowed to forget them, and to disappear into a sexless mass of academic records.[123]

It is highly unlikely that Starkie would have looked back on her own career as unaffected by her femininity. When she failed to secure an appointment in Sheffield in 1937, the Principal of Somerville, Helen Darbishire, had written consolingly: she had not wanted to lose Edith, and "obviously they wanted a man".[124]

Among the sources that can be used to explore the career experiences of women in the university world before 1929, autobiographies and biographies rank as particularly important, but these sources call for very careful reading and interpretation. Biographers often gloss over the less comfortable experiences of their subjects. Women are seldom comfortable with their own ambition, and acknowledgement of the drive to succeed, or of past ambitiousness, is rarely allowed to shape their autobiographical writing.[125] Stories of ambitions frustrated are as rare as narratives of success. To speak with authority can sound unfeminine, a dilemma that goes some way towards accounting for "the rhetoric of uncertainty" that one feminist scholar has identified as characteristic of women's autobiographical writing.[126] Only a few academic women have left autobiographies, and even where the writers were successful scholars of strong personality, these accounts are often surprisingly brief and modest, such as Jane Harrison's *Reminiscences of a student's life* (1925).[127] These sources rarely do more than hint at career difficulties, or experiences of discrimination. Margaret Murray, eloquent and humorous as she was about sexual divisions in University College London between the 1890s and the 1920s, says remarkably little about her later experiences, particularly in the years leading up to her retirement in 1925. We know from her own admission that the last years were difficult for her, and a completely different tone creeps into her autobiography at the end of Chapter IX:

When the bad times came at the end of my career at University College, and I ran down the Edwards Library stairs for the last time, I realised that my tears were flowing not for grief at leaving the place where I had spent so many happy years but because I was glad to escape from what was now a prison-house, full of bitterness and frustration.[128]

But as to the precise nature of this "bitterness and frustration" one can only speculate. There is little in the college archives to enlighten us. The question of funding a successor to Flinders Petrie appears to have been somewhat vexed because the college authorities seem to have decided that they were not able to appoint another full Professor while Margaret Murray, as Assistant Professor, remained in post. Murray had secured a waiver from the college, postponing her retirement, in 1933. Minutes of the college committee indicate a decision to appoint a full-time Reader in the meantime, at a salary of £600 p.a. (Murray was then receiving £450 p.a.). But these details, spare as they are, provide very little insight into the nature of what was apparently such an unhappy situation for Murray.[129]

Another case of a woman lecturer experiencing serious difficulties in her career comes from Bristol. Here again, the evidence is frustratingly inadequate. Geraldine Hodgson had been appointed head of the women's secondary training department in Bristol in 1902.[130] Hodgson had studied moral sciences at Newnham between 1886 and 1889. She had teaching experience and considerable skills as a scholar. She published prolifically during her life-time, supplementing research on education with books on religious subjects as well as four novels.[131] According to J. B. Thomas, Hodgson should be remembered as "one of the most distinguished of the teacher trainers appointed to universities before the First World War".[132] In view of this, it is somewhat surprising to learn that Hodgson was sacked by the university in 1916. J. B. Thomas has pieced together what evidence there is about the circumstances of her dismissal in an attempt to understand why. Her relationships with colleagues appear to have been strained. Hodgson had been unhappy about the status of secondary training in the university following the removal of her department from the Faculty of Arts to an association with elementary training, under the aegis of a professional teacher training board. She had engaged in a number of disputes with the Vice-Chancellor, Isambard Owen. Relations between the Vice-Chancellor and university staff in

Bristol were very strained in the period just before the First World War, and there had been protracted disputes over administration, lack of tenure, salary levels and dismissals.[133] In 1913 Hodgson allegedly complained that "certain unnamed persons" in the university had endeavoured "to undermine her position and make it impossible". Thomas concludes that,

> it is impossible to say whether Dr Hodgson was the victim of imagined slights or whether she was a genuine victim of academic and largely male jealousy and prejudice. What is certain is that the university lost one of the most distinguished woman academics of her generation.[134]

Difficult careers: the case of Edith Morley

We can learn more about some of the difficulties faced by women teachers in higher education from the career of Edith Morley in Reading. This is not to claim that Morley's career was in any way typical or representative. In some respects it was just the opposite: Morley, who became Professor of English Language in the new University College of Reading in 1908, claimed that she was "the first woman to obtain the title of professor at a British University or University College", and if we discount Mrs Mackenzie's title as head of the women's day training department in Cardiff in 1904, then this was indeed the case.[135] Morley's career nevertheless illustrates a number of themes; such as the ways in which a woman might find herself isolated among, and her authority undermined by, male colleagues; and also the ways in which determination in a woman might easily be represented as personal cantankerousness and eccentricity. Neither personal ambition nor determination were easily perceived as congruent with femininity. Even in self-representation, Morley disclaimed personal ambitiousness as a motive, insisting that she had always regarded the struggles of her career as her "contribution to the battle for fair dealing for women in public and professional life" rather than a matter of "personal gratification or pride".[136] No-one familiar with the obituaries of academic women can fail to be impressed by the frequency with which these women are described as "formidable" in personality.[137] There is indeed a sense in which any woman who achieved public recognition as a scholar in universities before 1939 could only have managed this through formidable persistence and application.

Edith Morley was certainly described as formidable by her colleagues, although, interestingly, her students seem to have remembered her rather differently, and even with sympathy and affection.[138] J. C. Holt, Reading University's historian, presents a somewhat unflattering picture:

> Of all the original staff at Reading Edith Morley is probably recalled as the least comfortable by all colleagues. She was likely to subject even the most casual of remarks about the weather to acid criticism. Her driving was memorable . . . and her driving was a direct expression of her character. She was provocative, disturbing, aggressive, intransigent; others kept their distance to avoid collision and damage. One colleague recalls her as "a robust socialist and a Fenian who tried to convert her students to it, and who pounded poor old Childs until he made her a professor"; if she succeeded in that she was formidable indeed.[139]

Holt continues in this vein, describing Morley as: "A Jewess and a resolute representative of her sex", "a very different sort of person" from her male colleagues, who "frightened" even "the most extrovert of men".[140] It is difficult not to read some closing of the ranks in these remarks, even if they are balanced, to some extent, by Holt's recognition of Morley's "humanity" ("She was ever ready to fight for the oppressed, especially if feminine") and her generosity and commitment to the university.[141]

There are a number of sources that enable us to reflect on the nature of Morley's difficulties in Reading. Holt has drawn upon the memories of colleagues and contemporaries but makes rather less reference to Morley's own account, which is included in her unpublished autobiographical piece, "Looking before and after; reminiscences of a working life", written in the 1940s and preserved in the university's archives. These archives also contain correspondence between the Principal, W. M. Childs, and de Burgh, the Dean of the Faculty of Letters, about Morley's position in the university college in the period 1908–12.[142] These were undoubtedly years of some crisis in Morley's career, but to understand why we need to go back to the circumstances of her original appointment in 1901–2.

Edith Morley had begun her academic education in the Ladies' Department of King's College London in the 1890s, where she and her friend Caroline Spurgeon had been encouraged by Lilian Faithfull, who became Vice-Principal in 1894, to read for the Oxford Honour School in English Language and Literature.[143] Although successful in their examinations the two women were not, of course, eligible for degrees. Unlike many of their contemporaries, they were unable to legitimate their success in the Oxford examinations by securing degrees *ad eundem* from Trinity College Dublin, because they had not "kept their terms" and taken the full course in Oxford or Cambridge.[144] Caroline Spurgeon proceeded to secure a doctorate from the Sorbonne, but Morley did not feel that she had the time or the money to attempt a higher degree overseas, and it was not until 1926 that Oxford conferred a degree on her, *honoris causa*. She later commented that:

> It may be thought that the absence of the right to a hood and to letters after one's name is a small matter in comparison with the enjoyment of a university education. So indeed it is, but it is nevertheless the cause of annoyance and pin-pricks of various kinds in academic life, and it is much easier to possess unquestioned the same status as one's male colleagues . . .[145]

Morley began her own teaching career in the Ladies' Department in Kensington, becoming a few years later, a "recognized teacher" in the college and also in the newly organized teaching University of London. When King's College for Women effectively came to an end in 1914, with the moving of the household science department to Campden Hill and the merging of the rump from Kensington into King's College in the Strand, she was offered a full time appointment, but tells us that she did not feel prepared to acquiesce in the new conditions.[146]

In 1901, Morley records that she was summoned to Reading to discuss a possible appointment in the college, of which she had no previous knowledge. Circumstances were hardly auspicious, for she remembered that:

> When I arrived at the station no-one was able to direct me to the College, so insignificant and unknown it still was to the man in the street. Consequently I was late for lunch and still remember the embarrassment I felt when shown into a Common Room full of men and with no other woman present. Of course it can't really have been the case, but my memory is of being offered the cruet by everyone at table and at any rate that lasting impression indicates my state of mind. One real occurrence remains. Lunch

was nearly over and many of the men had their unlit pipes in their hands. I could not know that, owing to the small size of the room, smoking was forbidden before 1.45, so I thought that they were politely waiting on my account. When therefore the Principal, (now Sir Halford Mackinder) offered me a cigarette for the first time in my life in public among strangers, out of sheer shyness I accepted and smoked it. To this day I remember my indignation when on my next visit to the College, I received a message from the authorities requesting me to refrain from smoking in Common Room.[147]

Nevertheless, in the interview that followed lunch Morley was asked if she would be prepared to teach Anglo Saxon and German for one afternoon a week in the college. The remuneration originally suggested was £30 for the three terms, to include rail fares from London. When she "indignantly rejected" these terms, "they were at once doubled without discussion", and she began the work in the week that followed.[148] The arrangements were relatively informal because the college was in what Morley described as "an embryonic condition" at the time. In 1901–2 what had originally been a University Extension Association changed its name to Reading College. This soon became Reading University College in 1903. W. M. Childs, who had originally been responsible for the teaching of English, replaced Mackinder as Principal in that session and Edith Morley became lecturer in English in his place. Between 1903 and 1912 she found herself solely responsible for the organization and almost all the teaching in the subject. By 1907 plans to reorganize the college on full university lines had crystallized and the staff learned that deans of faculty would be nominated, heads of department would become professors and faculty boards would be established. From an "embarrassed reply" to a "casual question" that she asked at this point, Morley tells us that she learned that an exception would be made in her case: she was the only lecturer in charge of a subject who would *not* receive the title of Professor.[149]

The situation was mortifying. Morley contended that "the whole business was conducted with considerable lack of tact and straightforwardness". She claimed that if she had been told openly what she believed to have been the truth, that is, that

a young and struggling institution with its reputation still in the making was afraid it might suffer if it risked being the first in the

British Isles to give to a woman the title of professor . . .
she would unhesitatingly have accepted the situation, "for I cared in-
tensely for the welfare of the College and had no illusions about my
own merits".[150]

Morley's resentment stemmed from the evasiveness of the authorities over their reasons for the slight:

> It was specifically denied that the omission of myself from the
> list of professors-designate was due to my sex, my youth, my
> lack of distinction or to any other cause. . . .[151]

and for the lack of sensitivity with which they handled the whole affair. Correspondence in the university archives allows the historian
another perspective. Childs stated unequivocally that Miss Morley
was not made a Professor in 1907 because in his judgement, "to which
I still firmly adhere", "she had not the requisite qualities for a Professor of English Literature".[152]

Morley's threat of resignation seems to have taken effect, and in
1908 she was granted the title of Professor, not of English Literature,
but of English Language. This was a compromise that failed to satisfy
anyone fully. Morley complained that this was the one branch of her
subject in which she had no intention of becoming a specialist.[153] The
authorities also made it plain that they intended to appoint a second
Professor, of English Literature, at some time subsequently, although
she claimed that she was reassured that this would not affect her
teaching of literature in the department.[154] Conflict erupted again in
1912, when the new Professor of English Literature, Mr Dewar, was
appointed. Morley considered Dewar to be her junior in terms of
scholarly achievement and teaching experience.[155] Correspondence
between the Dean of the Faculty of Letters, de Burgh, and Childs
shows that the former had little sympathy with her position. De Burgh
submitted that Morley was lacking in "judgement and discretion". He
felt that she "should be placed in definite subordination" to Professor
Dewar and that if she threatened resignation again, she should be allowed to carry out the threat. He conceded that he would be sorry to
lose her, because she was "a good lecturer, a very hard worker", and
"really attached to the College and to her students", but felt that anything was preferable "to a continuance of the protracted and undigni-
fied controversies" that had carried on "through a period of several
years".[156]

There can be little doubt that Morley felt her own position continually undermined. Although she was formally a Professor, some of the college clerks "probably with the connivance of their superior officer" persistently refused to use her title on official communications.[157] More seriously, the college authorities continued to regard it as unacceptable for a man to be responsible to a woman. When Morley interviewed and offered part-time teaching to a male assistant, it was proposed that he should be made responsible to de Burgh rather than to Morley.[158] In 1911 a newly appointed male lecturer in the department was assured (probably by de Burgh) that "he would not be long in the ignominious position of subordinate to a woman only" because of the intention to institute a Literature Chair in the following year.[159] Morley recorded that her personal difficulties "with one unreconcilable antagonist, who took every opportunity, public and private to humiliate me" continued over many years.[160] She herself may not have been the easiest of colleagues, and she was sensitive to slight, but not without reason.

Obstacles: careers versus marriage

Most of the women who taught in universities before the Second World War remained unmarried. Fernanda Perrone found that 79–85 per cent of women academics between 1884 and 1904 remained life-long spinsters, although this proportion had fallen slightly, to 67 per cent, by 1924.[161] This reflected the low rate of marriage among university educated women as a whole for the period, as well as the way in which single-sex women's colleges offered an alternative lifestyle outside the family for unmarried women.[162] Harsh representations and unflattering descriptions of celibate or lesbian women dons were plentiful in both popular fiction and contemporary polemic, particularly in the period between the wars.[163] But the tone of this criticism can be heard even earlier. Beatrice Webb, visiting Somerville College in 1896, came away with mixed impressions. She found the intellectual opportunities afforded by college life highly attractive, but was nevertheless impressed by the "narrowness" of the women teachers:

> The women dons were old maids – the type of boarding-school mistress. To my mind no woman should be accepted as a tutor who has not lived her life in the outside world. A man don is bad enough, but nowadays dons are married, and even in the old

days they were not presumably "celibates".[164]

Edith Morley observed that there was "no universal rule" relating to the employment of married women in co-educational universities before 1914. Even so, the issue was one that she identified as of great importance:

> Every lecturer who marries, can and ought to help to form the precedent that continuance of professional work is a matter for her own decision and is not one that concerns governing bodies.[165]

A small number of women managed to surmount the practical difficulties and to transcend the prejudices against combining university work with marriage before 1914. Only a handful of these women, of exceptional energy and spirit, managed to have children at the same time. May McKillop, who began teaching in King's College for Women in the 1890s had a son, as did Lilian Knowles at LSE. But many women who remained unmarried nevertheless shouldered a double burden of professional and family responsibilities, as did Edith Morley herself in taking care of elderly parents.[166] Morley submitted that the personal lives and dependencies of university women teachers were their own concern: employers had no right to interfere unless their work was suffering. Since women workers were as a rule "only too conscientious", she added, this contingency was "unlikely often to arise".[167]

The evidence suggests that in some universities at least, opposition to the employment of married women became more pronounced in the inter-war period. This was in parallel to the situation in school-teaching where many local authorities began to operate a marriage bar.[168] Elsie Phare, an ex-student of Newnham College who had failed to secure a fellowship in Cambridge, records that when she applied for a job at Southampton University College she was asked whether she was engaged or not. She answered, truthfully, in the negative, but when she subsequently became engaged to a young lecturer in classics in the college she was accused of having behaved deceitfully and warned that if she married she would lose her job:

> We married nonetheless, and I was sacked; married women were unemployable, our income £220 per annum, and for several years we lived largely on lentils. Amongst our wedding presents were two copies of *Sound catering for hard times*.[169]

Elsie Phare (now Duncan Jones) moved to Birmingham in the

1930s, where her husband had been appointed to a lectureship in philosophy. She managed to secure part-time teaching in the English department. She was pregnant, and wrote to the Vice-Chancellor,
Charles Grant Robertson, to indicate that she would be absent "for a
few days" in September:

> To my great surprise, Sir Charles . . . replied stiffly that leave of
> absence could most certainly not be granted, as a man would
> never ask for it on those grounds.[170]

Probably more surprising to the historian is the fact that Elsie expected otherwise. However, she records that her colleagues "stood
in" for her, particularly Helen Gardner, and "the Vice-Chancellor's
disapproval had no consequence".[171]

Difficult careers: the case of Margaret Miller

A controversy that erupted in Liverpool over the Vice-Chancellor's
attempts to impose a marriage bar in the 1930s had been much more
bitter in its development and outcome. In February 1933, following a
memorandum from the Vice-Chancellor Hector Hetherington and a
recommendation from Senate, Liverpool University's Council had resolved that women's contracts would automatically terminate on
marriage, and that they would have to reapply for their jobs should
they wish to continue in the university's service.[172] The Vice-
Chancellor explained to Council that it had been common practice
for women to resign on marriage before 1932, but that during that
year two women members of staff had broken with precedent, in that
they had married while intimating that they expected to retain their
posts. The women were Dr Margaret Miller, a lecturer in commerce,
and Dr Jean Wright, lecturer in French.[173]

We know little about what happened to Jean Wright, but a large
amount of evidence relating to Margaret Miller's role in the controversy has survived.[174] Miller's appointment in Liverpool dated from
1931; she had previously been an assistant lecturer in economics in
Manchester (1927–30). Her intellectual interests were in railway economics and Soviet public finance. She was an active member of the
British Federation of University Women and a committed feminist. In
1932 Miller married Mr Campbell, a colleague in the same department, writing to inform the Vice-Chancellor that her name would re-

main unchanged.[175] She was apparently quite unprepared for his hostile reaction to her intention of continuing in post. Hetherington insisted that the power of decision should lie with the university rather than the member of staff in such cases. Miller objected that she would never have contemplated marriage if she had realized that it would cost her her job. Her mother was economically dependent on her. She saw no reason why marriage should prejudice her work, indeed she had hopes that it would increase her productivity: she had already employed a housekeeper, and had plans for scholarly collaboration with her husband.[176]

Miller canvassed support from friends and colleagues, and from the British Federation of University Women. The BFUW reported that they had no cases on record of the dismissal of women from university appointments on marriage.[177] Eleanor Rathbone wrote a strongly worded letter to the Vice-Chancellor pointing this out, and suggesting that Liverpool avoid the invidious distinction of being the only university to institute a marriage bar. She herself regarded the resolution that he intended to put to Council "with dismay", and wondered whether it did not contravene the statutes. She had taken informal legal advice on the issue and had doubts whether a special condition such as celibacy for women employees could be imposed except through the rewording of the statutes.[178]

But this was all to no avail and Hetherington's resolution was accepted by Council in February 1933. The question of whether Miller's appointment should be extended or not was scheduled for consideration shortly afterwards. Hetherington seems to have advised her that her case would depend less on guarantees of continued efficiency than on the question of economic need. The increasingly desperate Miller wrote to the sympathetic Marie Adami:

> Can you imagine anything more humiliating, or more cruelly unjust, particularly in view of my extremely high record of efficiency? This is all the more astonishing if one considers the work of my own Professor, and the previous lecturer in the Department, Mr Dumbell. I consistently carried a heavier burden of lecturing work, both inside and outside the Department than they did, and nevertheless continued to produce research. The Professor's research record is precisely nil, and Mr. Dumbell produced two small articles in six years! I have no desire to be personal, but it is necessary to show what flagrantly different

standards it is proposed to apply to men and women, in an institution whose charter at least implies equality of status.[179]

She had little choice other than to accept Hetherington's terms, however, and in submitting her case for continued employment she (reluctantly) pleaded that her mother was ill, and that she had to provide for her support. Miller received a curt letter from her head of department, to tell her that he had supported a recommendation that her appointment be extended for another year. But he emphasized that this was *not* because he found himself in any way in opposition to university policy, with which after "careful consideration" he found himself in agreement, but because he sought "to mitigate the immediate effect of that policy" on Miller's personal situation.[180] In March the Vice-Chancellor wrote to inform her that Council had agreed to offer her an "upgraded" lectureship at a salary of £400 p.a. for the forthcoming session. This was accompanied by a warning. "If you accept this appointment", Hetherington wrote,

> the question of your future employment in the University will again rise in the course of twelve months. The position will then be entirely open, and it will be for the appointing bodies to take whatever course they think fit. But I think I ought to say to you that so far as my own personal view is concerned – and I think that that view is widely shared – it is unlikely, under present conditions, that the Council will appoint you again to a Lectureship in the Department of Commerce.[181]

This letter was written on the same day, 8 March 1933, as that chosen by the Vice-Chancellor for a personal meeting with the women teaching staff in the university, who had compiled a long and dignified letter of protest. Some inkling of the content of his address can be derived from notes made (probably by Margaret Miller herself) at the meeting.[182] Hetherington evidently maintained that marriage created "a new condition of life" for women, representing an undertaking of a different kind for a woman as compared with a man. Women "normally resigned" their jobs on marriage because of their "possible maternity" and because of "the burden of social obligation incidental to marriage". Marriage could be expected to interfere with mobility and efficiency "and was unlikely to be compatible with a full-time job". The university's legislation should be framed in accordance with "normal cases" although there might be exceptions. Hetherington conceded that he did not know much about practice in other universities "but he imagined that few would concede *without inquiry* that married women were *entitled* to retain their posts". He concluded by trying to reassure the women that "the University was not indifferent to personal cases", and that they "could rely on it to be generous".[183]

Not all of those present were reassured by these protestations of paternal benevolence. Margaret Miller was a fighter, and her case was taken up by women's organizations in the country at large. These worked together under the energetic lead of Monica Whately to organize a "Mass meeting for the Right of the Married Women to Earn" in Westminster in November 1933. Twenty-nine women's organizations, including the leading feminist groups – the Women's Freedom League, The Six Point Group, the National Council for Equal Citizenship, and so forth – expressed support. During the nine months between March and November 1933, Margaret Miller received sympathetic correspondence and letters of condolence from many well-known individuals including Emmeline Pethick-Lawrence, Winifred Holtby, and Beatrice Webb. There were well-known male academics who were equally hostile to Hetherington's position, such as Bernard Pares and Harold Laski, who both expressed support. Miller received a number of invitations to speak on her position, and her case became one of the *causes célèbres* scheduled for discussion at the Westminster meeting.[184]

According to a report in *The Daily Telegraph*, this meeting marked "the first united action of the entire feminist movement of Great Britain since the campaign to win the vote for women" of 21 years of age and over. Ethel Smythe led the community in singing "The march of the women", using the gold-collared baton that had been presented by the Women's Social and Political Union for the first performance of the song at a mass meeting in the Albert Hall in 1911.[185] Over 3,000 were alleged to have attended the Westminster meeting. Emmeline Pethick-Lawrence conveyed their strong resolution of protest to the Vice-Chancellor in Liverpool.

"I suppose you have heard . . . that Hector is 'worried'!!" May McKisack had written to Margaret Miller a couple of weeks earlier.[186] All this protest seems to have taken effect, and Liverpool University's Council suspended its offending rule, agreeing to receive a deputation consisting of two women members of staff (Frances Collie from education, and Margery Knight from botany) and four representatives of the BFUW. At the next meeting of Council in March 1934, the resolution was withdrawn.[187]

But where did this leave Margaret Miller? A letter she received from Hetherington in May 1934 indicates that the situation was far from happy. The Vice-Chancellor wrote that the university would shortly advertise her post:

> But since the vacancy arises because of the decision of Senate not to recommend your re-appointment in the ordinary way, there is a reasonable presumption that (unless the field should prove unexpectedly weak) another candidate will be preferred.[188]

He expressed concern that this would leave her in a difficult position, since she had indicated a year previously that she was committed to supporting her mother, at an (estimated) £150 p.a. He was therefore recommending that the university make her a grant of £150 p.a. for research work in her subject of Russian economics for a maximum of three years. The conditions on which she might hold this could be considered later. However, he would specify immediately that her "use of University buildings, and in particular the building of the Social Science Department, should be confined to the Library".[189] 1934 saw Margaret Miller looking for new jobs. She was 37 years old, with three scholarly books to her credit. In January she contemplated work in house property management. In June she applied for a job in an insurance society.[190] She kept her memories of the Liverpool affair (in a scrapbook stuffed with correspondence) for the rest of her life.

Networks of support

Reflecting on the nature and extent of social and professional support available to women academics in the early decades of the present century, it seems that women's groups were much more important than the Association of University Teachers (AUT). Margaret Miller was an active member of both the BFUW and the AUT, indeed, she is recorded as Vice-Chairman of Liverpool's branch of the AUT in 1933. Pressure from Liverpool, following the university's Council ruling in the spring of 1933 led to the AUT scheduling discussion of "the marriage question" at its central council meetings in May and December. Copies of a provisional statement on the issue were circulated to branches for "consideration and report". The wording was as follows:

> That this Council is of opinion that the adoption by University Authorities of any general policy of discriminating against the appointment or the continued appointment of women university lecturers because of marriage would not be in the best interests of universities or of the profession of university teachers.[191]

Twenty-two local associations indicated support, two gave qualified support, one expressed no opinion, and one expressed opposition.[192] Some of the women were disappointed: in Liverpool, Dora Yates wrote to Margaret Miller to complain that the resolution anyway "was not half strong enough".[193] But AUT members at the London meeting in December 1933 were reassured by the secretary's contention that most universities had married women on their staff, and that "in practice, the tendency was to consider cases on their merits".[194]

An article that appeared in *The Universities Review* in October 1933 caused some alarm in feminist circles. Under the guise of defending married women's desire to combine marriage with professional activity, E. H. Neville, from the University of Reading, suggested that women lecturers who married should be asked to serve a second period of probation, in order to demonstrate their continuing efficiency to the university.[195] Officers of the BFUW, Ida MacLean, Mabel Buer, Muriel Bond and Mary Ormerod, penned a swift response, objecting that such a system of "extra supervision" would be singularly open to abuse and would constitute a significant erosion of (women's) academic freedom.[196]

The AUT was headed by its first woman president, I. M. Bisson (née Maitland Smith) in 1933–4, herself a married woman (a lecturer in English, she had married a colleague who lectured in French at Birmingham). Her election address, in the year of Miller's trials in Liverpool, is interesting. Mrs Bisson indicated that she would refrain from

> marking the occasion by any discussion of the position of women in the universities, because she believed that it was a difficult problem which had passed the stage where statements of principle were of much value. It could best be solved by practical experience, with realism and wisdom and tact. The ardent theorist was a source of danger.[197]

Just as the National Union of Teachers around the same time was declaring itself "a Professional Organisation" and therefore "neither

Pro-Feminist nor Anti-Feminist" in its sympathies, the AUT seems to have avoided any identification of separate women's issues: feminism might be seen as quite incompatible with professionalism.[198] Indeed, there is evidence to suggest that in the minds of at least some AUT activists, aspirations towards raising the status of university teaching as a profession implied a masculine identity, and establishing as great a distance as possible between university *lecturing* and the more feminine (and lower status) occupation of school *teaching*. Dr J. W. McBain, a founding father of the AUT, never liked the appellation Association of University *Teachers*. In a letter to Laurie in 1918 he argued in favour of a union of "University Professors and Lecturers", to be free of the "stigma of teaching".[199] It is interesting to note that the association founded by McBain in Bristol in 1909, allegedly a precursor of the AUT, was "The Men Lecturers' Committee": women were not entitled to join.[200] A report published by this committee in 1909–10 shows that prominent concerns included the establishment of a "Men's Club" and an Officer's Training Corps.[201]

Women had their own clubs by the turn of the century, although the list of those they were excluded from was much greater. Writing about ladies' clubs in *The Nineteenth Century* in 1899, Eva Anstruther observed that women were still less "clubbable" than men. "May it not be", she pondered,

> that, whereas friendliness among women is more usual and counts for more in their lives than it does among men, the sense of good comradeship, should they chance to be thrown together, which men show one towards the other, which they have learnt at public schools and at college, is in a sense lacking, or at any rate, very undeveloped among women?[202]

Writing about the problems faced by professional women on the eve of the First World War, Phoebe Sheavyn mused on the implications of women being debarred from learning "from informal conversation in professional clubs, in smoking rooms, in dining-rooms, and at informal meetings".[203] Many of the learned societies, like male common rooms, were reluctant to admit women, and for similar reasons. Caroline Spurgeon, author of a noteworthy essay on Samuel Johnson, was not considered eligible for membership of the Johnson Club. G. H. Radford commented that:

> Our pious founders did not contemplate the admission of women, and I know not whether this omission is to be attrib-

uted to honest bigotry or to a notion that the air of punch and good fellowship which surrounds the club would be breathed by Ladies with difficulty.[204]

Kathleen Lonsdale, with Marjory Stephenson one of the first two women to be elected to the Fellowship of the Royal Society in 1944, recognized that although the Sex Disqualification (Removal) Act of 1919 had theoretically removed all legal barriers to women becoming members of any body having a royal charter, the system of proposing and nominating fellows had still served as an effective bar against change.[205] Even when admitted as members or fellows of learned societies, women could hardly feel other than "out of place". Beatrice Webb, the first woman to be elected to the British Academy (in 1932) recorded her first impressions of the Fellowship as "lifeless and derelict", "a funny little body of elderly and aged men".[206]

Sixty years later, the writer of a newspaper article on the University Women's Club in Mayfair recorded her impression that the premises were occupied by "elderly women", dozing "with their chins on their chests".[207] What was originally called the University Club for Ladies seems to have been the idea of Geraldine Elizabeth Mather Jackson, an ex-student and later Council member of Girton College, Cambridge. About 60 people attended a meeting at her home in Portman Square, London in 1883 to discuss the idea of setting up a club "to offer facilities of intercourse for women educated at the universities". Their names are not recorded, although we know that Louisa Lumsden took the chair.[208] It was decided that the entrance fee should be one guinea, and that the annual subscription should be the same. The club would offer rooms and facilities in central London. Admission would be by ballot, following nominations by a proposer and seconder. The club opened its doors (originally at 31, New Bond Street) in 1887 with a membership of 212 women.[209]

Various minute books and other records have survived from 1886 to the present and these enable a reasonably full reconstruction of the club's history.[210] The University Club for Ladies was renamed the University Women's Club in 1921, the year in which the club moved from premises in George Street to its present home in Audley Square. Activities were governed by a management committee, which included representatives from the Oxford and Cambridge women's colleges and from London. Women who were eligible for membership included graduates, registered medical practitioners, students who had kept residence in Oxford or Cambridge colleges for at least three terms, undergraduates of any university who had passed examinations "next after matriculation", and students of the London School of Medicine for Women who had passed their first professional examinations. A category of special membership was introduced for women who had played a leading role in the development of women's education, and this brought women such as Lady Stanley of Alderley, Madame Bodichon, Emily Davies and Elizabeth Wordsworth into the club.[211] The minutes give the impression that the membership continued to be dominated by women from Oxford, Cambridge, and London. There were a few women connected with the Scottish universities: in 1889 Miss Houldsworth, Miss Dundas and Lady Aberdeen were proposed and accepted as special members, as was Miss Struthers two years later. Even so, in 1895 Charlotte Carmichael Stopes submitted that Scottish women were under-represented in the membership and on the committee, and it was decided that "copies of the rules of the Club, etc., should be sent to Secretaries of the Women's University Classes in Glasgow, Edinburgh, St Andrews and Aberdeen".[212] Rather fewer women from the newer universities seem to have availed themselves of club membership. In 1888 Edith Wilson of Owens College was proposed for special membership, but no decision is recorded.

A concern for exclusivity vied with the desire to increase membership throughout the club's history, and the minutes indicate that the committee were often unsure of the status of qualifications and continuing new developments in the provision of higher education for women. The question of whether the possession of the LLA certificate from St Andrews University qualified women for membership seems to have caused some perplexity, for instance. In 1905, on the advice of Miss Anstruther, it was decided that it did not. Although headmistresses of the stature of Miss Beale and Sophie Bryant were regarded as distinguished members, a suggestion, in 1891, that all headmistresses of high schools should be eligible for ordinary membership was forcefully rejected by the general meeting. A category of associate membership was later introduced for those who were not technically qualified for full membership. This was for women in education, "the higher branches of public service", and those involved in the pursuit of arts, science, or literature. The number of associate members was limited and they paid a reduced subscription. They were not entitled to vote on any issue concerning the organization of the club's affairs. The category of associate membership was widened in 1908 (partly in response to the financial deficit of that year), and those involved in "some definite philanthropical work" were deemed eligible.

The University Women's Club had about 1,000 members in the 1920s. It constitutes an interesting example of an organization that was in part devised in response to women's needs and in part as an attempt to emulate the gentlemen's clubs of the day. References in the minutes to women bringing in their own food to eat on club premises, or controversy over whether children were welcome, suggest that the male model was not appropriate for all members. Like The Pioneer (a ladies' club founded in 1892) and Sesame Club (for both sexes, founded in 1895), both of which the University Women's Club shared hospitality agreements with at various times, the club provided its members with convenient facilities and opportunities for meeting, networking and friendship. The political tone was that of respectable, almost intellectual establishment feminism. As early as 1890 Dr Clarinda Body was given leave to display a petition in support of the "Women's Disabilities Removal Bill" for signature, although "the permission was not to be considered a precedent".[213] Women who lived outside London (a special category of country membership with reduced rates of subscription was introduced in 1931) made use of the club's provision for overnight accommodation. There is no doubt that the perception of belonging to a self-defined élite of educated women was important to many members, some of whom rarely used the club's facilities. In reporting the resignation of Miss Welsh, Mistress of Girton in 1903, Miss Jackson observed that Miss Welsh had never set foot in the club, even though she had subscribed since its inception.[214]

The British Federation of University Women

A much more important source of support for women working in the universities, particularly outside Oxford, Cambridge and London, was the British Federation of University Women. The origins of the Federation in Manchester, in the first decade of the present century, were described earlier in this chapter. Although the BFUW aimed to recruit widely, from all women with a university education who were concerned with the status and involvement of women in public life, its central organization and activities before 1939 were very much dependent on a network of women in university posts. The early concerns of the Federation with research opportunities and women's representation in academic life reflected this. One of the first actions of the executive committee meeting in London in 1910, for instance, involved a resolution to canvass the organizers of a conference proposed on the theme of "the modern universities" over discussion of subjects of particular interest to women. Margaret Tuke and Hilda Oakeley were deputed to raise three issues: the first was the vexed position of domestic economy in the university curriculum; the second, the relationships between a university and its halls of residence; and the third, the advisability of teachers in training attempting a full degree course in addition to professional training without a lengthening of the period of study in which to undertake this double load.[215] At the committee meeting that followed in March 1910 it was reported that the project of a "Modern Universities Congress" had fallen through, but the episode demonstrates the alacrity of the Federation in adopting the role of watchdog in relation to women's interests in the universities. Two years later the BFUW sent a letter to the secretary of the Imperial Universities Congress asking what opportunities were to be offered to "women of standing in the academic world" to share in discussions of matters affecting female students.[216]

As early as 1912 the Federation saw fit to appoint a small standing subcommittee to keep an eye on appointments, particularly in respect of cases where men were appointed to senior posts in women's colleges. This followed complaints from members who were uneasy about posts in Bedford College and the London School of Medicine for Women that had gone to men in 1911–12.[217] There was also controversy over the Chair of Chemistry at Royal Holloway College in 1913, as discussed earlier in this chapter.[218] The BFUW committee was particularly concerned with the wording of advertisements in such cases, communicating with interested parties in an attempt to ensure that job descriptions were worded in such a way as not to discourage women from applying for non-resident posts.[219]

It is clear that individual women experiencing career difficulties, particularly in relation to what they perceived as discriminatory treatment in their posts, turned to the BFUW for support. One of the most widely reported controversies in higher education during the war with a clear sexual-political dimension erupted in Leeds in 1916, not in the university, but in the municipal training college. Winifred Mercier, who had been Vice-Principal of the college, resigned in that year, driven to a pitch of frustration by difficult relationships with the male Principal of the college and particularly the Secretary for Education in Leeds, James Graham, both of whom she experienced as having undermined her authority and obstructed her policy at every turn.[220] Mercier's resignation was followed by that of nine of the women tutors in the college, all of whom felt that their position had become untenable.[221] Mercier was a woman of high principle with academic standing and a well-developed, liberal set of attitudes towards teacher education. She received a great deal of support from fellow educationalists (Professor Findlay in Manchester, for instance, and Sadler in Leeds), as well as in the local and national press.

Mercier was president of the Leeds and District branch of the BFUW, which responded immediately with sympathetic support. An emergency meeting of the central executive was held in London in July 1916, to discuss the situation in Leeds and the Federation added its voice to the chorus of those urging the Board of Education (successfully) to institute a full inquiry.[222] The report of this inquiry, fully exonerating Mercier and the nine women tutors from blame, was not published, and Mercier experienced two "difficult and uncertain" years, a hiatus in her career before her appointment as Principal of Whitelands College in 1918.[223] According to her biographer Lynda Grier, Mercier was particularly touched by the support of the BFUW during this period. Her fellow members in Leeds penned an eloquent and sensitive appreciation of the aims and ideals that had both brought her into conflict with the authorities in the first place, and sustained her through the difficulties.[224] But neither formal tributes nor minute books can record the full importance of informal networks and friendships with women who might have shared similar experiences in the workplace. Mercier continued to live in Leeds during the year following her resignation from the training college: as a result of Sadler's generosity she received "harbourage" in the education department at the university, although hopes that this would lead to a permanent appointment were not realized. It is interesting to note that Mercier shared a house with Alice Silcox, headmistress of Thoresby High School during this year.[225] A few years later (1921–

31) Miss Silcox was installed as Dean of Women Students in the University of Leeds, destined to experience problems not altogether dissimilar to those that had confronted Mercier.[226] When Mercier's hopes of an appointment in Leeds faded, she accepted a post in the Education Department of Manchester University. During the year she spent in Manchester she lived with Phoebe Sheavyn, an old friend from Somerville, Senior Tutor to Women Students in the university, a founder member of the BFUW, and a woman whose own departure from academic life appears to have been bound up with the frustration of sexual politics.[227]

The strength of the BFUW can be judged from the speed with which it developed a network of local branches. The Manchester branch continued to be very active, and inspired similar groups of women to come together in London, Cambridge and Bangor. By 1932 there were 25 local associations in England and Scotland, with a total of 3,500 members.[228] The Federation published regular newsletters (later *The University Women's Review*) from 1919. It was particularly active during the 1920s, a decade characterized by the raising of funds in connection with the acquisition of the Federation's new headquarters in Crosby Hall, London, which opened in 1927. This ambitious project aimed to provide residence for 40 postgraduate women students: it was envisaged that Crosby Hall would serve as a clubhouse and as a "research mecca" for women scholars from England and abroad who were working in London. The initial cost was estimated at £35,000.[229] Donations came from a variety of sources in England and from abroad. Anyone giving £1,000 was entitled to "name" a room, and the first residential wing, opened in 1927 by Queen Mary, included a number of these "named" rooms donated by Associations of University Women in Britain and elsewhere, as well as individual members of the University and City Association of London.[230]

The growth of the International Federation of University Women was another important development of the 1920s. Tradition has it that the idea of establishing an International Association came from a conversation between Caroline Spurgeon, Rose Sidgwick, and Dean Virginia Gildersleeve of Barnard College about the war, which had just ended in 1918. Gildersleeve recorded the conversation:

> "We should have", said Miss Spurgeon, "an international federation of university women, so that we at least shall have done

all we can to prevent another such catastrophe."

Miss Sidgwick and I looked at each other. "Then I guess I must rally the Association of Collegiate Alumnae," I said. Rose Sidgwick added, "And we must go back and talk with the British Federation of University Women."[231]

In fact the idea of international co-operation between university educated women went back earlier, and was not least inspired by the International Congress of Women, which had gathered at The Hague in an attempt to prevent further international conflict in 1915.[232] The BFUW established a Committee on International Relations in 1919. A conference held in Bedford College London in July 1920 brought together representatives of eight national federations of university women as well as delegates from seven other countries (where national associations were formed shortly afterwards). Professor Winifred Cullis and Dean Gildersleeve presided jointly, and Professor Spurgeon was elected first president of the newly established International Federation of University Women.[233]

The International Federation was to have its headquarters in London. This was originally in a room provided by the Universities Bureau of the British Empire, until 1927 when the British Federation was able to offer accommodation in Crosby Hall. By 1929 the International Federation embraced 33 separate national organizations. It had close links with the League of Nations, particularly through the Committee on Intellectual Co-operation and its sub-committee on universities. The Federation worked energetically to establish research fellowships which would allow women to combine study with travel abroad in an attempt to further intellectual community and international understanding.[234] As Eileen Power commented in the 1930s, the organization functioned as "a special sort of travel agency" for its members, who offered hospitality and welcomed fellow scholars into their homes. She contended that there was

> no more powerful means of binding nations together than by the infinite multiplication of these tiny invisible threads of personal contact and mutual understanding.[235]

Regular conferences were held, and in 1932 the British Federation hosted the Sixth International Conference in Edinburgh. The subject of the conference was "Does a university education fit the modern woman for life?" There was an elaborate programme of lectures, receptions, discussion sessions and excursions.[236] George Watson's Ladies' College, in George Square, and the Edinburgh University Women's Union allowed their buildings to be used for conference delegates. The conference literature proclaimed that "new, experimental methods of discussion" would be introduced, in order to maximize opportunities for members to express their opinions. Speakers included Amy Johnson, pioneer aviator and an ex-student of Leeds University; Dr Harriette Chick, the nutritionist; Mrs Corbett-Ashby who spoke on disarmament; Professor Johanna Westerdyk, a plant pathologist, as well as a number of other established women scholars from abroad. Some of the speakers – Harriette Chick, for instance, and Joan Evans, the art historian – addressed the question of whether women could make a distinct contribution to intellectual work.[237] The reports of the conference give a clear impression of a sense of intellectual community among academic women, particularly in relation to a shared commitment to the idea of knowledge and research as having potential for advancing social welfare, international understanding, and peace.[238]

The conference in Edinburgh was accounted a success by many of the participants: according to local press reports, upwards of 500 women had attended, "all of them without powder or lipstick". The BFUW newsletter quoted the latter observation with amusement, demurring that it was "not *quite* true", and protesting that it had been "no assembly of mere bluestockings".[239] But the optimistic visions of a peace wrought through knowledge and understanding were soon to be clouded. The October 1933 edition of the British Federation's newsletter carried a plea by the above mentioned Professor Westerdyk to "Help the German university women", describing pressure on Jewish academic women to relinquish their university posts.[240] Refugees were already beginning to seek refuge in Crosby Hall, and one of the most formidable tasks undertaken by the members of the Federation in the later 1930s, that of finding asylum for the displaced intelligentsia of Nazi Germany, was gathering momentum.

Notes

1. J. Sondheimer, *History of the British Federation of University Women, 1907–1957* (London, 1957), p. 9.
2. "Report of committee on the Yates professorship of archaeology", 14 De-

cember 1888, adopted by Senate, 17 December 1888, and by Council, 12 January 1889; note of dissent by Beesly, 15 December 1888 (University College London). Cited by N. B. Harte, *The admission of women to University College London, a centenary lecture* (London, 1979), p. 19.

3. Minutes of the University Court, 12 March 1894, p. 325 (University of Edinburgh).
4. *Ibid.*
5. See her entry in *Girton College Register, 1869–1946* (Cambridge, privately printed, 1948), p. 640.
6. For Ethelwyn Lemon see obituary in *University of Edinburgh Journal* 12, 1942–3. Miss Lemon "spent more than forty years in Edinburgh as a very successful classical coach, numbering among her pupils some of the family of the late Lord Oxford and Asquith, and of the Haldanes of Cloan, and she was also for twenty years Assistant in Scottish History in the University, and acted as an Inspector for the Scottish Education Department". She was not listed among staff in the Edinburgh University calendar. The first woman to appear therein was Alice Brown Lennie, listed as an assistant in geography for 1912–19.
7. University of Edinburgh, *Calendars*, 1912–21.
8. L. Moore, *Bajanellas and semilinas: Aberdeen University and the education of women, 1860–1920* (Aberdeen, 1991), p. 51.
9. E. J. Morley, "Women at the universities and university teaching as a profession", in *Women workers in seven professions*, E. Morley (ed.) (London, 1914), p. 18.
10. I. B. Horner & E. A. Haworth, *Alice M. Cooke: a memoir* (Manchester, 1940), p. 9.
11. *Ibid.*, pp. 13–14.
12. This was in spite of the sentiments that had been expressed by Mrs Albright-King in 1902: see her correspondence with Oliver Lodge, cited in n. 54, Chapter 2 of this volume.
13. E. Huws-Jones, *Margery Fry, the essential amateur* (London, 1966), p. 79.
14. See Chapter 2.
15. Minutes of the day training committee, University College of North Wales, vol. I, 9 May 1894 to 8 May 1907. See entry for 11 May 1898 (University College of North Wales, Bangor).
16. *Ibid.*
17. J. B. Thomas, "University College, Bristol: pioneering teacher training for women", *History of Education* 17(1), pp. 59, 67, 1988.
18. M. F. Pease, "Some reminiscences of University College, Bristol", unpublished typescript, 1942 (Bristol University), p. 15.
19. S. B. Chrimes (ed.), *University College, Cardiff: a centenary history, 1883–1983* (Cardiff, 1983), pp. 279–80, and p. 68, note 79.
20. *Ibid.*, p. 68; J. B. Thomas, "Students, staff and curriculum in a day training college: a case study of University College, Cardiff, 1890–1914", *Paeda-*

gogica Historica 2(25), p. 288, 1985.
21. A. H. Halsey & M. Trow, *The British academics* (London, 1971), p. 140.
22. University Grants Committee, *Returns from universities and university colleges in receipt of Treasury grant for the academic year 1930–31* (London, 1932), p. 26.
23. W. H. Dawson (ed.), *Yearbook of the universities of the Empire (of the Commonwealth)* (London, annually from 1914, not published 1941–46).
24. *The directory of women teachers and other women engaged in higher and secondary education* (London, 1913); see also editions published in 1914, 1925, and 1927; *Hutchinson's woman's Who's Who* (London, 1934).
25. *Ibid.*, pp. 647–60.
26. Completed questionnaires "On the position of women on the teaching staff of the universities or other equivalent institutions of higher education in Great Britain", circulated by the British Federation of University Women, for return by 25 January 1931 (BFUW archives).
27. M. Rendel, "How many women academics, 1912–1976?" in *Schooling for women's work*, R. Deem (ed.) (London, 1980), p. 148.
28. *Ibid.*
29. F. Perrone, "Women academics in England, 1870–1930", *History of Universities* XII, p. 343, 1993.
30. *Ibid.*
31. British Federation of University Women, *Annual report*, 1930–1, pp. 35–6.
32. Rendel, "How many women academics, 1912–76?", pp. 144–55.
33. *Ibid.*, p. 150.
34. Morley, "Women at the universities and university teaching as a profession", pp. 15–16.
35. P. Sheavyn, *Higher education for women in Great Britain* (International Federation of University Women, pamphlet No. 2, London, n.d.), p. 17.
36. Morley, "Women at the universities and university teaching as a profession", p. 22.
37. Rendel, "How many women academics, 1912–76?", p. 150.
38. Morley, "Women at the universities and university teaching for women", pp. 17–18; Sheavyn, "Higher education for women in Great Britain", p. 17.
39. Morley, "Women at the universities and university teaching for women", pp. 16–17.
40. *Ibid.*, p. 18.
41. *Ibid.*
42. *Ibid.*, p. 23.
43. F. Perrone, *University teaching as a profession for women in Oxford, Cambridge and London, 1870–1930*, DPhil (University of Oxford, 1991), p. 200; C. Bingham, *The History of Royal Holloway College, 1886–1986* (London, 1987), p. 148.
44. Minute books, 1909 – British Federation of University Women; see report of meeting on 27 March 1915 (BFUW archives).

45. Morley, "Cost and duration of courses for the first degree in the faculties of arts and science, together with scholarships in those faculties available for women at the universities and university colleges of the United Kingdom", Table 1 in *Women workers in seven professions*, pp. 82–136.

46. I. Smedley MacLean, "A short account of the British Federation of University Women", presidential address delivered to annual general meeting of council of BFUW, June 1935 (BFUW archives), pp. 1–2; Sondheimer, *History of the British Federation of University Women*, p. 1.

47. Sondheimer, *History of the British Federation of University Women*, p. 1.

48. Minute books, 1909 – BFUW, report of first meeting on 9 October 1909 (BFUW archives).

49. *Ibid.*

50. Smedley, "A short account of the British Federation of University Women", p. 2.

51. *Ibid.*, p. 5.

52. See annual reports of BFUW, and printed newsletter, from April 1930 (after no. 22, *The University Women's Review*).

53. Applications for BFUW Fellowships, including Rose Sidgwick Memorial Fellowship (BFUW archives).

54. Perrone, *University teaching as a profession for women in Oxford, Cambridge and London*, pp. 203–5.

55. Minutes of Gilchrist Educational Trust, 1874 onwards (Trust archives, Mary Trevelyan Hall).

56. Papers relating to Shaw Research Scholarships, 1900 (archives, LSE).

57. Correspondence, Mrs C. F. Shaw to Miss McTaggart, 17 and 30 April 1911; and advertisement for Shaw Studentship May 1911, in papers relating to Shaw Research Scholarships (archives, LSE).

58. C. F. Shaw to Miss McTaggart, 23 July 1915; see also Mrs Shaw's memorandum to W. P. Reeves suggesting subjects for research, 8 June 1911 (archives, LSE).

59. Papers relating to Hutchins' research studentship, 1898 (archives, LSE).

60. See typescript note from Miss McTaggart, 8 November 1938, referring to Hutchins' women's studentship (archives, LSE); B. L. Hutchins & A. Harrison, *A history of factory legislation* (Westminster, 1903); and B. L. Hutchins, *Women in modern industry* (London, 1915).

61. List of those awarded Hutchins' research studentships, 1926–46 (archives, LSE).

62. K. Lonsdale, "Women in science: reminiscences and reflections", *Impact of Science on Society*, XX, p. 55, 1970.

63. *Royal Commission on university education in London* (Haldane Commission) (London, 1911), vol. 13, appendix to third report with minutes of evidence, Cd. 5911, paras. 7189 to 7192.

64. *Ibid.*, paras. 7189–7190.

65. "Report of committee on the proportion of women on the staff", 10 November 1911, bound in with reports of the council of the University of Liv-

erpool, vol. 3, 1911 (archives, Liverpool University).
66. A. Walton, "Attitudes to women scientists", *Chemistry In Britain* (May 1985), p. 465.
67. K. Lonsdale, "Women in science", p. 46.
68. A. Walton, "Attitudes to women scientists", p. 465; L. A. Hall, "Chloe, Olivia, Isabel, Letitia, Harriette, Honor and many more: women in medicine and biomedical science, 1914–45", in *This working-day world: women's lives and culture(s) in Britain 1914–45*, S. Oldfield (ed.) (London, 1994), p. 196.
69. R. Love, "'Alice in Eugenics-land': feminism and eugenics in the scientific careers of Alice Lee and Ethel Elderton", *Annals of Science* 36, pp. 145–58, 1979.
70. *Ibid.*, p. 157.
71. *Ibid.*
72. D. Weston, *Clio's daughters, change and continuity: the question of the role of women academics in the "old" and "new" women's history*, MA thesis (Thames Polytechnic, 1987).
73. *Ibid.*, pp. 47–8.
74. M. Berg, "The first women economic historians", *Economic History Review* XLV(2), pp. 309–329, 1992.
75. *Ibid.*, p. 314.
76. *Ibid.*, pp. 315–16.
77. *Ibid.*
78. *Ibid.*, pp. 319–20; see also article on Lilian Knowles in *Clare Market Review* VI(1), pp. 16–17, 1925.
79. Berg, "The first women economic historians", p. 322 ff.
80. *Ibid.*, pp. 320–321.
81. L. Grier, *The life of Winifred Mercier* (Oxford, 1937), p. 81.
82. *Ibid.*
83. M. Ellman, "Academic women", in *And Jill came tumbling after: sexism in American education*, J. Stacey, S. Béreaud, J. Daniels (eds) (New York, 1974); "The damned tribe of scribbling women", in M. Proctor, *The English university novel* (Berkeley & Los Angeles, 1957); "Barbarous women", in I. Carter, *Ancient cultures of conceit: British university fiction in the post-war years* (London, 1990).
84. Correspondence, E. Power to G. Coulton, 23 December 1920 (Power papers, archives, Girton College). Quoted in Berg, "The first women economic historians", p. 325.
85. See Chapters 2 and 3 of this volume.
86. M. Murray, *My first hundred years* (London, 1963), pp. 97–8.
87. *Ibid.*, p. 98.
88. J. Richardson, *Enid Starkie* (London, 1973), p. 102.
89. E. M. Butler, *Paper boats* (London, 1959), p. 113; see also the same author's *The tempestuous prince* (London, 1929).
90. Butler, *Paper boats*, p. 115.

91. C. Collet, *Educated working women: essays on the economic position of women workers in the middle classes* (London, 1902), p. 58.
92. Murray, *My first hundred years*, p. 154.
93. Love, "Alice in Eugenics-land", p. 148; cf. also the position of Violette Lafleur in the department of Egyptology at UCL in the 1930s, R. M. Janssen, *The first hundred years: Egyptology at University College London, 1892–1992* (London, 1992), pp. 35–6.
94. Love, "Alice in Eugenics-land", p. 157.
95. *Ibid.*
96. From UGC report, cited in *Key profession*, H. J. Perkin (London, 1969), p. 79.
97. A. Temple Patterson, *The University of Southampton: a centenary history of the evolution and development of the University of Southampton, 1862–1962* (Southampton, 1962), p. 152; Contracts book, 1900–1929 (archives, Southampton University).
98. Questionnaires returned to BFUW in 1931, see note 26.
99. Correspondence, James Graham to Dr Baillie, 18 May 1931 (archives, central filing office, Leeds University).
100. *Ibid.*
101. Memorandum on Tutor to Women Students, 28 July 1931 (archives, Leeds University).
102. J. Baillie, "Notes on the appointment of a successor to Miss Silcox", 18 May 1931 (archives, Leeds University), pp. 6–7.
103. See categories designated on BFUW questionnaires, 1931 (BFUW archives).
104. BFUW annual report, 1930–1, pp. 35–6; see also correspondence, Miss K. Johnston to Lady Simon, 20 May 1932 (BFUW archives). The 16 women professors were *in London*: Doris Mackinnon (King's, zoology); Hilda Johnston, (Royal Holloway, history); Winifred Cullis (London School of Medicine for Women, physiology); A. Louise McIlroy (Royal Free Hospital School of Medicine for Women, obstetrics and gynaecology); Mary Lucas Keene (Royal Free, anatomy); Ada Levett (Westfield, history); L. Susan Stebbing (Bedford, philosophy); Lilian Penson (Bedford, history); Helen Gwynne-Vaughan, (Birkbeck, botany); Eva Taylor, (Birkbeck, geography). *Outside London*: Helen Wodehouse (Bristol, education); Edith Morley (Reading, English language); Olive Wheeler (Cardiff, education); Mary Williams (Swansea, French); P. Sargant Florence, (Birmingham, commerce); and L. P. de Castelvecchio (Birmingham, Italian).
105. Morley, "Women at the universities and university teaching as a profession", pp. 20–21.
106. Love, "Alice in Eugenics-land", p. 152.
107. File on M. Murray (records office, University College London).
108. *Ibid.*
109. University Grants Committee, *Report for academic year 1923–4*, p. 21.
110. *Ibid.*
111. L. Moore, *Bajanellas*, p. 73.

112. M. Murray, *My first hundred years*, pp. 158–9.
113. *Ibid.*, p. 159.
114. *Ibid.*, p. 160.
115. Gwyn Jones, "The colour of then", in *Fountains of praise: University College Cardiff, 1883–1983*, G. Jones & M. Quinn (eds) (Cardiff, 1983), p. 190.
116. M. Stocks, *My commonplace book*, (London, 1970), p. 179.
117. *Ibid.*, p. 180.
118. I. Sommerkorn, *On the position of women in the university teaching profession in England: an interview study of 100 women university teachers*', D.Phil (LSE, 1967), pp. 166–84.
119. J. Bernard, *Academic women* (Pennsylvania, 1964), cited in Sommerkorn, p. 166.
120. Sommerkorn, *On the position of women*, p. 166.
121. *Ibid.*, p. 170.
122. *Manchester Guardian*, 12 February 1960 (cited in *Enid Starkie*, J. Richardson, p. 218).
123. *Ibid.*
124. *Ibid.*, p. 115.
125. For a useful discussion of these themes see C. Heilbrun, *Writing a woman's life* (London, 1988), pp. 23–25.
126. *Ibid.*, p. 23.
127. J. Harrison, *Reminiscences of a student's life* (London, 1925); see also L. Lumsden, *Yellow leaves*; and J. Marcus, "Invincible mediocrity: the private selves of public women" in *The private self: theory and practice of women's autobiographical writings*, S. Benstock (ed.) (London, 1988), pp. 139–41.
128. Murray, *My first hundred years*, p. 166.
129. See file on M. Murray (records office, University College London). See also R. M. Janssen, *The first hundred years: Egyptology at University College London,* p. 28ff. Janssen's account suggests that Margaret Murray's attitude to Petrie's successor, Glanville, could be less than co-operative at times: "Her unwavering devotion to Petrie proved awkward on the advent of a new régime, although, according to eye-witnesses, the new Reader was as considerate to her as possible and acknowledged her strong points. Nonetheless, she once reported him to the Provost because he sometimes stayed behind after hours with a few of his female students when she was not there to chaperone them. Actually such late stays occurred in order to sort out the collection at a quiet time of the day". (Janssen, p. 30).
130. J. B. Thomas, "University College Bristol: pioneering teacher training for women", p. 67.
131. See entry for Geraldine Hodgson in *Newnham College register*, vol. I, 1871–1923, p. 89.
132. Thomas, "University College Bristol", p. 68.
133. See references to Bristol in ED 119/5, Public Records Office.
134. Thomas, "University College, Bristol", pp. 66–8.

135. E. Morley, "Looking before and after: reminiscences of a working life", unpublished typescript (archives, Reading University, n.d., *c.*1940–6), p. 120. For Professor Mackenzie see note 19.

136. Morley, "Looking before and after", p. 118.

137. For a useful selection of such obituaries see *Appendices* in Weston, "Clio's daughters".

138. J. C. Holt, *The University of Reading: the first fifty years* (Reading, 1977), p. 90.

139. *Ibid.*, pp. 88–9.

140. *Ibid.*, p. 89.

141. *Ibid.*

142. Correspondence relating to Edith Morley's position on the staff, 1910–12 (Box 239, archives, Reading University).

143. Morley, "Looking before and after", p. 23ff.

144. *Ibid.*, p. 59. Between 1904 and 1907 nearly 700 women took advantage of Trinity College Dublin's offer to confer degrees on women who were in all but name graduates of Oxford or Cambridge. These women were locally known as "the steamboat ladies" because most of them arrived in Dublin by ferry the night before graduation. See S. Parkes, "Trinity College Dublin, and 'the steamboat ladies', 1904–1907", unpublished paper (Conference on women and higher education, University of Aberdeen, 1994).

145. Morley, "Looking before and after", p. 60.

146. *Ibid.*, p. 84.

147. *Ibid.*, pp. 93–4.

148. *Ibid.*, p. 95.

149. *Ibid.*, pp. 96–100; pp. 114–16.

150. *Ibid.*, p. 115. Morley could be scrupulous in self-assessment: "I was a successful lecturer and teacher; I possessed the makings of a tolerable scholar and I was already engaged upon research work of importance. But I knew that I had no claim to outstanding intellectual gifts and that it was beyond my power to produce original work of a high order". (p. 116).

151. *Ibid.*, p. 115.

152. Handwritten memorandum by Childs, June 1912 (Box 239, archives, Reading University).

153. Morley, "Looking before and after", p. 116.

154. *Ibid.*, p. 117.

155. Correspondence, Morley to Childs, July 1912 (Box 239, archives, Reading University).

156. Memorandum from de Burgh to Childs on Professor Morley's position, 20 June 1912 (Box 239, archives, Reading University). See also correspondence, Childs to de Burgh, 18 June 1912.

157. Morley, "Looking before and after", p. 118.

158. *Ibid.*, p. 119.

159. *Ibid.*

160. *Ibid.*, p. 124.

161. Perrone, "Women academics in England, 1870–1930", p. 360.

162. Alice Gordon, examining the histories of 1,486 ex-students of women's colleges in 1895, reported that only 208 of her sample had married. See A. Gordon, "The after careers of university educated women", *The Nineteenth Century* XXXVII, pp. 955–60, 1895. On alternatives to marriage for educated women see M. Vicinus, "'One life to stand beside me': emotional conflicts in first generation college women in England", *Feminist Studies* 8(3), pp. 603–628, 1982, and the same author's *Independent women: work and community for single women, 1850–1920* (London, 1985).

163. C. Haldane, *Motherhood and its enemies* (London, 1927), p. 148; R. Lehmann, *Dusty answer* (London 1927). "Clemence Dane's" (Winifred Ashton's) *Regiment of women* (London, 1917), represents the best-known attempt to "pathologise" the lesbian-spinster teacher in the literature of the period, although the setting in this novel is that of a school rather than a college. Dorothy Sayers' *Gaudy night* (London, 1935), preys upon the protagonists' (and readers') stereotypes about sexually frustrated women dons only to demolish them. For background to the scapegoating of lesbian teachers see S. Jeffreys, *The spinster and her enemies: feminism and sexuality, 1880–1930* (London, 1985), and L. Faderman, *Surpassing the love of men: romantic friendship and love between women from the Renaissance to the present* (London, 1982).

164. B. Webb, *Diary,* entry for 1 March 1986, in *All the good things of life, the diary of B. Webb,* vol II, *1892–1905,* N. & J. Mackenzie, (eds) (London, 1983), pp. 91–2.

165. Morley, "Women at the universities and university teaching as a profession", p. 23.

166. Responsibilities that Morley discussed in "Looking before and after", p. 71.

167. Morley, "Women at the universities and university teaching as a profession", pp. 23–4.

168. On the marriage bar in school teaching see A. Oram, "Serving two masters? The introduction of a marriage bar in teaching in the 1920s", in *The sexual dynamics of history,* The London Feminist History Group (eds) (London, 1983).

169. E. E. Phare, "From Devon to Cambridge, 1926: or, mentioned with derision", *The Cambridge Review* (26 February 1982), p. 149.

170. *Ibid.*

171. *Ibid.*

172. Liverpool University Council minutes, 21 February 1933 (archives, Liverpool University).

173. *Ibid.,* see also T. Kelly, *For advancement of learning: the University of Liverpool, 1881–1981* (Liverpool, 1981), p. 207.

174. Margaret Miller's private papers, correspondence and scrapbooks relating to the events of 1921–34 are currently held by Mrs J. Bhatt, and will eventually be lodged in Liverpool University's archives. Copies of some of these letters have already been deposited (D. 384, archives, Liverpool Univer-

sity).

175. Correspondence, M. Miller to Hector Hetherington, 16 October 1932 (M. Miller papers).

176. Correspondence, M. Miller to Mrs Adami, 11 December 1932; Hector Hetherington to M. Miller, 15 December 1932; M. Miller to Hector Hetherington, 13 February 1933 (M. Miller papers).

177. Correspondence, K. Johnson (Secretary of the BFUW) to M. Miller, 31 October 1932 (M. Miller papers).

178. Correspondence, E. Rathbone to Hector Hetherington, 12 December 1932 (M. Miller papers).

179. Correspondence, M. Miller to M. Adami, 11 December 1932 (M. Miller papers).

180. Correspondence, H. Hetherington to M. Miller, 8 March 1933 (M. Miller papers).

181. Ibid.

182. "Notes on statement made by Vice-Chancellor to women members of the teaching staff", 8 March 1933 (M. Miller papers).

183. *Ibid.*

184. Scrapbook with notices of meetings, press reports, and correspondence (M. Miller papers).

185. *The Daily Telegraph*, 13 November 1933, press cuttings in scrapbook; correspondence, Monica Whately to M. Miller, 31 October 1933 (M. Miller papers).

186. Correspondence, May McKisack to Margaret Miller, 26 October 1933 (M. Miller papers).

187. Kelly, *For advancement of learning*, pp. 207–8.

188. Correspondence, H. Hetherington to M. Miller, 22 May 1934 (M. Miller papers).

189. *Ibid.*

190. M. Miller, letter of application for employment with United Women's Insurance Society, 15 June 1934; and correspondence, Alice Samuel to M. Miller, 22 January 1934 (M. Miller papers).

191. Minutes of 36th meeting of the central council of the Association of University Teachers held on Friday, 26 May 1933; item 15, in minutes of AUT Council, 1919–1975 (Modern Records Centre, Warwick University).

192. Minutes of 37th meeting of the central council of the AUT, Thursday, 14 December 1933; item 9, minutes of AUT Council (Modern Records Centre, Warwick University).

193. Correspondence, Dora Yates to M. Miller, 22 November 1933 (M. Miller papers).

194. Minutes of 37th meeting of central council of AUT (Modern Records Centre, Warwick University).

195. E. H. Neville, "The misdemeanour of marriage", *The Universities Review* VI(1), p. 7, October 1933.

196. I. Smedley Maclean, M. Buer, M. Bond, M. Ormerod, reply to E. H.

Neville printed in *The Universities Review*, pp. 180–1, April 1934.
197. I. M. Bisson, "Presidential address", 14 December 1934 (uncatalogued AUT papers, Modern Records Centre, Warwick University) quoted by Perrone, *University teaching as a profession for women*, p. 245.
198. Leaflet issued by NUT, 1931 (archives of National Union of Women Teachers, Institute of Education library, University of London). Reproduced in P. Owen, "'Who would be free, herself must strike the blow': the National Union of Women Teachers, equal pay, and women within the teaching profession", *History of Education* 17(1), p. 93, 1988.
199. Correspondence, J. W. McBain to D. Laurie, 18 March 1918 (AUT archives, MSS 27/3/2, Modern Records Centre, Warwick University).
200. See note on "Men lecturers' committee" (DM 219, special collections, Bristol University).
201. "Second report of the men lecturers' committee, 1909" (DM 219, special collections, Bristol University).
202. E. Anstruther, "Ladies' clubs", *The Nineteenth Century* XLV, p. 611, 1899.
203. P. Sheavyn, "Professional women", in *The position of woman: actual and ideal . . . papers delivered in Edinburgh in 1911 with a preface by Sir Oliver Lodge* (London, 1911), p. 99.
204. Correspondence, G. H. Radford to Caroline Spurgeon, (n.d.) (archives, Royal Holloway College), cited by Perrone, *University teaching as a profession for women*, p. 209.
205. Lonsdale, "Women in science", p. 51.
206. Quoted by Sir Mortimer Wheeler in his book *The British Academy, 1949–1968* (Oxford, 1970), p. 6.
207. E. Oxford, "The comfort of a frumpy chair" *The Independent*, 13 August 1992, p. 10.
208. A. G. E. Carthew, *The University Women's Club: extracts from fifty years of minute books, 1886–1936* (Eastbourne, 1985), p. 1.
209. *Ibid.*, pp. 1–7.
210. *Ibid.*, see also archival material (including house committee minute books, minutes of annual general meetings, and album of distinguished members compiled by Grace Thornton), University Women's Club, 2, Audley Square, London. The following information has been derived from these sources.
211. Carthew, *The University Women's Club*, p. 7.
212. *Ibid.*, p. 24.
213. *Ibid.*, p. 14.
214. *Ibid.*, p. 34.
215. Minute book, 1909–, entry relating to second meeting held on 3 January 1910 in Russell Square, London (BFUW archives).
216. *Ibid.*, entry for 30 March 1912.
217. *Ibid.*, entries for 19 October 1912, and 31 December 1912.
218. F. Perrone, *University teaching as a profession for women*, minute books (BFUW).

219. Minute book, 1909–, see entry for 31 December 1912 (BFUW).
220. L. Grier, *The life of Winifred Mercier* (Oxford, 1937), especially Chapters 7 and 8.
221. *Ibid.*, p. 122.
222. Minute book, 1909–, note on emergency meeting of executive committee, 29 July 1916 (BFUW).
223. Grier, *Life of Winifred Mercier*, pp. 150–7.
224. *Ibid.*, p. 142.
225. *Ibid.*, p. 152.
226. See Chapter 2 in this volume.
227. Grier, *Life of Winifred Mercier*, pp. 153, 252, and see Chapter 2 in this volume.
228. BFUW, annual report, 1931–2 (BFUW archives).
229. Sondheimer, *History of the British Federation of University Women*, Chapter 6.
230. M. Bowie-Menzler, *Founders of Crosby Hall* (London, 1981).
231. E. Batho, *A lamp of friendship, 1918–1968: a short history of the International Federation of University Women* (Eastbourne, 1968), p. 1.
232. G. Bussey, & M. Tims, *Pioneers for peace: Women's International League for Peace and Freedom, 1915–65* (London, 1965); S. Oldfield, "England's Cassandras in World War One", in *This working-day world: women's lives and culture(s) in Britain, 1914–45*, S. Oldfield (ed.) (London, 1994).
233. Batho, *A lamp of friendship*, pp. 1–5.
234. *Ibid.*, pp. 1–24.
235. E. Power, typescript of (untitled) paper for Sixth International Conference of International Federation of University Women to be held in Edinburgh, 1932 (BFUW archives).
236. Files relating to organization of conference with promotional literature and programmes, in BFUW archives. These also house a copy of the Pathe news film that recorded the events of the conference in July 1932.
237. *Ibid.* Typescript summaries of papers in BFUW archives.
238. G. Hudson, "Unfathering the thinkable: gender, science and pacificism in the 1930s", in *Science and sensibility: gender and scientific enquiry in England, 1780–1945*, M. Benjamin (ed.) (Oxford, 1991).
239. BFUW *Newsheet*, No. 8, November 1932, p. 7.
240. BFUW *Newsheet*, No. 11, October 1933.

Chapter Five

Student life

"Penetration" and "acceptance": thinking about change

Most of the historians who have considered the impact of women's admission to the universities between 1880 and 1939 have drawn a distinction between the early period of the pioneers, who established a right to entry, and a later period of acceptance and integration. The first chapter of Mabel Tylecote's history of women at Manchester University was entitled the "Period of penetration, 1872–1899", and was followed by a chapter on "Growth and consolidation, 1899–1914".[1] In her Fawcett Lecture on "Women and the universities: a changing pattern" in 1963, Dame Kitty Anderson spoke of the period between 1880 and 1902 as one of "spearhead attack", and of "dedicated zeal of the pioneering spirit". The "second stage", she suggested, ran from 1902 to 1944, and might be designated as "the broadening front, consolidation following the break-through".[2] Sheila Hamilton's study of women in the Scottish universities before 1939 follows a similar pattern, with its second chapter headed "Integration and acceptance: the first two decades".[3]

Helpful though it can be, there are also problems with this kind of approach. First, any tendency towards a narrative of steady progress makes it more difficult to account for the conflicts of the 1920s and 1930s, except in simple terms of backlash or stagnation.[4] Secondly, patterns of accommodation and institutional developments of the early period might survive and indeed develop their own momentum well beyond that time. The institution of special officerships such as superintendents, censors and advisors to women students at the turn of the century could affect provision for women up to the Second

World War, for instance. Thirdly, questions about the degree of integration achieved by women students through the period are not straightforward, and indeed can be argued to be much more complex than some writers have allowed.

In 1928 Margaret Tuke argued that the "semi-cloistered seclusion" that had characterized women's experiences of university life earlier in the century was a thing of the past: she claimed that men and women students could now "meet freely", run unions and activities jointly, and that "easy intercourse and co-operation" prevailed in colleges across the country.[5] But there were other observers who told a different story. An editor of Reading University's student magazine *Tamesis*, contended in 1932 that "the relations between the sexes here are for the most part either relations of open or veiled hostility", and that there was little camaraderie.[6] There were separate men's and women's unions in most universities, and informal segregation as manifested in shared refectories or common rooms bisected by an invisible line, with men seated to one side, women to the other, is a frequent theme of reminiscences and memoirs.

Segregation versus assimilation: interpreting the evidence

Perceptions of segregation and distinction, like those of discrimination, were to some degree subjective and relative. Even more importantly, as was suggested in the Introduction, patterns of segregation between the sexes could carry different meanings and have always to be considered in their specific historical context. Some forms of separation – such as the housing of women students in halls of residence at a distance from male hostels – could be so taken for granted that they barely aroused comment. Segregation might reflect a deliberate policy on the part of authorities keen to protect women from men, or men from women. It might be a result of male exclusiveness, or it might be a consequence of women's own self-conscious desire to foster their interests in a patriarchal community. Women-only societies might or might not be associated with explicit feminism, and the degrees of feminist awareness might, and indeed did, vary considerably through time. Even a cursory glance at the history of Manchester University's student unions will illustrate some of these complexities. Tylecote tells us that the women students formed their own union in

Manchester in 1899 with some reluctance, since they were excluded from membership of the men's union.[7] Relationships between the two unions were characterized by "mutual antagonism" before 1918, and both opposed any attempts to institute a joint union in the 1920s and early 1930s.[8] In Edinburgh, members of the Association for the Higher Education of Women seem to have taken it for granted that women students would need their own union, the establishment of which was originally connected with that of Masson Hall as a residence for women.[9] In 1939 the university's Rector envisaged the construction of a joint union – the women approved, but the proposition was opposed by the men.[10] Even the women students' proposal for temporary amalgamation in 1940 to save expense fell on stony ground, since the men "considered that they had not yet been reduced to admitting women within their sacred portals".[11] As late as 1966 a distribution of 800 questionnaires by the men's union in Edinburgh showed a majority of 85 per cent opposed to admitting women.[12]

With these complexities in mind, and in spite of the reservations expressed about any simple division of the period into stages of "penetration" and "consolidation", I will nevertheless approach the subject of student experiences chronologically, and look first at the reception of women in university communities before 1914. As was described in Chapter 2 this was a period in which almost all universities established posts of special responsibility for women students. It was also the period in which women's hostels and halls of residence were established, partly in connection with the universities' expanding role in teacher education during these years.

The late nineteenth-century debates over whether higher education would cause intellectual strain and even physiological damage to women seem to have fuelled less controversy in the provincial universities than in Oxford and Cambridge, at least outside medical circles.[13] Two of the leading proponents of the claim that intellectual exertion could seriously damage women's health were Henry Maudsley of University College London, and John Thorburn, who was Professor of Obstetrics at Owens College Manchester in the 1880s.[14] Thorburn's lectures on *Female education from a physiological point of view* were published in 1884, coinciding with the trial period of women's admission to the college. Tylecote tells us that when Annie Eastwood, who was one of the first female students to register, died of tuberculosis before completing her studies, Thorburn contended publicly that her death was connected with "over-education".[15] However, Dr Cullingworth, who succeeded to Thorburn's Chair in 1885, thought differently, maintaining that women's health was more likely to be undermined by lassitude than by overwork.[16] The university authorities insured themselves by requiring a written statement from parents or guardians of women embarking on degree work to the effect that they believed study would not prejudice health, but this practice was abandoned in 1903.[17] Testimony against the dire prognostications of Maudsley and Thorburn had been collected (separately) by two feminist scholars, Emily Pfeiffer and Mrs Sidgwick, in the 1880s. Pfeiffer's conclusions were embodied in her essay on *Women and work*, which was published in 1888;[18] Mrs Sidgwick's *Health statistics of women students of Cambridge and Oxford and of their sisters* appeared in print two years later.[19] Writing on "Women and the universities" in the *Contemporary Review* in 1890, the educationalist J. G. Fitch contended that these studies "made plain to all who study the evidence" that there was "no antagonism" between serious study and the healthy development of womanhood.[20]

Protecting women from men, or men from women?

The concern to protect women students stemmed more from notions of propriety than from anxieties about feminine health or physiology. As emphasized earlier, there was the need to reassure parents and guardians, which went hand-in-hand with the desire to avoid scandal. Much has been written of the elaborate systems of chaperonage that restricted women's freedom to associate with members of the opposite sex in late Victorian Oxford and Cambridge. Mary Paley Marshall remembered the social anxiety that might surface in response to the idea of women moving freely in public: even as a young tutor it was considered somewhat risky for her to travel to London alone.[21] These restrictions disappeared slowly, and were certainly in evidence right up until the First World War. Joan Evans, who became a student of St Hugh's in Oxford in 1914 recalled that:

> Regulations were numerous and old-fashioned: I remember going to the Vice-Principal for leave to go to look at Oxford architecture by myself, as there was a rule which said that students

should not go for expeditions in the city alone. Similarly, when I went to a class given in New College by Professor Myres, an old family friend, the central organisation of the women students provided a chaperon for me at 1s.6d. an hour. She sat and knitted, to Professor Myres' irritation; and startled me considerably by leaving me to walk home in the dark by myself. All these regulations had a certain justification: they reflected home discipline, and naturally reflected with it a certain time-lag; and they were drawn up in the fear of those who wished to keep women out of the university.[22]

Regulations of this kind were certainly not peculiar to Oxford and Cambridge. In Manchester the "lady students" had to submit to a "terribly severe code of rules" in the 1880s and 1890s:

It would have been the height of impropriety to enter the library and demand a book in the hardened manner now usual . . .

wrote one early student, in 1901:

No, we had to "fill up a voucher", and a dear little maid-of-all-work, aged about 13, went to the library with it. If we were not quite sure of the volume required, she might have to make the journey ten times, but it was never suggested that she should be chaperoned.[23]

Clearly as "lady students" became "women" this particular rule faded, but others remained in force. The first official joint ramble between men and women students took place under the auspices of the Students' Representative Council in 1904, with the Professor of Education, J. J. Findlay as chaperon.[24] Tylecote tells us that chaperonage requirements persisted until the end of the war in Manchester, although they could be evaded by the simple expedient of not advertising meetings and excursions on the college notice board.[25]

In Durham, women students had to contend with an extremely elaborate code of discipline that posed additional obstructions to their participation in what was a particularly male-dominated community. Records of the Women Students' Association, which was formed in 1899, indicate that the question of women's co-operation with the Students' Representation Committee (SRC) was a vexed issue at the turn of the century.[26] This was partly because the women felt that the SRC was only concerned with "the men's interests" and that it was near impossible for the women to speak at meetings. But Bessie Callender, as "Senior Woman" student, also pointed out that it was difficult for the women students to attend meetings of the SRC, which were held in the evenings, and that they were obliged to be accompanied by a chaperon, which altered the character of a meeting that was supposed to consist of students alone, without the presence of university officials of any kind. In view of these difficulties the women unanimously voted *against* sending representatives to SRC meetings.[27]

The records indicate that women in Durham were becoming increasingly impatient with the rules about chaperonage, which were often opaque in their complexity. In 1907 they held a meeting to discuss the Junior Proctor's ruling that women who illicitly "walked or talked" with male students were liable to be sent down. They noted that the interpretation of this rule was in the hands of the women censors and asked them to clarify the situation.[28] In June 1907 it was recorded that:

> Replies . . . were read from the Censor of Abbey House and the Censor of the Home Students. They agreed that women students should not walk or talk with the men except on special occasions, which were, according to the Censor of Abbey House, when the woman student was accompanied by her parents, Censor, or the Wife of a Don; but according to the Censor of Home Students, when she was accompanied by a Parent, or guardian, or a relative or friend recognized by Parents or Guardians as an adequate chaperon, or her Censor or the wife of a Don. Both agreed to lay any case of repeated or deliberate defiance of this rule before the Proctors.[29]

Not surprisingly, the students were somewhat confounded by this, and persisted, in a lengthy series of correspondence, to seek further clarification.[30]

Arrangements like this were not restricted to the older universities: chaperonage requirements and disciplinary codes were equally complex in Wales. As we have already seen, women students in Cardiff were assiduously protected from the dangers of joint dramatic productions, or "mixed pic-nics".[31] In Bangor, the ill-fated Frances Hughes zealously endorsed a rigid system of chaperonage. Gwynn Williams tells us that at one meeting of the debating society a speaker made reference to socialism: Hughes "immediately arose, her charges dutifully trooping after her to the safety-zone of the Women's Hall".[32] Bangor's Principal, Reichel, his nerves scorched by the incident involving Miss Hughes and Violet Osborn in 1892, became almost fanatical in his desire to avoid further scandal, but destiny ordained otherwise. In 1901 two couples left the college Eisteddfod by a side entrance, and the women in question failed to return to hall until after ten o'clock at night.[33] The women were punished by being confined to hall from five o'clock in the afternoon onwards, while the two men were sent down for the rest of the term. The students were outraged by this and planned a strike. Senate responded by prohibiting all meetings of students.[34] Meanwhile two more students were spotted holding hands in Anglesey. They were expelled.[35]

A good deal of unwelcome newspaper publicity followed, with *The Daily Mail*, *Punch*, and the *The Manchester Guardian* devoting space to the events.[36] Gwynn Williams has described how the college's regulations and prohibitions became even more explicit in consequence. Men students were not to meet women students by appointment, to walk with them to and from college, in college grounds, or indeed anywhere, and they were not to visit them in lodgings. The frontiers of the permissible were also firmly delineated: "reasonable intercourse" between men and women students was permitted:

(a) at authorized social meetings within the college;
(b) on the college field during the progress of matches;
(c) in the college itself for business connected either with college societies or with class work.[37]

Aberystwyth had also attracted unwelcome attention in the press for what was similarly referred to as a "Romeo and Juliet" incident in 1898. This was the episode that the young Olive Marsh had eagerly reported in a letter to her fiancé in October of that year.[38] In response to some whistling from below, an inmate of Alexandra Hall had committed the heinous offence of calling out to a male student from an open window of the hall. Miss Carpenter, the Warden, who had already identified the girl in question as a troublemaker, insisted that she leave the hall. The girl was sent down, although later she was allowed to return on condition that she lodged with the family of a member of Senate.[39] The offending male was rusticated for two terms. He was popular among his fellows, a large gathering of whom assembled in a mock funeral procession to see him off. There was considerable outrage in the town at what many considered a draconian punishment, and at one stage a riot seemed likely and the police were involved.[40] Olive Marsh's letters indicate that she felt considerable sympathy for the male student and also, interestingly, for Miss Carpenter. She had less time for the girl, whom she considered "fast" and guilty of calling Miss Carpenter "some pretty bad names".[41]

Miss Carpenter had worse to contend with. Olive Marsh reported a rumour that on 5 November the townspeople intended to burn her in effigy outside Alexandra Hall.[42] These were certainly troubled years for those responsible for disciplinary codes. Resentments simmered and another revolt was reported in 1904, when Miss Carpenter reported that Senate "wished the resident women students to have as little intercourse as possible with any men outside college buildings".[43] On this occasion the members of Alexandra Hall's Council responded with a statement of lofty tone. They declared that, while they were grieved at the evident lack of confidence that the authorities manifested in their ability to discipline themselves, they hoped that:

> Worthiness and true womanliness, refinement and true manliness will so pervade the atmosphere of our College life, that the Authorities will recognise our high ideals for mixed education.[44]

Poor Miss Carpenter had had enough and shortly afterwards she resigned. But, as was recounted in Chapter 3, her successor, Helen Stephen, was soon embroiled in a much more bitter series of conflicts over discipline. The matter of the "escort rule", allowing male students to accompany women to and from college events, was an early bone of contention, and it was Miss Stephen's insistence on limiting this right that precipitated the deterioration in her relationships with students in Alexandra Hall, culminating in the revolt of 1907 and her own resignation.[45]

The notorious "escort rule" stipulated that:

> When outside College, men students are not allowed to escort women students. Conversation between men and women students outside College is forbidden, except at public meetings, at athletic matches, at tennis, and at such social functions as are sanctioned by the Warden of Alexandra Hall.[46]

Its interpretation was a constant source of conflict and resentment in Aberystwyth before the war, as evidenced by a lengthy, bitter editorial in the student magazine *The Dragon* in 1914.[47] By this time all three colleges of the University of Wales had earned a reputation among the student population in Britain generally for the stringency with which they enforced their disciplinary regulations. Lindy Moore tells us that the Welsh colleges were mocked for their "grandmotherly legislation" by students in Aberdeen.[48] Similarly, Gwynn Williams notes that a Welshman from Warwick, with six children who had between them experience of various universities in England, Wales and Scotland, wrote to *The Manchester Guardian* asserting that regulations were far more effective in Scottish universities, where chaperons did "just sufficient to satisfy Mrs Grundy" and where there was far less "espionage and suspicion".[49]

The discussion so far has focused mainly on the ways in which university authorities reacted to the admission of women students before 1914. What was the response of male students? Several of the student debating societies had earlier discussed the question of the higher education of women and opponents had often carried a vote against it. In Aberdeen the debating society had discussed and rejected the higher education of women three times in the 15 years prior to their admission.[50] In St Andrews an article in the student magazine *College Echoes* in December 1897 expressed the hope that the discussions chaired by Bryce in London would hasten the institution of a women's university.[51] The writer pointed out that men in the debating society had recently voted overwhelmingly *against* the idea of mixed classes. Men felt their dignity compromised by co-education: a woman's university would protect "the unimpaired virility of Scottish university life".[52]

Articles in student magazines around the time of women's admission tended to be characterized by a tone of satire or nervous ridicule. Women students were labelled by jokey diminutives such as "bajanellas and semilinas", or "bejantinas" (in Scotland), "doves" (in Durham) or "sweet girl graduates" elsewhere. They were represented as being more obsessed by frivolous matters of dress in relation to the colour of hoods and styles of gown and mortar board than by the weightier concerns of academe. Alternatively, they were caricatured as "swots" and as unimaginative "goody-goodies" who attended every lecture punctiliously and faithfully transcribed everything that the lecturers said. Their presence was held to be distracting. In St Andrews, *College Echoes* declared that "the degree aspirant" would need to become "a recluse" if he wanted to concentrate less on the "coming troops of lady students" than on his studies.[53] The element of nervous insecurity that can be detected in these representations increased when women did particularly well in examinations, or were successful in securing bursaries. The October 1892 edition of *College Echoes* featured a humorous poem, "An admonition", addressed to male students who were urged to "gird their loins" and redouble their efforts on hearing that a young lady had come third in the bursary competitions ("A Girl is third! Hangs every Bejant head/Save two . . .").[54]

In Durham, as one historian has observed, women, "simultaneously cherished and feared . . . were kept at arm's length with a mincing courtliness that seems strange, and a little distasteful, to a more liberated age".[55]

The *Durham University Journal* responded to the admission of women with an editorial in March 1898 nailing its colours to the mast under the heading "Thus far shalt thou go and no farther". The author congratulated the union on its staunch refusal to admit women to membership, submitting that this represented a particular form of chivalry inherent "in refusing to place women in positions which we conscientiously believe to be unbecoming to their sex".[56]

The following year the same journal carried an editorial on "The intellectual inferiority of women", the gist of which reassured men that they had nothing to fear from "the much vaunted successes of female students since the universities were thrown open". They should take reassurance from history, which amply demonstrated women's lack of real distinction and the fact that the best of them would always seek fulfilment in marriage and motherhood.[57]

How did women students respond to representations of this kind? They were by no means wholly passive. A few brave women tried to engage in argument, but found it difficult to strike the right note. In "A woman's reply" to the above-mentioned article on "The intellectual inferiority of women", for instance, one female student in Durham countered that scholarly women were "none the less true and tender" than their less educated sisters and could not be caricatured generally as belonging to "the shrieking sisterhood". Learning might "ennoble and elevate" women, who seldom exhibited the "same bombastic dignity" and capacity for "pompous address" as men.[58] An attempt to occupy the high ground of moral earnestness was very common, although this often represented a retreat from, rather than any engagement with, argument and ridicule. When Edinburgh's student magazine scoffed at meetings of the Women's Debating Society in the 1890s (reporting a debate on "whether potatoes should be boiled in their skins?" for instance), the women students complained and threatened to cease sending notices to its editors on account of the wearing derisiveness of their tone.[59] There was a similar episode in University College London in 1904. Minutes of the Women's Union Society record that when the women took offence to an article lampooning them in the college's *Gazette*, they promptly returned their copies of the magazine and declared that they would no longer submit notices of their activities.[60] Withdrawal or retreat were often deemed preferable to the public exposure that would accompany any active riposte with male satirists. When the student magazine in St Andrews featured "a scathing indictment of university women" in 1912, accusing them of "stale conventionality" and a "lack of any real mental breadth", a woman *was* stung into reply. She pointed out that "the average woman student" was "terrified to give free play to her thoughts and actions", lest she find herself "the subject of unflattering discussion in the Men's Union".[61] Contributions such as this were rarely signed or even initialled, appearing anonymously as the offering of "A Woman Student", or under some pseudonym. The fear of male gossip could be an effective guarantee of silence.

A willingness to speak out, and to risk public exposure might be accounted as typically unfeminine, although the fear of visibility exhibited generally by those in minority or token positions has been much discussed by institutional theorists. R. M. Kanter has emphasized that

> it is often at those moments when a collectivity is threatened with change that its culture and bonds become exposed to itself; only when an obvious "outsider" appears do group members suddenly realise aspects of their common bond as insiders.[62]

Tokens or minority groups cannot be assumed to share the tacit understandings of an existing group, and their presence

> can lead dominants to exaggerate both their commonality and the tokens' "difference". They move to heighten boundaries of which, previously they might not even have been aware.[63]

It is in this way, Kanter has argued that the presence of a minority group can serve to under*line* rather than to under*mine* majority culture. Faced by token women in American corporate structures, men responded with heightened camaraderie and sometimes exaggerated displays of masculinity, particularly on informal occasions where the presence of women provided "both occasion and audience". Women who were bent on avoiding conflict and ridicule often responded by trying to keep a very low profile.[64]

Masculinity redefined: male ideals of fellowship and performance

Insights of this kind provide one way of looking at patterns of interaction between the sexes in university life. At the time that women were beginning to make their presence felt in university communities, assumptions about the membership of certain societies, or about the nature of male fellowship, were suddenly made explicit. This might take the form of deliberate exclusion. In Glasgow, for instance, the students' Dialectical Society altered its constitution to limit membership specifically to *male* students.[65] In several universities what had earlier been known as "the students' union" gradually became referred to as the "men's union". In Bangor we learn that a secret society, the Thirty (XXX) Club, was instituted in 1908: it was intended originally for all men students in their third or subsequent year as well as "leading men" in their second year, although later the membership was restricted still further to a total of 30.[66] There were many examples of what one might see as "a heightening of boundaries" to exclude women. We have seen that in Durham, the Union Society voted overwhelmingly against the admission of women students in 1898. The *Durham University Journal* reported the decision with some satisfaction, its editor opining that

> we fail to see how the admission of women to a club existing for the recreation of men is a logical conclusion of admitting them to a general scholastic education.[67]

A perceptible heightening of self-conscious masculinity is detectable in the union's activities thereafter in Durham, and not just in the short term. A historian writing in 1952 described the union's functioning thus:

> When a young man comes into residence in Durham, in seven cases out of ten he decides to become a member of the Union society. If he does so, he finds himself a member of the chief debating club in the University, and, indeed, as some would aver, in the North of England. And he is then in the succession of many whose first experience in oratory and official administration, gained in the Union Debating Hall and clubrooms, has stood them in good stead for the rest of their lives.[68]

Women were held at arm's length throughout the 1950s, although they were allowed in on "Ladies' Nights". (There were times when the women boycotted these occasions, such as 1912–13, when their attempts to secure representation on the SRC were rebuffed).[69]

The aura of masculinity was strong in Durham where before 1914 it has been observed, "muscular Christianity was the fashion, sport was king, and 'swots' were regarded as dangerous deviants".[70] An aura of maleness certainly pervades the student magazine *The Sphinx*, the pages of which celebrate "excellence in manly sports", "double palatinates", and an endless succession of "Men of Mark" and "splendid fellows" throughout the first two decades of this century. Women are rarely referred to, except in a jokey or condescending vein. In 1908, for instance, the reader (inevitably assumed to be male) is informed that:

> December 1st is to be a great Female Festival. A Suffragette meeting in the Assembly Rooms at 3 pm and a Ladies' Night in the Castle Hall at 8.15! The Chief Constable is importing a special squadron of police and . . . mice.[71]

Sport has received much attention from social historians who have emphasized the importance of games playing and athleticism in the construction of masculinity in late Victorian Britain.[72] Sporting activities in the universities were seen as possessing the same educational advantages for young males as their equivalents in the curriculum of the boys' public school. As Kate McCrone and others have emphasized, women's involvement in sporting activity was highly controversial and symbolically loaded, since it challenged both biological and social conventions about feminine frailty.[73] A transition from gentle callisthenics and dancing to more vigorous and competitive activity is evident in girls' schools after the 1880s. McCrone has argued that this came about through the influence of the first generation of college-educated women who had learned the importance of games in Oxford, Cambridge and London.[74] Although Lady Margaret Hall and Somerville had banned hockey and cricket in the mid 1880s, and rules surrounding women's riding of bicycles had been legion, she points out that by 1914 the women's colleges generally had become more confident, and a variety of athletic and sporting activities were well established. On balance, she contends, there was remarkably *little* controversy in the universities, and "the collegiate sportswoman appears to have been accepted as readily as the lady wrangler".[75] This last observation begs a few questions, of course. However, McCrone's suggestions that controversy was lessened by women's scrupulous observance of behavioural rules, and by the way in which femininity and propriety were emphasized by keeping play within the confines of college or private grounds, are more convincing.[76] In the oft-quoted expression coined by Frances Dove in 1891, the women aspired "to play like gentlemen, but to behave like ladies".[77] Most important of all, the women maintained their separation from, and avoided any challenge to, men's sport. Boundaries were crucial.

Men and women had separate clubs. Men were jealously territorial about their sporting facilities and grounds. In Manchester, women students of the 1880s and 1890s "tried to content themselves with playing squash-ball in the back yard of Brunswick Street".[78] Suggestions that they might have occasional access to the men's courts were not well received. One or two of the more chivalrous professors offered the women the use of their own courts.[79] When a women's hockey club was founded in 1896 its members had to use the asphalt playground of the local girls' high school.[80] Things improved after 1898, when the women were "rewarded" for their help in raising funds for the new college sports ground in Fallowfield by being allotted space for hockey and a share in the use of the pavilion.[81]

Mixed tennis playing was countenanced in most places by 1914. In Bangor, it was first licensed by Senate in that year, but only on certain days. The students' handbook commented that this was a privilege not yet extended to the playing of any "sinister winter game".[82] A heightened awareness of male clubbery and physical culture often went hand-in-hand with a nervous paternal protectiveness on the part of college authorities anxious to circumscribe women's activities, particularly in a mixed sex environment.

Boat-racing, women and sport

Reading University's archives contain some fascinating correspondence over the question of boat racing for women in 1917. Reading's Principal, W. M. Childs, was constantly anxious about discipline and student welfare, particularly where women students were concerned.[83] A series of detailed memoranda to the wardens of the women's halls show him much exercised by questions such as late leaves, student absences from dinner, and the wearing of caps and gowns.[84] In 1917 Childs appointed a committee consisting of Edith Morley, the Warden of St Andrews Hall, and the Censor of Women Students to help him investigate the vexed issue of the suitability of "rowing, racing and sculling" for women students.[85] They were to inquire into practice in other university colleges, and were asked to report on the kind of safeguards that other authorities might have adopted "in the interests of women students". Detailed question-naires asking for information about the kind of costumes that women might be required to wear, and whether "sliding seats" were thought appropriate in watercraft, were accordingly dispatched to Bedford, Westfield, Royal Holloway and the vice-chancellors and principals of universities and colleges elsewhere in the country. Some of the replies have been preserved. Sir Isambard Owen reported that boating was not really an issue in Bristol since the river was so un-suitable. Nevertheless, he added his own opinion, "as a physician", that rowing in races could hardly be considered a suitable form of exercise for young girls.[86] There were others who echoed this view, although Dr Aldrich Blake, from the London School of Medicine, adopted a different tone. Rowing was a healthy sport, in her opin-ion, and racing could do little harm to those of sound disposition: why not leave the boating club itself to make its own rules? Nothing could have been further from Childs' mind. Elaborate rules were for-mulated. A woman would need a medical certificate, her parents' permission, and the go-ahead from the Censor of Women Students before embarking on any training on the river. There was to be no racing for more than half a mile, and no competition with men. These regulations remained in force through the 1920s and were re-iterated by Sibley, Childs' successor, in 1931: "under no circum-stances" were a crew of women students "to race, or in any way compete with" a crew of men.[87]

There were many examples of such restrictions coming into force, even after 1914. Mindful of the problems associated with any overly simple model of history as progress, one might suggest *especially* af-ter the war. Both the threat and the experience of war brought con-siderable realignment of sexual divisions as men became absorbed in military activities and women moved into new territory at home. When male students and ex-servicemen returned there were prob-lems of readjustment in the universities as elsewhere.[88] Anxieties about women having invaded the male domain were strong, leading to some self-conscious assertions of masculinity in the 1920s. Tylecote mentions that there was a revival of athletic activity among women students in Manchester after the war, and that several new clubs (netball, lacrosse, badminton and athletics) were formed, but that much disapproval was voiced over the female interest in athletics, in particular, in that decade.[89] In Aberystwyth, Mrs Guthkelch, the Senior Warden of women's halls, nervously legislated against women's participation in "sack and potato races" at any athletic events, these activities being considered particularly compromising of femininity.[90]

The history of sporting activities among the women at King's College London is interesting, since it allows one to consider the implications of the transition from a single-sex to a co-educational milieu. According to Edith Morley, the King's College hockey club was one of the earliest London hockey clubs for women. The "sight of a hockey stick in a girl's hands" was sufficiently unusual "to subject her to cries of 'new woman' from passers-by or bus-conductors" in the 1890s, and she and her fellow enthusiasts were self-conscious and inordinately proud of their uniform.[91] The students were much encouraged by Lilian Faithfull, who was a keen player herself. Morley tells us that:

> Miss Faithfull's method of collecting players resembled her ways of obtaining examination candidates. Anyone became a student at King's by enrolling herself for a single course of lectures for a whole or even a half-term. The cheapest lectures were those in Divinity, since this was a compulsory subject for matriculated undergraduates at King's College, a C of E foundation. Consequently prospective hockey players without intellectual leanings were, I regret to say, encouraged to pay for half-a-term's course of Divinity Lectures, I think at the cost of 5/3, in order that they would be entitled to rank as students of King's and therefore to join the Hockey Club. . . . In this fashion we secured some of our foremost players. . . ..[92]

Morley insisted that it was the hockey club that really cemented friendships in the Women's Department and created a strong sense of belonging to a corporate body:

> I am inclined to think . . . that the training in sportsmanship in its widest sense . . . contributed something to our development which girls with our individualistic upbringing could have got in

no other way from a non-residential college.[93]

Bicycling was equally important. Like countless others of her generation, Morley recalled the gift of a bicycle as epoch making in the freedom it brought her to go about town on her own and to make long expeditions and tours in the country. A college bicycle club was formed in King's College for Women in 1897.[94]

Enthusiasm for sport seems to have waned among female students after the Women's Department became absorbed by King's College in the Strand. Minutes of the committee of the women's common room in the 1920s show a few energetic individuals trying to rouse their apathetic colleagues. In January 1922, for instance, it is recorded that:

> Miss Fisher Parker then addressed the women on the subject of sports. She said that it was important that they should take a much livelier interest in the athletic life of the college.[95]

The spur to a "livelier interest" was at hand. In March 1922, the minutes record that the professorial board in King's had decided to impose a ban on mixed sports and that the women students would not be allowed to participate in the annual sporting events of that year.[96] This decision seems to have aroused some of the more sedentary spirits and even Miss Plumer, the Women's Tutor, thought the ban somewhat peremptory. She took it upon herself to investigate the reasoning behind the board's decision.[97] The following day the Principal himself, Ernest Barker, came to explain the situation to the women. According to the minutes, the Principal explained that the professors objected to the idea of mixed sporting events for three reasons. First, on account of the physical differences between masculine and feminine physiology, "athletic excellence was only obtainable in sports for men". Secondly, they feared that the annual sports days were degenerating into mere social events. Thirdly, there was the question of the "decency of women's costume" and "of their participation in the tug-of-war", which several considered unseemly.[98] Some animated discussion followed. Miss Plumer expressed her opinion that no exception need be taken to the idea of mixed sports if they were properly conducted. Might they not take place that year as a test? She tactfully assured the Principal that if they came to believe "that the good of the college was endangered" by such events then the women, "being the smaller body", would be ready to give way. The Principal agreed to re-open the discussion with the professors.[99] The women do seem to have participated in King's fiftieth annual sporting events at Mitcham that May. But the women students' enthusiasm for athletics was short-lived. In May 1933, Miss Sawyer "proposed that the women's sports should be allowed to lapse altogether".[100] This was *not* judged to be a good idea and so female participation limped on through the 1930s.

Speaking out: women's debating societies

Sport remained one of the most gendered of student activities. Sexual divisions were also marked in debating societies. In the older universities these societies ranked among the longest established and most prestigious student organizations. They provided opportunities for men to sharpen their wits in political argument, and to practise and perfect those skills in oratory that would stand them in good stead for public positions in later life.[101] They were quintessentially arenas of masculine performance. We have seen how some of these societies had discussed and rejected the idea of women being admitted to the universities earlier, in the late nineteenth century. By the turn of the century, women were sometimes allowed into the debating halls as members of the audience. In Aberdeen in the 1890s, one woman student remembered that the women sometimes attended special debates "sitting in the galleries reserved for our use like medieval ladies at a tournament".[102] They were not permitted to sit in the lower part of the hall, where the seats were reserved for members. The formation of women's debating societies marked an important stage in the growth of the women students' self confidence. Speaking in public carried quite different implications for women schooled in feminine modesty and propriety: indeed it should be remembered that many Victorian girls' schools had traditionally discouraged any involvement in politics and controversial issues among their pupils.[103]

One of the earliest debating societies to be founded by women students was at University College London, and it came about largely through the initiative of Ada Heather Bigg in 1878. Records from the early years of this society show that the women were highly self-conscious about their activities. They were well aware of being in the public eye (early debates were reported in *The Queen*, and in a periodical called *The Alexandra*) and anxious to observe rules and proper procedures lest they incur disapprobation or ridicule from male students and professors.[104] Millicent Fawcett was chosen as Honorary President of the society, a position that she occupied between 1878 and 1883, when she was succeeded by Anna Swanwick. There was an early fracas over procedure when "after some slight irregularities . . . regarding the calling of a committee meeting" in 1879 the Secretary, Miss Murton, alleged that she received "sixty-five letters complaining of the mismanagement of the society". It was alleged that "many of the Professors in the College" disapproved of the women's activities, and Miss Murton decided to resign. But a majority of the members protested that no definite charges had been made against the women or their activities, and that there were other professors who looked favourably upon the venture, and so the society survived. The early debates were serious in tone, addressing social and political matters as well as literary subjects. Hardly surprisingly, many of the discussions focused on issues of particular concern to women, such as women's status on the schoolboards, "the industrial position of the sexes", and the entry of women into the professions. The 1880s saw debates on Home Rule, dress reform, the education of domestic servants, and Tennyson's poem *The Princess*. Clara Collet became an active committee member in the late 1880s and her interest in social and political matters was reflected in the subjects chosen for debate, especially after she became Vice-President of the society in 1887. Women like Collet, Heather Bigg, Mary Petrie and Ottilie Hancock were convinced of the need to encourage women to speak in public, seeing this as one of the most important components of a university education. As early as 1880 it had been suggested that members of the society who had kept silent for four consecutive meetings should be liable to a fine.[105] The society's activities were varied, including impromptu addresses, the reading of prize-winning essays, play readings, and mock-elections, as well as formal debates. Inter-collegiate debates were held from the 1880s onwards, both with the other women's colleges in London and also, in spite of the initial qualms of the Tutor to Women Students, with the men in UCL.

For a short period in 1918–19 the women in UCL seem to have decided to hold all their debates in collaboration with the men, but according to an account of the women's society written in the 1920s, "this arrangement proved to be unsatisfactory . . . and was discontinued".[106] Annual "foundation debates" were organized under the auspices of a joint committee, and the minutes from the 1920s indicate a concern that the chair on these occasions should sometimes be occupied by a woman. It was always more difficult to find women speakers when debates on political subjects were held in conjunction with men. When in 1926 it was proposed that the Women's Debating Society should amalgamate experimentally, for one year, with the men's society, there was considerable opposition on the grounds that many women felt it easier to speak in woman-only discussions.[107] The proposal was carried nonetheless, although the minutes indicate that the women were meeting separately again, at least on some occasions, by 1928. In January of that year we learn that the women received some special coaching in public speaking from a Miss Fogerty, who urged them to make use of what she considered "women's particular gifts in speech": allegedly their sense of order, their retentive historical memory, and their distinctively feminine powers of persuasion. "Women's Debating Societies should not be a mimicry of men's," insisted Miss Fogerty.[108] In March of the same year the Women's Debating Society proudly celebrated its fiftieth anniversary, the President pointing out that it represented the oldest women's society in UCL.[109]

Separate women's discussion groups and debating societies came into existence in a number of other universities in the late nineteenth and early twentieth centuries. Bristol had separate debating societies at least until the First World War. Women's debating societies were founded in Aberdeen (in 1896), in Leeds (in 1903) and in Glasgow and Edinburgh. There were separate societies in Manchester, too: although women were first invited to take part in debates organized by the men's union in 1895, Tylecote records that they showed fluctuating interest in such joint activities before 1914. Ellen Wilkinson, the future Labour politician, served as a Debates Secretary in 1912 and she inveighed against the women's apathy, nervousness, and lack of "speechcraft" in the university magazine of that year.[110] In 1907 the men's and women's unions in Manchester came together to debate the enfranchisement of women and the suffragists carried the vote, but Tylecote observed that "the debate, a noisy one, was not regarded as of high quality" and that many of the men had left before the vote was taken.[111] In debates among themselves or with women from other universities, the subjects chosen were even more likely to reflect women's concerns, such as their entry into the professions, the influence of university education on motherhood, or the desirability of economic independence for women. The ethics of vivisection was another subject commonly debated among women, and the first meeting of the Women's Debating Society in Leeds focused on this topic in 1903.[112] The subject was one that had long exercised advocates of women's entry into higher education, particularly in connection with the study of science.[113] But this is not to suggest by any means that topics of a broader political or social character were neglected by the women students who joined debating societies in the early years of the century.

There was a particularly strong tradition of women debating a broad range of social, political, feminist and literary subjects in Edinburgh, where a Ladies' Debating Society, (originally the "Edinburgh Essay Society") had been founded in 1865.[114] This society flourished under the aegis of Sara Elizabeth Siddons Mair and remained in existence until 1935. It was not formally connected with the university, although its members included many of the middle-class ladies who were prominent in the activities of the Edinburgh Ladies' Educational Association and the movement for women's entry into higher education both at the local and the national level. A history of this society, *Ladies in debate*, edited by Lettice Milne Rae, was published in 1936. Lists of members, together with a full list of the subjects debated throughout the society's existence, were printed as appendices in the volume. These provide a fascinating catalogue of the changing range of issues and controversies that exercised the minds of educated women throughout this period.[115] The Edinburgh Women Students' Debating Society, founded in 1893, inherited something of this tradition. Cognisant of the importance of schooling women in the arts of public speaking, the society advertised its advantages in the student handbook thus:

> If you wish in after life to be able to head an insurrection, give a public lecture, conduct the business of a sewing meeting, or dismiss cook with perfect ease – here you may learn the art.[116]

Something of a common pattern is discernible in the fate of these women's debating societies after the war. There was a tendency towards more co operation, if not amalgamation with the men's societies, but this might be checked, as in University College London, by the women's renewed appreciation of the difficulties involved in speaking in a mixed-sex milieu. The Edinburgh University Women's

Debating Society seems to have survived the war but to have disappeared by 1924.[117] A "Talking Women" society appeared shortly afterwards. This was an exclusive society, the membership of which was limited to 40 women who assembled "dressed in long black evening gowns", debating on occasion with an equally select men's society.[118] Margaret Laurence, who was a member of the Talking Women Society, also remembered representing Edinburgh's women students "at a king's speech form of political debate" with women from other universities in Scotland and Northern England.[119] Women were neither allowed to participate nor even to attend debates in the Edinburgh University Union before 1936. In October 1929, a particularly misogynistic writer in *The Student* had commented that union debates were now the only functions where women were properly "muzzled", "and, please God, we will keep them so".[120]

In 1936 the debates committee decided to break with tradition and to invite women to participate in a debate over the legalization of abortion.[121] Agnes McLaren, a final-year medical student, was invited to speak against Ian MacQueen, Senior President of the SRC. The union's committee of management promptly produced a regulation barring women from all parts of the building, including the debating hall. The invitation to Agnes McLaren was accordingly cancelled, and a male speaker substituted. MacQueen objected, announcing that he and McLaren would hire a hall and hold their debate as originally intended. The outcome was a compromise: the men would assume the speakers' roles but women would be invited into the hall and they would be allowed to take part in the debate. A recent historian of Edinburgh's union considers it

> a matter of history that the first participation from the floor of the House was a vigorous criticism by Agnes McLaren of parts of MacQueen's address.[122]

Some months later the union debates committee was replaced by a university debates committee, its members nominated by the SRC, and both men's and women's unions.[123]

The students of King's College Ladies' Department had established a literary and debating society by 1900. Edith Morley congratulated members on the progress they were making in the art of public speaking: contributions were becoming "less prolix", the repartee was much sharper, and "written speeches were being replaced by short notes and impromptu remarks".[124] The reorganization of the college on the eve of the First World War brought about the disruption of many of the women's societies. Women students in the Strand were allowed to join the King's College Union, although they had their own common room, and many of them chose not to. The women's common room committee soon busied itself with new initiatives, which included the formation of a new women's debating society in June 1921.[125] The women participated in inter-collegiate debates, but the reports of these activities in the *King's College Review* indicated that they were often nervous of speaking where men were present. Reporting a debate that had taken place in 1919, for instance, one writer asked:

> And the women – shy, were they? Only Miss Greenwood faced the ordeal of speaking.[126]

Male contributors to the *Review* continued to adopt a fairly derisive tone in commenting on the women's activities throughout the 1920s and 1930s. Women were represented as rather pathetic creatures who found cocoa parties "simply thrilling" and whose performance in sport and public debate was rarely better than execrable. In November 1933 for instance, one male wit parodied the "girlish" tone thus:

> A lot of us attend Union Society Meetings, and last year one girl got up and made a speech. This year it is hoped to arrange for a girl to ask a question in a Union Society meeting but it is *frightfully* difficult to think of something to ask. However, a temporary committee has been set up and questions are *heartily* invited. Come along, now, girls, and do your bit towards the cultural life of the College! We are also appealing for a girl to volunteer to ask the question when we have thought of it.[127]

Small wonder that the women were often reduced to silence.

Gender and misrule: women and the college "rag"

The passage quoted above appeared in a rag issue of the *King's College Review*. Most universities established a tradition of annual "rag weeks", characteristically involving elements of pantomime, carnival and general festivity. These were legitimized in terms of fundraising for union facilities or charitable purposes such as the support of local hospitals and infirmaries. In the Scottish universities a tradition of charivari and misrule was associated with rectorial elections, occa-

sions when the university authorities were often hard put to distin-
guish between licensed disorder and outright rowdyism or vandalism.
A certain amount of horseplay fuelled by heavy drinking could be
considered part of the *rite de passage* into adult manhood. Female students found themselves in an uneasy position in relation to such activities. Their women tutors urged them to keep their distance, and to
avoid anything that might smack of impropriety or attract public attention. In most cases, particularly before the First World War, they
needed no such warning. Enid Hamer (née Porter) who had been a
student in Liverpool between 1917 and 1922, remembered that on
"Panto Night", a forerunner of Rag Day, a cohort of male students
wearing fancy dress (those studying medicine particularly prominent
among them), would drag a disorganized procession of floats through
the city, collecting for local hospitals. "The participants were nearly
all men", she recalled, "and women students merely onlookers".[128] A
woman student from Queen Margaret College, Glasgow, around the
turn of the century, described her experience of rectorial elections in
an article for *King's College Magazine*, produced by the Ladies' Department in South Kensington:

> Every third November is a time of wild carnival to the students.
> Nobody does any work; we all canvass each other; the two po-
> litical committees shower on us all pamphlets and circulars, se-
> rious and skittish. The men entertain us at the Union, or selected
> speakers from the two clubs come down and somewhat sheep-
> ishly address us at QMC. Finally, on the day of the election, the
> students cast aside the last shred of self-control. The men turn
> out in strange costumes of red and blue, armed with pea-shoot-
> ers and riding in brakes. There are free fights round the voting-
> places; no ballot acts regulate the Rectorial elections. We too
> adorn ourselves with red and blue badges, caps or hat-bands; we
> too ride in brakes, and the more important members of commit-
> tee have hansoms at their disposal; but we refrain as a general
> rule, from pease-meal and free fights. . . . In the evening the men
> had a torchlight procession, but in this we naturally had no
> share.[129]

Similarly in Aberdeen, Lindy Moore observes that the women students refrained from participating in the general *brouhaha* of rectorial elections, although their approval might be considered important:
in 1909 for instance, some of the female students offered to help to

raise funds to pay for the cost of a carriage that had been smashed by their male counterparts.[130] Women were in effect part of the *audience* for effuse displays of masculine high spirits.

Things were slightly different in the 1930s when it seems that a growing self-confidence among women less inclined to be inhibited by traditional notions of feminine decorum required those in authority to exercise more vigilance. The minutes of the women's common room committee in King's College London for 1933 record the chairman's anxiety over a "rather free and easy" behaviour among the women, who were urged to try to "keep out of rags".[131] In Durham around the same time we find the students in St Hild's College who were also members of the university much exercised about their role in rag activities: was it "proper" for them to dress up or not? It was decided in the end that this was *not* a good idea but that the women should throw their energies into making costumes for the men.[132]

A double standard remained much in evidence in the 1920s and 1930s. In Aberystwyth for instance, the college's vexed disciplinary regulations, which were described earlier in this chapter, came in for particular challenge after the war, not least because of the registration of a sizeable contingent of ex-servicemen in the college. As E. L. Ellis has commented,

> Men . . . who had endured the horrors of the Somme or the dangers and privations of life at sea were not intimidated by the pop-gun power of the college social regulations. Prohibitions, including entering public houses, were simply ignored.[133]

A new era was ushered in by the "Compact of 1919", which suspended rules prohibiting conversation between men and women students, at least within a three-mile radius drawn around the town clock in Aberystwyth and during daylight hours.[134] There was even a concession towards joint consultation between Senate and the SRC over discipline. But *women* students were to stay out of this: it was not thought fitting that they should play any role in judging the behaviour of ex-servicemen.[135] Women students were granted official permission to participate in the student rag in Aberystwyth for the first time in 1931, an event that prompted one (male) writer to complain that the women "behaved like boys" and the men like "ninnies in trousers". He ridiculed the men on this occasion for having failed to summon sufficient energy to stage "a successful and virile Rag".[136]

Male contempt for the disciplinary arrangements in women's halls of residence generated regular satirical features in the student magazines of the inter-war period. Women occasionally joined this offensive, particularly those whose experience of war work had widened their horizons to a point where regulations seemed unreal in their pettiness. This was the tone of a poem, "Advice to women students", which appeared in Reading University's magazine, *Tamesis* in 1919, a representative verse of which read:

> When you think of long nights spent
> Making bomb and shot and shell
> Or of hectic nights when bent
> On filling forms and typing well
> Forget it, there is this dilemma
> Your lights go out at 10 pip emma.[137]

Women usually had more to lose by complaining or attacking the regulations than men, although this was not always the case. It is worth remembering an incident in Oxford in 1924 when Gerald Gardiner (a future Lord Chancellor) was sent down for co-operating with Arthur Tandy and the young Dilys Powell over the publication of "an offensive yellow leaflet" entitled *The truth about Somerville*, which lampooned the disciplinary provisions of the college.[138] The leaflet, which seems harmless enough today, was declared a "detestable and mischievous production" by the college Principal, Emily Penrose. According to Gerald Gardiner, in a letter of apology to Miss Penrose, the Vice-Chancellor had acknowledged that the pamphlet had been "written as a rag", but nevertheless maintained that it could be misconstrued outside Oxford, and had stated further that there "had been too much criticism by the *Isis* of the Women's Colleges, and that it must stop". He was under injunction "to leave Oxford by midnight".[139] Dilys Powell, who had earlier fallen foul of the authorities by being caught receiving a leg-up over the college wall after hours, had already been banished, and shorn of her Exhibition in college.[140]

But on the whole, male students were allowed, and took advantage of, a much greater degree of licence than women in the 1920s and 1930s. The female incumbents of halls of residence generally contented themselves with playing tricks on their fellow residents such as the ritual disordering of other students' rooms and the construction of apple-pie beds. Men were rather bolder in their misdeeds. In Reading, the students of Wantage Hall, for instance, had their annual celebration of "Sheep Night". This dated from 1928 when one student, rebelling against the Warden's habit of locking the hall gates at a regular time every evening, had discovered that a garage key in his possession served as a master key to these gates, and had driven a flock of sheep into the quadrangle to be discovered the following morning.[141] There was also an occasion when some drunken latecomers lit a bonfire outside the Warden's lodgings and, dancing round banging tin trays with pokers, called upon the Warden to come out to be burnt. Someone else broke into the clock tower and caused the clock to strike rather more times than it should have done at midnight. The neighbours called out the fire brigade. The students were eventually fined ten shillings each for their misdemeanours.[142] Boisterous initiation rites involving the buttock-blacking of freshers were a source of disturbance to the authorities in the 1930s, causing the Vice-Chancellor to warn that instances of "molestation" would lead to expulsion.[143]

Late nineteenth-century educational authorities often expressed the rather hopeful conviction that the presence of women students would cause men to modify their behaviour and guard against the tendency to excess. R. D. Anderson mentions that in Aberdeen the influx of "lady students" did indeed have a calming effect initially, and

> their presence inhibited rowdiness in class, leading to a decline
> in "passing up" and the rougher forms of ragging and gown-
> tearing.[144]

The student from Queen Margaret College, Glasgow, whose observations were quoted earlier, remarked that the women had been given to understand

> that the presence of girls (had) worked a great reform in the cos-
> tumes of the class. Formerly, I believe, it was by no means rare to
> see a man clad in a long overcoat, minus a collar, and looking
> somewhat slim. He had probably jumped out of bed five min-
> utes before the lecture and would go back afterwards to dress
> and breakfast.[145]

But the civilizing influence of feminine refinement was not always regarded as beneficial, and there were some male observers who resented the "petticoat invasion" as emasculating, or as sapping the virility of the nation's manhood.[146] It is interesting that R. D. Anderson observes that student drunkenness and hooliganism "seem to have reached new levels in the 1890s" in Aberdeen, in spite of having previously emphasized the calming effects of the early women students.[147]

This may be interpreted as an instance of "boundary heightening", with the men keen to proclaim their distance from the women.

Conviviality or misogyny?

The fact that masculine student culture and male conviviality might be hallmarked by elements of misogyny, even tantamount to what we would now regard as sexual harassment, could leave women students in a difficult position. R. D. Anderson has described the Aberdonian celebration of "bursary night" in the later nineteenth century. This took place in February:

> When the bajans were expected to emerge from their shells, and bursars, flush with money, would "visit the shrines of Venus or Bacchus". The "Shrines of Venus" were probably not brothels, but the local girls' schools, which it was the custom to besiege: the last day of the session in 1889, noted Bulloch, "the police . . . were out in all their strength to defend the ladies' seminaries in the city which our Bajan friends love to visit at this season".[148]

The offensive may not have amounted to very much, probably not much more than drunken singing and catcalls. But as was the case with the frequently observed tendency for men to array themselves in drag for rag-time pantomimes and carnivals, there could be elements of aggression in the display of masculinity that positioned women as objects of ridicule or as targets. The late-nineteenth-century sieging of ladies' seminaries had its twentieth-century counterpart in the developing tradition in many universities of the late night processions of men who descended on women's halls or hostels, culminating in drunken serenades and catcalls.[149] Thefts of door-knockers, seized as trophies, were the bane of lady wardens everywhere. The minute books of Masson Hall in Edinburgh contain more than one weary reference to "the removal of the doorplate" by gangs of male students, who could not always be prevailed upon to return it.[150] Depredations could sometimes take a more serious form. In June 1933, Marjorie Rackstraw wrote to the university Secretary complaining that "some of the Cowan House men" had broken into Masson Hall leaving a trail of scattered books and broken china and stealing the dinner-gong.[151] It was partly the experience of incidents of this kind that underlay the opposition of some of the wardens of women's halls (such as Marjorie Rackstraw herself, and May Staveley in Bristol), to schemes involving the construction of male halls of residence in close proximity to the women.[152]

Women's suffrage

The more misogynistic elements latent in male student culture often surfaced around suffragist activities in the universities between 1906 and 1913. In Aberdeen, the University Women's Suffrage Association planned a meeting in 1908 at which Rosemary Gawthorpe and Helen Fraser were scheduled to speak. Lindy Moore has described how this event "led to the type of pandemonium more often reserved for the rectorial contests".[153] Those who had tickets for this meeting (both men and women) were admitted to a room in Marischal College, but

> about fifty other male students gathered outside spoiling for a fight. They found a substitute for a battering ram and, bursting the doors in, invaded the meeting armed with handbells and whistles . . . a fight nearly started and a smoke bomb was let off.[154]

This event was not unusual. In Liverpool two years earlier, Charlotte Stopes had addressed a meeting of the University Women's Suffrage Society in the zoology lecture theatre. According to the *Liverpool Daily Post*, a group of male students had

> amused themselves by lighting cigarettes, throwing them half-smoked among the audience, howling, shouting and singing comic songs to the accompaniment of stamping feet[155]

The meeting had broken up in disarray.

The rectorial election of 1908 in Aberdeen was fraught with significance for suffragists since Asquith, a determined opponent of "the cause", was standing as one of the candidates. The more determined supporters of women's suffrage lent their support on this occasion to the Conservative Unionist, Edward Carson.[156] Temperatures ran high and when Asquith was returned his rectorial address was interrupted by a male student dressed as a woman.[157]

Some women students were also involved in militant and disruptive activities. In Liverpool, Margaret Ker, a student member of the Women's Social and Political Union who had set a pillar box on fire, spent her Christmas vacation and part of the following term in Walton

Gaol.[158] She was sent down, although the Vice-Chancellor allegedly visited her in prison and brought her books, and she was subsequently allowed to resume her studies in the university. Her mother was a well-respected doctor.[159] The majority of women students, even those who felt strongly over the issue of suffrage, were careful to avoid militancy, particularly in view of their need to keep their reputations clear for a future career in teaching.

However, the authorities in most universities became understandably nervous. In 1907, when students in Nottingham planned a lecture at which Mrs Pankhurst would speak about "Votes for Women", the college Council protested and two members were "so indignant" that they resigned.[160] The event had to be arranged off premises. Tensions mounted in the year before the war. In St Andrews, suffragists were suspected of involvement in a fire at the Getty Marine Laboratory in June 1913, although the local branch of the National Union of Women's Suffrage Societies (NUWSS) emphatically condemned the damage.[161] When the Scottish branch of the NUWSS wanted to hold its annual summer school in the women's hall of residence in St Andrews in 1913, some of the members of the University Court were hostile.[162] There followed an attempt to limit the terms on which the premises could be made available: none of the buildings could be used for "political propaganda" and only residents of the hall could attend meetings. The records reveal some anxious correspondence between Miss Dobson, Warden of the women's hall, Florence Hilliard, the organizer of the summer school, and Dr Elsie Inglis, who urgently vouched for the "law-abiding" character of the women.[163]

In October 1913, Bristol University's athletics ground pavilion at Coombe Dingle was destroyed in a fire that was popularly attributed to suffragettes. Whatever the facts of the situation, the male undergraduates of the university "took swift and effectual action". According to a report in the *Illustrated London News*:

> At 5 pm the next day a body of students, estimated at from 300 to 500, dashed out of the university and made for the Suffragette Offices (the Bristol Headquarters of the WSPU) in Queen's Road, which they completely wrecked. The furniture was thrown into the street and burnt. One suffragette, who was on the premises, escaped by a back way. Further attacks were made on the Saturday.[164]

Men were also implicated in episodes of suffrage vandalism in Aberdeen in 1913, when medical students cut the slogan "Release Mrs Pankhurst" in 12-foot high lettering in the turf at Duthie Park.[165]

There were suffrage societies in most universities in the period from 1906 to 1913, and several of them admitted men as well as women as members. In Scotland, as Sheila Hamilton has described, interest in the suffrage campaign was heightened by the struggles of a group of women graduates in Edinburgh who tried to establish their right to vote in the 1906 election.[166] The Universities of St Andrews and Edinburgh were represented by a joint parliamentary seat and "persons of full age and not subject to any legal incapacity" were eligible to vote, the university franchise being based on an educational rather than a property qualification. Five women graduates of Edinburgh – Frances Melville, Frances Simson, Elsie Inglis, Margaret Nairn and Chrystal MacMillan – applied for voting papers, and when these were not forthcoming, contested the decision in the Scottish Court of Session. Lord Salvesen's decision in June 1906 went against the women, who promptly appealed. When their appeal failed, they resorted to the House of Lords. In spite of some dignified pleading by Chrystal MacMillan and Frances Simson, the Lords dismissed the case in December 1908, and the women had to pay costs.[167]

The publicity surrounding these events stimulated interest in the suffrage question in universities in Scotland and Northern England. In Glasgow, a Queen Margaret College Suffrage Society came into existence in 1907, publishing a magazine, *Jus Suffragii Alumnae*. This seems to have recruited 60–70 members (out of a total of 600 matriculated women in the university) by 1913.[168] Edinburgh's Student Suffrage Society, with its magazine, *The Only Way*, was established two years later: Chrystal MacMillan and Elsie Inglis served as Honorary Vice-Presidents.[169] Aberdeen University's Women's Suffrage Association dated from 1908.[170] The suffrage societies in Edinburgh and St Andrews established their own libraries of literature on the subject. Donations of books and pamphlets seem to have come from all over the country. The minutes of the Women's Representative Committee in Edinburgh record that in 1906 Lady Wright, in Reigate, Surrey, sent pamphlets on the suffrage question, and that she had offered to donate complimentary copies of *The subjection of women*, "bound in art linen with the crest of the University" embossed on the cover, to all women graduands that year.[171] The offer was repeated in the following year. In St Andrews the house committee of the Women Students'

Union record a concern with the location of "The Suffrage Library", the contents of which were allegedly becoming rather "shabby and unsightly" by 1913, possibly as a result of being well used.[172]

Tylecote records that the Scottish women graduates' attempt to secure the vote in 1906 provoked a mixed response in Manchester, where an unofficial meeting of students (including representatives from Leeds and Liverpool) had voted *against* sending an expression of sympathy to the women involved in the struggle.[173] The *Manchester University Magazine* in 1905 carried an editorial deprecating the activities of the "Shrieking Sisterhood".[174] Interestingly, this roused the ever-diplomatic Edith Wilson into defending the women, in a letter that she wrote from her retirement in Italy.[175] A special general meeting of the Women's Union resolved to send a message of "hearty sympathy" and offer of financial support to the Scottish women graduates.[176] In Manchester, as in Edinburgh and Glasgow, student suffragists were encouraged by the support of many of their women tutors, as well as other women prominent in the intellectual, social and political life of the community.[177]

Women students' involvement in suffrage societies and their related activities provides only one measure, and that rather less than satisfactory, of the extent of feminism in the universities. Although many of the activists emphasized their preference for law-abiding tactics and were keen to dissociate themselves from militarism, there were many women, their sights often set on the sober prospect of a career as schoolmistresses, who preferred to keep out of the public eye altogether. One should remember that, in any case, the proportion of students active in university societies generally was always rather low. The vast majority were preoccupied with the daily realities of studying and survival. Brian Simon estimated that before 1939 rather less than 25 per cent of the student body at any particular time could be designated as "active in student affairs" and noted that

> any student officer was, up to the outbreak of war, prepared to talk at length about the general "apathy" of the student body, and of the difficulty of getting them to take part in activities.[178]

This view was echoed by "Bruce Truscot" whose study of the *Redbrick university* was published in the same year (1943) as Simon's *A student's view of the universities*. Truscot contended that it was comparatively easy to divide undergraduates into "the apathetic and the

keen", judging it "probably not an exaggeration to put the proportions at five to one".[179]

Women students and the community:
settlements and social work

One of the areas of student activity in which gender differences were
apparent, at least to some extent, was that of community and social
work. The nineteenth-century tradition of women's involvement in
philanthropy developed in new directions through the work of the
universities and their settlements from the 1880s onwards. Some of
the earliest societies formed among women in the universities were
devoted to charitable and philanthropic activity. Students of the
Women's Department in Manchester in the 1880s involved themselves in work with local mill-girls, and many enrolled as helpers in
the Clarendon Street Girls' Club and similar ventures well before the
university established its own settlement in 1895.[180] Two years later
Alice Crompton, a graduate in classics, was appointed Head of the
Manchester Settlements' Women's House. Some interesting research
was initiated by the women involved with the settlement in the 1890s,
who investigated the conditions of local women homeworkers, and
the employment of girl school leavers (in association with the National Union of Women Workers, in 1899).[181]

There were similar developments in Glasgow and Bristol. In Glasgow, the women students of Queen Margaret's College undertook social work in the Anderston district in the 1890s: the Queen Margaret
Settlement Association, with its own settlement house, was founded
in 1897.[182] It remained until 1935 a women's venture, although the
constitution was changed in that year to allow men to become members. (Both of the settlements organized by men in the university were
defunct by that time.[183]) In Bristol, a "Women's Guild" was founded
in 1899, at the suggestion of Miss Earle, who was then Tutor to
Women Students. As in Manchester and Glasgow, members concentrated their efforts on the welfare of women and children in the district, and worked closely with local girls' clubs.[184] The university
settlement in Bristol, initially conceived as a venture that would in-
volve both men and women students, developed effectively as a wom-
en's settlement.[185] The energy and initiative for social and community

work in Bristol came largely from the women tutors in the university, especially May Staveley and Hilda Cashmore. Staveley, Tutor to Women Students, a part-time lecturer in history, and Warden of Clifton Hill House, had considerable experience of social work. She had been Warden of the Women's Settlement in Birmingham between 1899 and 1905, and had subsequently lectured on "The Practice of Charity" in Liverpool University's School of Training for Social Work. Hilda Cashmore, like Staveley, a historian from Somerville, was Warden of the university settlement in Bristol between 1911 and 1926. Prior to this she had taught history in the day training department in Bristol, where she seems to have fired large numbers of women students with a zeal for social work. By 1911, 105 out of a total of 130 students in the department had enrolled in the Women's Guild for Social Service, which had been established by Rosamund Earle.[186] The Students' Guild was a highly active body, which organized an impressive series of lectures and discussions on the social issues of the day. Early speakers included Cecile Matheson, Warden of the Women's Settlement in Birmingham, who spoke on the position of women industrial workers; Mrs Townshend, on the subject of the Children's Act; and Seebohm Rowntree, on poverty.[187]

Bristol's university settlement had close links with the university's two-year "Testamur" course of training for those intending social work.[188] Indeed, connections between the voluntary involvement of women students in community work, the university settlements, activities of the Charity Organisation Society, and the gradual involvement of the universities themselves in the training of social workers, were apparent in London (with the establishment of the School of Sociology in 1903 at the London School of Economics), and in Liverpool, Birmingham, Bristol, Manchester, Leeds, Glasgow and Edinburgh.[189] The numbers of those qualifying with certificates or diplomas in social work before 1918 at least were small, but this area of the university curriculum was important in that a comparatively high proportion of those involved in the teaching of the subject were women.[190] This was one area of activity where women tutors and students sometimes took the lead in initiating new developments, rather than simply imitating men, and what began as voluntary activities might be gradually formalized, having some degree of impact on the university curriculum.

Martha Vicinus has explored the ways in which settlement work exerted such a strong appeal for college-educated women in turn-of-the century Britain. Work of this kind "emphasized the womanly virtues of public life".[191] The students of Lady Margaret Hall established their own settlement house in Lambeth in 1897, and Newnhamites were particularly active in the work of the Women's University Settlement, which had been instituted earlier as a co-operative venture by the women's colleges in 1887.[192] Exploring the work of university settlements outside London highlights the activities of a wider network of women, many of whom had first encountered each other at college, and who shared similar backgrounds of educational and work experience. Many of these women followed careers in which they moved easily between appointments as wardens of university women's halls of residence and hostels and settlement houses, often supplementing these with part-time lecturing work. Both kinds of appointment gave scope for close personal and often tutorial relationships with women students, partly in the context of residential community life. These women played an important role in shaping the aspirations and experiences of women students in the universities before 1939.

Feminine subcultures and feminism

All in all, these networks of relationships and activities concentrated in, but reaching beyond the halls, hostels and settlements associated with universities across the country, constituted an important part of what we may indeed designate a "women's culture", or at least, a "feminine subculture" on the margins of university life. This feminine culture, moreover, was often strongly imbued with feminism. Women students were actively building their own traditions. Associations of women graduates, and the old-girl's networks based on the women's halls, were part of this. A sense of indebtedness to the women pioneers of the 1890s was not uncommon, even after the First World War. Although there were undoubtedly women who took their access to the universities for granted, there were others who still identified themselves as pioneers, and who were highly conscious of the fact that their qualifications carried uncertain status in the labour market, especially outside teaching.

There was a consciousness of women having a separate history in the universities, and clear evidence of their desire to hold on to this

223

separate history. It is interesting to observe the women students in King's College London in the 1920s expressing their desire to learn more about "the old, pre-Strand days", and agreeing to mount an exhibition of the photographs of past senior students in the women's common room.[193] They determined to compile a short history of the women's institutions in the college.[194] Anniversaries commemorating the entry of the first women students, or the foundation of the women's halls and hostels, were celebrated in most university communities, and these events generated a crop of published histories. In 1926, for instance, the women students in Edinburgh celebrated the twenty-first birthday of the Edinburgh University Women's Union with the publication of a miscellany of essays, entitled *Atalanta's Garland.*[195] Among the better-known contributors were Virginia Woolf and Naomi Mitchison, and the collection also included essays on pioneer medical women and women's contribution to the arts in Scotland. In their preface, the editorial committee emphasized their desire "to pay tribute" to the first generation of university women, and to draw public attention to the breadth of their achievement.[196] A few years later, in 1933, women in the University of Manchester celebrated the jubilee of their admission. The women graduates raised around £2,000, which they donated to the university in token of their gratitude. Sara Burstall, Eileen Power and Harriette Chick received honorary degrees.[197] We owe Mabel Tylecote's scholarly, feminist history of women's education in the university at least in part to the women graduates of the jubilee committee: the book was written at their instigation and they defrayed some of the cost of its publication in 1941.[198]

Thinking about the extent of feminism among women university students before 1939 involves grappling with definitions as well as problems of historical interpretation. Do we take feminism to mean a clear consciousness of women's comparative subordination in university life, together with some kind of commitment to working to lessen this? Or should we adopt a broader definition, which would encompass an awareness of difference, a consciousness of the fact that women's experiences and interests might be distinct from men's, possibly finding expression in a separate women's culture? Here we return to some of the problems, both conceptual and methodological, which were outlined at the beginning of this chapter. The interpretations of historians will differ according to the construction that they put on patterns of segregation and difference. Some will take the existence of separate women's societies, or the sheltered community life that grew up around women's halls of residence before 1939, as signifying the limits of women's assimilation into university life generally: others will view the same phenomena differently, representing them as oases of women's culture, nurturing confidence and feminist awareness in a desert of educational patriarchy.

On the basis of interviews with second and third generation women graduates and other evidence, Sheila Hamilton has suggested that the cohorts of women students who followed the pioneers in the Scottish universities tended to take their access to these universities for granted.[199] They were aware of little discrimination in educational provision at the formal level. Patterns of segregation persisted in student social life but

> Women's unions, SRC committees and societies were not in the vanguard of a great feminist movement within the universities to challenge for greater equality and rights.[200]

In so far as these institutions reflected the views and outlook of women students, Hamilton describes them as "passive vehicles of feminist thought", but she expresses doubts about the applicability of a feminist interpretation of history in this context:

> One has to judge . . . whether it is correct to impose a feminist perception and language on events which from oral evidence and other sources did not initially appear to those involved to be strongly feminist.[201]

But while a feminist perspective on history requires some exploration of sexual divisions, and will need to take cognisance of the outlook and attitudes of women in the past, its validity does not depend on the self-conscious identification of these women as feminists.

The relationship between the recorded memories of individuals and historical social analysis is rarely straightforward. Elspeth Huxley, who studied agriculture at Reading in the 1920s, responded to questioning about feminist awareness thus:

> I'm afraid I can be of little, or no help to you on the question of feminist studies or teachers. It would, of course, be absurd to say that feminism didn't exist in those days. . . . But I don't think I heard the word until many years later – the 1960s probably – and so far as I know, it wasn't an issue at least at Reading then. . . . But then I have never been a political animal; there may have been groups etc., discussing feminism but I never heard of them.

As female students, we didn't feel oppressed in any way; in fact
the reverse in agriculture, the ratio of men to women was very
favourable from the women's point of view.[202]

Nonetheless, there were fairly clear patterns of sexual division
among students in Reading at the time. A women students' union had
been founded in 1906, separate from the men's union, "The Shells",
and these organized separate functions, and had their separate common rooms.[203] Women were subject to separate disciplinary arrangements, both in their halls of residence and in the university generally.
The reminiscences of student life that appeared in Elspeth Huxley's
autobiographical *Love among the daughters* (published in 1968)
make reference to many aspects of sexual difference. She records that
pubs were "out of bounds" to female students, and that her female
contemporaries were often poorer than the male students, whose
scholarships were more ample, and whose families "rightly regarded"
the education of their sons as a better investment than that of their
daughters.[204] Men and women opted for different courses of study,
too: not least in view of the fact that their career options varied so
widely. Elspeth Huxley was aware of her own conspicuousness as a female student of agriculture, and recognized that she would have been
much less conspicuous had she chosen a course in dairying or horti-
culture.[205] In view of all this, and mindful of the well-developed feminist consciousness and activities of women staff such as Edith Morley
and Mabel Buer in Reading between the wars, the historian arrives at
a rather more complex picture.

The fact that sexual segregation was so often taken for granted in
patterns of university social life needs careful attention from historians. Rather than seeing the women's societies as duplicate bodies, as
simply imitative of their male counterparts, or even as passive vehicles
of feminist thought, the historian needs to recognize that these societies could carry multiple meanings, some of which were historically
specific and liable to shift through time. Women often set up their
own societies in the 1890s in response to being excluded by the male
groups; later, they might operate and defend their own forms of exclusiveness. As Marjorie Knight, Warden of Liverpool's University
Hall for Women, commented, a sense of isolation could be strong
among the early women students, who frequently felt "in danger of
being overlooked and submerged under the overwhelming numerical
superiority of men".[206] When some of the women associated with

Mason College in Birmingham established a "Ladies' Social Circle" in the 1890s, their feminist activities elicited a satirical diatribe from a male contributor to the *Mason College Magazine*:

We are anxiously awaiting the near approaching lady-millennium, when Mason's will follow Holloway and Girton and Newnham, and then the man-student of the day – Macaulay's New Zealander, perchance, can stay if he likes, and take service as a "gyp". . . . Then from the new Ladies' College in the Midland Metropolis some female Jupiter will launch her thunderbolts to undermine the whole fabric of man's supremacy.[207]

This evoked a defence from one of the women, who signed herself "CMB", and protested that "The real object of the new society is not, as the writer seems to suppose, to shut out men, but to welcome women."[208]

The activities of the "Ladies' Social Circle", as reported in the same magazine, seem to have been more demure than feminist. About 80 women are alleged to have attended the first meeting: they took tea, and entertained themselves with a "graceful little play". Flowers were presented and "some games followed".[209] Many of the early women's societies were of this kind. In Bristol a Women's Literary Society was established in 1898. A number of professors' wives were active on the committee. As the name of the society implies, its discussions were primarily, though not exclusively, on literary subjects. This society changed its constitution to admit men in 1905.[210] Societies of this kind often met in the drawing rooms of "Lady Hostesses", who were commonly the middle-class supporters of the movement for the higher education of women in the locality. Lower down the social scale, and somewhat less elevated in tone (but often equally important in offering a life-line to the lonely) were the women's "tea-clubs", such as that initiated by women students in Nottingham in 1896. This was for the benefit of "those girls who have lectures in the evening and cannot go home". Members contributed twopence each for tea, bread and butter. Professor Bumby graciously donated a tea-service.[211]

Such prosaic and modest origins were not uncommon, and women's societies often grew out of a shared attempt to secure basic facilities, such as cloakrooms, a kettle, or a common room. A more political interest in women's representation, or the allocation of resources, could easily follow. In Edinburgh, the early minutes of the

Women Students' Representative Committee between 1895 and 1899 show members much preoccupied with the state of lavatories and cloakrooms. Several of the women complained about chairs in the reading room, which allegedly "bristled with nails, and inflicted damage on the dress".[212] But they soon moved on to weightier matters, such as the establishment of Masson Hall, the question of "petitioning parliament re the opening of all university bursaries, prizes and scholarships to women students", and the efforts of the Association of University Women Teachers to secure adequate salaries for women graduates.[213] Under the lead of Ethelwynn Lemon and Frances Melville there was concern about how best to secure the representation of women's interest in the university. Those with no particular views on the issue were apt to be strongly chided for their apathy. When two members of the committee sent their apologies to a meeting in 1897, explaining that they were unable to attend "on the score of pressure of university work",

> Miss Jacob moved that this was not a sufficient excuse, the present meeting being also university work, and all members of committee being likewise busy with class work.[214]

Her motion was carried.

Women's societies were important in universities, serving a range of needs that differed through time, and according to overt and covert goals. Meeting in settings where women might feel at home – often in private houses, halls of residence, teashops or women's common rooms – such societies provided a space in which women students might explore their own preconceptions and develop their own interests. Even a cursory survey of the lists of subjects discussed or debated by these groups before 1939, or of the papers presented by guest speakers, will indicate that the women's interests often differed significantly from those of their male peers. In this context women gained experience of public speaking, committee work and administration, an important contribution to the informal education of those actively involved in the organization of these groups. Not surprisingly, the question of women's suffrage stands out as a key area of interest before the First World War: issues surrounding women's work, careers and professions, and the impact of higher education on femininity, loomed large in discussions, both before and after the war. Discussions on these themes allowed women students to explore personal aspirations and the (often contradictory) social expectations and pressures surrounding their future lives: subjects that the formal curriculum of the university usually ignored.[215]

Notes

1. M. Tylecote, *The education of women at Manchester University, 1883–1933* (Manchester, 1941).
2. Dame K. Anderson, *Women and the universities: a changing pattern* (London, 1963), p. 4.
3. S. Hamilton, *Women and the Scottish universities c. 1869–1939: a social history*, PhD thesis (University of Edinburgh, 1987).
4. For further discussion of the problems inherent in the whiggish approach, see C. Dyhouse, "Storming the citadel or storm in a tea-cup? The entry of women into higher education, 1860–1920", in *Is higher education fair to women?* S. Acker & D. Warren Piper (eds) (Guildford, 1984).
5. M. Tuke, "Women students in the universities", *Contemporary Review* 133, p. 74, 1928.
6. *Tamesis* (Autumn 1932), cited in *The University of Reading: the first fifty years* (Reading, 1977), p. 74.
7. Tylecote, *The education of women*, p. 58.
8. *Ibid.*, p. 124.
9. W. Boog Watson, "The story of the Women Students' Union", *University of Edinburgh Journal* 24, p. 186, 1970.
10. *Ibid.*, p. 190.
11. *Ibid.*, p. 191.
12. I. Catto (ed.), *"No spirits and precious few women": Edinburgh University Union, 1889–1989* (Edinburgh, 1989), p. 78.
13. For this debate generally see J. N. Burstyn, *Victorian education and the ideal of womanhood* (London, 1980), pp. 84–99.
14. H. Maudsley, "Sex in mind and education", *Fortnightly Review* XV, pp. 466–83, 1874; J. Thorburn, *Female education from a physiological point of view* (Manchester, 1884).
15. Tylecote, *The education of women*, p. 31.
16. *Ibid.*
17. *Ibid.*
18. E. Pfeiffer, *Women and work: an essay* (London, 1888).
19. Mrs H. Sidgwick, *Health statistics of women students of Cambridge and Oxford and of their sisters* (Cambridge, 1890).
20. J. G. Fitch, "Women and the universities", *Contemporary Review* 58, p. 252, 1890.
21. M. Paley Marshall, *What I remember* (Cambridge, 1947), p. 21.
22. J. Evans, *Prelude and fugue: an autobiography* (London, 1964), p. 70.
23. Miss E. Lang, quoted by Tylecote, *The education of women*, p. 33.

24. Tylecote, p. 71.

25. *Ibid.*, p. 72.

26. Durham University Women Students' Association (later Women's Union Society), minute books of general meetings, 1899–1908 (Durham University); see reports of discussions on issue of women's representation on SRC, 3 December 1900 and 23 January 1901.

27. *Ibid.*, entry for 23 January 1901.

28. *Ibid.*, report of meeting on 4 June 1907.

29. *Ibid.* report of meeting on 18 June 1907.

30. *Ibid.*, see also report of meeting on 20 June 1907.

31. Minutes of Ladies' Hall Committee, 13 December 1887 (archives, Aberdare Hall, Cardiff). See also Chapter 3 in this volume.

32. J. Gwynn Williams, *The University College of North Wales: foundations, 1884–1927* (Cardiff, 1985), p. 308.

33. *Ibid.*, p. 309.

34. *Ibid.*

35. *Ibid.*

36. *The Daily Mail*, 19 February 1901; *Punch*, 27 February 1901; *The Manchester Guardian*, 23 and 28 February 1901, as cited by J. Gwynn Williams, *The University College of North Wales*, p. 310.

37. J. Gwynn Williams, pp. 310–11.

38. "Life at Aberystwyth and Alexandra Hall at the end of the nineteenth century . . . being extracts from the letters of Lady Stamp, (née Olive Marsh), 1898–1900", extract from letter dated 24 October 1898 (University College of Wales, Aberystwyth).

39. E. L. Ellis, *The University College of Wales, Aberystwyth, 1872–1972* (Cardiff, 1972), p. 125.

40. *Ibid.*

41. "Life at Aberystwyth and Alexandra Hall", letters dated 3 and 17 November 1898.

42. *Ibid.*

43. "The truth about the 'revolt'", *University College of Wales College Magazine* XXVII(1), p. 18, 1904.

44. *Ibid.*

45. E. L. Ellis, "Alexandra Hall, 1896–1986", in *Alexandra Hall, 1896–1986*, E. Ellis (ed.) (Aberystwyth, 1986), pp. 10–11.

46. "Leave of escort", *The Dragon* XXXVI, p. 190, 1914.

47. *Ibid.*

48. L. Moore, *Bajanellas and semilinas: Aberdeen University and the education of women, 1860–1920* (Aberdeen, 1991), p. 70.

49. *The Manchester Guardian*, 23 and 28 February 1901, quoted by J. Gwynn Williams, *The University College of North Wales*, p. 310.

50. L. Moore, *Bajanellas*, p. 84.

51. *College Echoes* IX(9), p. 66, 1897.

52. *Ibid.*

53. *College Echoes* 4 (11), p. 81, 1893.
54. *College Echoes* 5 (3), p. 22, 1892.
55. H. Tudor, *St Cuthbert's Society, 1888–1988* (Durham, 1988), p. 29.
56. "Thus far shalt thou go and no farther", *The Durham University Journal* (5 March 1898), p. 25.
57. "The intellectual inferiority of woman", *The Durham University Journal* (13 May 1899), pp. 265–6.
58. "A woman's reply", *The Durham University Journal* (10 June 1899), pp. 281–2.
59. *The Student* 8, p. 300, 1894, cited in S. Hamilton, *Women and the Scottish universities*, p. 167.
60. University College London, minutes of the Women's Union Society, 1903–37, entry for March 1904 (records office, University College London), pp. 6–10. The offending article was "Corridor confidences, No. II", *The University College Gazette* III(50), p. 384, 1904.
61. *College Echoes* XXIII(15), p. 249, 1912. (The article accusing women of "stale conventionality" appeared in XXIII(14), p. 233, 1912.)
62. R. M. Kanter, *Men and women of the corporation*, (USA: Basic Books), p. 222.
63. *Ibid.*, pp. 222–3.
64. *Ibid.*, pp. 219–224.
65. "Women students at the Scottish universities", *King's College Magazine* (Lent Term, 1902), p. 13 (K SER 17/16 archives, King's College, London).
66. J. Gwynn Williams, *The University College of North Wales*, p. 324.
67. "Thus far shalt thou go and no farther", *The Durham University Journal* (5 March 1898), p. 25.
68. P. D. A. Campbell, *A short history of the Durham Union Society* (Durham, 1952), p. 5.
69. Tudor, *St Cuthberts' Society*, p. 55.
70. *Ibid.*, p. 30.
71. *The Sphinx* III(11), p. 193, 1908.
72. J. A. Mangan, *Athleticism in the Victorian and Edwardian public school: the emergence and consolidation of an educational ideology* (Cambridge, 1981).
73. K. McCrone, *Sport and the physical emancipation of English women, 1870–1914* (London, 1988); J. A. Mangan & R. J. Park (eds), *From "fair sex" to feminism: sport and the socialisation of women in the industrial and post industrial eras* (London, 1987).
74. K. McCrone, "Play up! Play up! And play the game! Sport at the late Victorian girls' public schools", in *From "fair sex" to feminism*, Mangan & Park (eds), p. 103.
75. *Ibid.*, p. 106.
76. *Ibid.*
77. F. Dove, "Cultivation of the body", in *Work and play in girls' schools*, D. Beale et al. (London, 1891), p. 407, cited in J. Hargreaves, "Victorian

familism and the formative years of female sport", in *From "fair sex" to feminism*, Mangan & Park (eds), p. 142 and note 50. See also J. Hargreaves, "'Playing like gentlemen while behaving like ladies': contradictory features of the formative years of women's sport", *British Journal of Sports History* 2 (1), pp. 40–52, 1985.

78. Tylecote, *The education of women*, p. 39.
79. *Ibid.*, pp. 39–40.
80. *Ibid.*, p. 40.
81. *Ibid.*, p. 78.
82. J. Gwynn Williams, pp. 318–9.
83. See *Correspondence on questions concerning women students, 1917–43* (Box 253, archives, Reading University).
84. *Ibid.*
85. Memoranda and correspondence on "Boat racing for women, 1917–21" (Box 253, archives, Reading University).
86. Correspondence, Sir Isambard Owen to W. M. Childs, 12 October 1917 (Box 253, archives, Reading University).
87. F. Sibley, "Memorandum on boat racing for women" (Box 253, archives, Reading University).
88. For extensive discussion of this theme see M. R. & P. Higonnet, "The double helix", in *Behind the lines, gender and the two world wars*, M. R. Higonnet et al. (eds) (Yale, 1987); and S. Kingsley Kent, *Making peace: the reconstruction of gender in interwar Britain* (Princeton, 1993).
89. Tylecote, *The education of women*, p. 129.
90. Correspondence, Mrs. Guthkelch to Vice-Principal of University College, Aberystwyth, 1 May 1922 (Alexandra Hall archives, University College of Wales, Aberystwyth).
91. E. Morley, "Looking before and after, reminiscences of a working life", (*c.*1940–6), unpublished typescript (archives, Reading University), p. 44.
92. *Ibid.*, p. 45.
93. *Ibid.*, p. 47.
94. *Ibid.*, pp. 48–49.
95. Minutes of women's common room committee, 1920–39 (KU/WCR/M1–3, archives, King's College London), see report of meeting on 27 January 1922.
96. *Ibid.*, report of meeting on 20 March 1922.
97. *Ibid.*, report of meeting on 21 March 1922.
98. *Ibid.*, report of meeting on 22 March 1922.
99. *Ibid.*, report of meeting on 22 March 1922.
100. *Ibid.*, report of meeting on 12 May 1933.
101. A theme reflected rather well in the subtitle of David Walters' history of Oxford University's Union, *The Oxford Union, playground of power* (London, 1984).
102. R. Annand Taylor, "The coming of the women students" in *Alma Mater*, 1906, p. 56, quoted by Moore, *Bajanellas*, p. 84.

103. C. Dyhouse, *Girls growing up in late Victorian and Edwardian England* (London, 1981), p. 54.
104. Minutes of Women's Union Debating Society (UCL MEM III/C 4, and MS ADD 78, 123–5, University College London). The following information has been derived from these sources.
105. *Ibid.*, report of meeting on 13 January 1880.
106. Short account of the history of the Women's Union Debating Society, *c.*1924 (UCL MEM III/C 4, University College London).
107. Minutes of Women's Union Debating Society, UCL, report of meeting on 26 February 1926.
108. *Ibid.*, report of meeting on 23 January 1928.
109. *Ibid.*, report of fiftieth anniversary debate, 15 March 1928.
110. *Manchester University Magazine* (May, 1912), pp. 179–80; and (December 1912), p. 34, cited by Tylecote, *The education of women*, pp. 65–6.
111. Tylecote, *The education of women*, p. 66.
112. *The Gryphon* (Summer 1953), p. 26.
113. C. Lansbury, *The old brown dog: women, workers and vivisection in Edwardian England* (Wisconsin, 1985). For aspects of Frances Power Cobbe's involvement in the controversy in Oxford see "Somerville Hall: a misnomer, a correspondence with notes" and other documents (Maitland file, archives, Somerville College, Oxford).
114. L. Milne Rae (ed.), *Ladies in debate; being a history of the Ladies' Edinburgh Debating Society, 1865–1935* (Edinburgh, 1936).
115. *Ibid.*, pp. 71–116.
116. *Student handbook*, 1914–15, Edinburgh University.
117. S. Hamilton, *Women and the Scottish universities*, p. 359.
118. M. Laurence, "Anecdotage, 1927–1931", *University of Edinburgh Journal* 28, p. 127, 1977.
119. *Ibid.*
120. "Boanerges", "I don't like women!", *The Student* (22 October 1929), pp. 29–30.
121. I. Catto, *"No spirits and precious few women: Edinburgh University Union 1889–1989* (Edinburgh, 1989), p. 27. (The account that follows is derived from this source.)
122. *Ibid.*
123. *Ibid.*
124. *King's College Magazine* IV(2), p. 29, 1900 (K SER 17–, archives, King's College London).
125. Minutes of women's common room committee, entries for June 1921 (archives, King's College London).
126. *King's College Review* XX, p. 7, 1919.
127. "Burblings from Bayswater", *Odds and Ends*, the rag issue of *King's College Review* XXXV (1), p. 8, 1933.
128. E. Hamer (née Porter), typescript reminiscences of years at Liverpool University, 1917–22 (D 255/3/3, archives, Liverpool University).

129. "Women students at the Scottish universities", *King's College Magazine* (Lent Term, 1902), p. 15 (K SER 17/16, archives, King's College London).
130. Moore, *Bajanellas*, pp. 106, 109.
131. Minutes of women's common room committee, entries for March 1933 (archives, King's College London).
132. Minute books of St Hild's College University Students' Society, 1920–, 2, (20 March 1931), archives, Durham University.
133. E. L. Ellis, "Alexandra Hall, 1896–1986", p. 14.
134. *Ibid.*, see also typescript of "College regulations" and map of Aberystwyth showing "the three mile limit" defined in these regulations (Alexandra Hall collection, archives, University College of Wales, Aberystwyth).
135. See "Hall notes", *The Dragon* XLII(3), p. 155, 1920.
136. Letter from W. C. (Sam) Davies, BSc in *The Dragon* LIV(1), pp. 30–31, 1931.
137. "Advice to women students", *Tamesis* XIX(1), p. 19, 1919.
138. J. Howarth, "Women", in *The history of the University of Oxford*, vol. VIII, *the twentieth century*, B. Harrison (ed.) (Oxford, 1994), p. 362; see also discipline file (archives, Somerville College).
139. Copies of pamphlet and correspondence in Somerville College archives, discipline file (Somerville College).
140. *Ibid.*
141. J. C. Holt, *The University of Reading, the first fifty years* (Reading, 1977), p. 68.
142. *Ibid.*
143. F. Sibley, notice warning undergraduates against "molestation", dated 19 January 1937. All male students were required to sign, indicating that they had read this and noted its contents (discipline file, archives, Reading University).
144. R. D. Anderson, *The student community at Aberdeen, 1860–1939* (Aberdeen, 1988), pp. 61, 63.
145. "Women students at the Scottish universities", *King's College Magazine* (Lent term, 1902), p. 13.
146. The phrase is from J. M. Gibbon, writing in *Alma Mater* 18, p. 4, 1900–1 (Aberdeen University), cited by Moore in *Bajanellas*, p. 93.
147. R. D. Anderson, *The student community at Aberdeen*, p. 69.
148. *Ibid.*, pp. 19–20.
149. There were many examples. Robert Smart notes that the annual "bejant smoker" in St Andrews, (an initiation rite for first year students dating from early in the present century, which sometimes "got out of hand") was concluded by a serenade of University Hall (letter to author, 15 September 1993).
150. See minutes of house committee, Masson Hall, entry for 10 February 1926 (Da 64 MAS 4, archives, Edinburgh University).
151. Correspondence, M. Rackstraw to Mr. W. A. Fleming, 17 June 1933, in uncatalogued papers (Masson Hall archives, Edinburgh University).

152. For Marjorie Rackstraw's concern with this issue see minutes of Masson Hall committee, 9 June and 26 October 1926, (Da 64 MAS 4, archives, Edinburgh University). For May Staveley's opposition to a plan to use Goldney House as a men's hall of residence in Bristol, (Goldney House being very near to the women's residence in Clifton Hill House) see E. E. Butcher, *Clifton Hill House: the first phase, 1909–1959* (Bristol, n.d.), pp. 8–9.

153. L. Moore, *Bajanellas*, pp. 94–5.

154. *Ibid.*, p.95.

155. Quoted in T. Kelly, *For advancement of learning: the University of Liverpool, 1881–1981* (Liverpool, 1981), p. 168.

156. L. Moore, *Bajanellas*, p. 95.

157. *Ibid.*, p. 98.

158. T. Kelly, For *advancement of learning*, p. 169.

159. *Ibid.*

160. A. C. Wood, *A history of the University College Nottingham, 1881–1948* (Oxford, 1953), p. 65.

161. Dobson/Suffrage file, University Hall papers, 1 May 1913 to 31 December 1914 (St Andrews University). See also E. King, *The Scottish women's suffrage movement* (Glasgow, 1978), cited by S. Hamilton, *Women and the Scottish universities*, pp. 302–3.

162. Dobson/Suffrage file, University Hall papers (St Andrews University).

163. *Ibid.*, correspondence F. Hilliard to Miss Dobson, 24 and 30 June 1913, Elsie Inglis to Miss Dobson, July 1913, Alice Crompton to Miss Dobson, 8 July 1913.

164. *The Illustrated London News*, 1 November 1913, from book of press cuttings, April 1913–February 1914 (special collections, Bristol University).

165. Moore, *Bajanellas*, p. 98.

166. S. Hamilton, *Women and the Scottish universities*, pp. 362–6.

167. *Ibid.*, pp.365–6.

168. *Ibid.*, pp. 368–70. There is a copy of *Jus Suffragii Alumnae* for January 1909 (233/2/16/8/1, archives, Glasgow University).

169. Hamilton, *Women and the Scottish universities*, pp. 370–72.

170. Moore, *Bajanellas*, p. 94.

171. Edinburgh University Students' Representative Council, women's committee minute book, No.1, 1899–, entries for 15 March 1906, 9 March 1908 (Masson Hall papers, Edinburgh University).

172. Minute book, Women Students' Union, entry for 10 November 1913 (UY908, St Andrews University).

173. Tylecote, *The education of women*, p. 68.

174. *Manchester University Magazine* (February 1905), p. 103, and (April 1906), pp. 145–6, cited by Tylecote, p. 68.

175. Tylecote, p. 69.

176. *Ibid.*

177. There was a particularly strong interest in, and level of support for, suffrage activities in Ashburne Hall under Phoebe Sheavyn's leadership. See, for instance, *Yggdrasill* (Autumn term, 1909).

178. B. Simon, *A student's view of the universities* (London, 1943), p. 88.

179. B. Truscot, *Redbrick university* (London, 1943), p. 162. "Bruce Truscot" was the pseudonym of E. Allison Peers, Gilmour Professor of Spanish at Liverpool University, 1922–52. (My thanks to Adrian Allan for this information.)

180. Tylecote, *The education of women*, pp. 41–2.

181. J. R. Harrow, *The development of university settlements in England, 1884–1939*, PhD thesis (London School of Economics, 1987), p. 341.

182. O. Checkland, *Queen Margaret Union, 1890–1980, women in the University of Glasgow* (Glasgow, 1980), p. 8.

183. *Ibid.*, see also C. Kendall, "Higher education and the emergence of the professional woman in Glasgow, *c.* 1890–1914" *History of Universities* X, pp. 199–223, 1991.

184. E. M. Keen, M. K. Cope, E. C. Fortey, "The Women's Guild", *The Magnet* (21 February 1900), pp. 106–7 (Bristol University).

185. J. R. Harrow, *The development of university settlements in England, 1884–1939*, p. 410.

186. *Ibid.*, p. 389; see also *Hilda Cashmore, 1876–1943*, n.a., privately printed with an introduction by Marian Pease (Gloucester, 1943, copy in Bristol University).

187. See regular reports of the Guild's activities in *The Magnet*.

188. Harrow, p. 410.

189. R. G. Walton, *Women in social work* (London, 1975), pp. 56, 61.

190. *Ibid.*, p. 63.

191. M. Vicinus, *Independent women: work and community for single women, 1850–1920* (London, 1985), Chapter 6.

192. *Ibid.*, pp. 221–2.

193. Minutes of women's common room committee, entry for 6 June 1924 (archives, King's College London).

194. *Ibid.*

195. *Atalanta's Garland, being the book of the Edinburgh University Women's Union* (Edinburgh, 1926).

196. *Ibid.*, pp. v–vii.

197. Tylecote, *The education of women*, pp. 139–40.

198. *Ibid.*, p. vii.

199. S. Hamilton, *Women and the Scottish universities*, p. 336.

200. *Ibid.*, p. 381.

201. *Ibid.*, pp. 380–1.

202. E. Huxley, correspondence with author, 11 November 1990.

203. Entries for "The Women Students' Union" and "The Shells" in Reading University College's *Student handbooks*, 1907–8 and 1908–9.

204. E. Huxley, *Love among the daughters* (London, 1968), pp. 48, 122.

205. *Ibid.*, pp. 48–9.
206. M. Knight, "A seed which grew and the tree into which it developed" *Liverpool University Hall Association, fiftieth anniversary bulletin*, 1952, p. 16.
207. *Mason College Magazine* X(4), pp. 78–81, 1892.
208. *Mason College Magazine* X(5), pp. 116–17, 1892.
209. *Ibid.*, p. 113.
210. Minutes of the Women's Literary Society, 1898–1905 (special collections, Bristol University).
211. L. Wright, "The Tea Club", *The Gong* 2(1), p. 7, 1896.
212. Minutes of Women's Representative Committee, 1895–9 (entry for 30 January 1896) (Masson Hall archives, Edinburgh University).
213. *Ibid.*, entries for 6 January 1898, 7 June 1898.
214. *Ibid.*, 6 March 1897.
215. These issues were also brought into focus and discussed in the popular literature of the period. There are many examples, but see especially "Graham Travers" (Margaret G. Todd), *Mona Maclean, medical student* (Edinburgh & London, 1892); A. Stronach, *A Newnham friendship* (London, 1901); I. Compton-Burnett, *Dolores* (Edinburgh & London, 1911); V. Brittain, *The dark tide* (London, 1923); and M. Redlich, *Cheap return: portrait of an educated young woman* (London, 1934).

Conclusion

The historian will find no consensus among those who have attempted to measure the progress women had made in establishing their position as students or teachers in British university life by 1939. Contemporary observers, like those who looked back, supplied a range of perspectives and some sharply divided judgements.

Discordant and contradictory messages are communicated even within the covers of a single volume. Vincent and Hinton's history of the University of Birmingham, published in 1947, provides a good example. The authors contended that:

> It is a virtue of modern education that we have nowhere had occasion to write with specific differentiation of women's position in the University of Birmingham. It was open to either sex from the start of Mason College. All the long struggle over women's entrance into education had been fought and won generations earlier. Now men and women share in the common life with complete identity.[1]

As we observed in Chapter 2, the writers had somehow lost sight of, or they had chosen to overlook, the separate provision that Birmingham had made (since the beginning of the century) for its women students. Moreover, the messages transmitted by the book as a whole belie these contentions. Lavishly illustrated, the plates feature an endless succession of male worthies bedecked in their academic regalia and adorned with badges of institutional and civic office. A feminist reader will inevitably recall Virginia Woolf's impassioned attack (with its illustrations) on "the procession of the sons of educated men" with their gowns and furs, ribbons and maces in *Three guineas*, published ten years earlier.[2] There are one or two photographs of women in Vincent and Hinton's volume: they relate to different kinds of property. Lady Barber appears, as an important benefactress of the university. The photograph is of her portrait by Sir James Shannon and it shows her in rustling silk and pearls, wearing a picture hat. She nestles under a tree with two little terrier pups wearing ribbon-bows on their heads.[3] Femininity is further manifested in some of the *objets d'art* in the university's possession. There are photographs of a Virgin, painted by Botticelli, and of a torso of Aphrodite (headless), from the studio of Praxiteles.[4]

Women's position in Oxford and Cambridge, between the wars, remained characterized by considerable uncertainty. Oxford conceded its degrees to women in 1920, and it was widely expected that Cambridge would follow suit. As is well known, Cambridge failed to do so, and in October 1921 the university's rejection of the women's case unleashed scenes of undergraduate rowdyism revealing a bitter misogyny among undergraduates and echoing those that had accompanied Cambridge's earlier rejection of the women's claims in 1897. On this previous occasion, students had lowered an effigy of a woman wearing ample breeches ludicrously stuffed and padded out with straw and riding a bicycle, from a window outside the Senate House.[5] In 1921 a mob of undergraduates descended on Newnham with catcalls and chants of: "We won't have women". They barged the bronze memorial gates of the college with a handcart, causing serious damage to the lower panels.[6] Some of the young men involved in the fracas of 1921 were severely reprimanded, and copious apologies followed. But it was widely rumoured that there were senior members of the university who had not been altogether untinged by complicity in the onslaught.[7]

Cambridge's reaction caused heart-searching in Oxford, particularly among those haunted by a vision of the university being flooded by women students. The Royal Commission of 1922 (the Asquith Commission) sanctioned Cambridge's determination to remain "mainly and predominantly a 'men's university', though of a mixed type". It was recommended that the number of women students should not exceed 500, which would fix the proportion of women to men at around 1:10 of the student body.[8] This decision strengthened the determination of those who pressed for a similar limitation of the number of women students in Oxford. Joseph Wells, Warden of Wadham, contended that it was "a law of nature" that as the numbers of women "indefinitely" increased, "our young men will prefer the other place". It was "not encouraging", he added darkly,

> to observe what is happening in an Ancient University in Scotland where the number of women-students is becoming equal to the number of the men.[9]

A rising proportion of female students might threaten the loss of male control. Wells appealed to his colleagues with a warning that:

> We can only maintain and carry forth the high ideals of this place if it remains predominantly a man's university with the management and teaching mainly in male hands: and this is what the younger women-students themselves desire and prefer. For certain fundamental reasons a woman-administered university could never achieve a high success.[10]

The debate over the question of whether the numbers of women students in Oxford should be limited by statute was fought out in the Sheldonian in June 1927. Margery Fry, as Principal of Somerville, spoke for the women and against the statute. It was "a very nervous occasion", she later reported to Lady Fry, and "I was wobbly with fright".[11] Eloquent and capable as she was, the vote went in favour of the statute. Oxford was determined to reassert itself as master in its own house: a total of 840 students was determined as the limit for the five women's "societies" (not yet permitted the status of "colleges"), fixing the proportion of women at about one-sixth that of the number of men.[12]

Universities elsewhere in Britain were not uninfluenced by events in Oxford and Cambridge, and, as we have seen in the preceding chapters, there is a good deal of evidence to suggest that sexual divisions were reasserted after 1918 and that the map of gender was being redrawn. There are a number of ways of representing these events and tendencies in the years between the wars. The period can be seen as one of backlash, where the foothold women had gained in the universities was increasingly challenged in the context of unemployment and the slump. Or one might question the foundations and solidity of earlier increments of progress, emphasizing instead the heightening of tensions and divisions that had never effectively been resolved. As was shown in Chapter 5, any notions of steady assimilation or easy integration tend to disappear in the face of the detailed historical evidence.

It can certainly be argued that universities outside Oxbridge had come to depend on the presence of a sizeable contingent of female students. During the 1914–18 war, the government's attitude had been to emphasize the need for a continuing supply of teachers and trained professional workers. Women undergraduates were persuaded to stick to their studies, as part of the national war effort. There were important gains while the men were away. In Birmingham, for instance, we may note that the Guild of Undergraduates elected three women presidents between 1914 and 1917.[13] In Edinburgh, as we saw in Chapter 2, women became much more assertive in their demands for space and sympathetic tutorial arrangements during the war years. But the reaction after the war could be equally sharp. No other women are listed as Presidents of Birmingham's Guild of Undergraduates between 1917 and 1950.

Ina Brooksbank, a student at St Hugh's in Oxford in 1917, vividly remembered the resentment displayed by male students who returned to the university after the war, and who felt that a "regiment of women" had taken over "their" university. This attitude had been shared by some of the dons:

> We went down that term expecting only the lifting of a few restrictions, but on our return we found a different world. The city was full of men, bicycles and motor bicycles, often ridden in carpet slippers. We went to our usual lecture at Magdalen and found the hall full of men, seated, and women standing or sitting on the floor. Professor Raleigh entered, saw the situation and postponed the lecture at once. Another don rejected one brave young man's proposal that the men and women should change places, spoke for a quarter of an hour and then dismissed us all. Another announced that he didn't lecture to women, so out they had to go.[14]

The notion that women students "sapped the virility" of a university and undermined its status had not entirely disappeared. In Scotland, Professor Leask had inveighed against the destruction of "the old manly atmosphere" of Aberdeen by the introduction of a "pestilential miasma of a flabby hermaphroditism". This was in 1911, and he had failed to rouse very much support for his views at the time.[15] But as Lindy Moore's account of the education of women in the university indicates, there were a number of observers who continued to complain of the university as "infested" by women.[16] In Edinburgh, a student magazine published an article by an angry male undergraduate in 1929, who expostulated that:

> Each time I pass through the Old Quad, I am moved to bitter speech. To say that women have spoiled our University in no way overstates the case.[17]

An undercurrent of misogyny lingered on, and occasionally surfaced in more sustained and seriously argued attacks, such as the much publicized and controversial contention in the 1930s that higher education was wasted on women, who would marry and fail to make use of their degrees.

Attacks of this kind forced women on to the defensive, and there is evidence to suggest that both teachers and students judged their position uncertain in the 1920s and 1930s. A correspondence between Phoebe Sheavyn as Senior Tutor to Women in Manchester and Frances Melville, Mistress of Queen Margaret College in Glasgow in the 1920s, makes this clear. Dr Sheavyn had written to her colleague suggesting that it might be a good idea to investigate the health of women students in co-educational institutions, since:

> Women have had perforce to gain an entry into these great universities, established for men, and largely managed by men; and some of us would like to know how it is answering.[18]

Dr Melville delayed before replying in March 1924 that after having given the matter serious thought, she felt that such an enquiry would be "premature" and likely to concede hostages to fortune. She was uneasy about the attitudes of medical men, and feared that:

> If an enquiry such as you describe were to be mooted here now, it would be seized upon at once as not only confirming the view of the conservatives that the strain of university work would certainly prove too much for women, but as showing that the women themselves are vereing [sic] to that point of view. I fear that the women in this University are not sufficiently regarded as a matter of course to make it safe to begin an investigation on them.[19]

In spite of the fact that 30 years had passed since women had first been admitted as students in Glasgow, their presence was still regarded "as in an experimental stage", and "in addition, we are now in the midst of a period of abnormal reaction in the University, where women are concerned."[20]

In view of this, Melville judged that any attempt to "take stock" of the effects of women's admission to the universities should be covert, "for our private edification": to invite public debate could only run the risk of courting reaction.[21]

Melville hoped that the reaction would prove transient. But ten years later, and in the context of the slump, the forces of reaction had, if anything, gathered momentum. The Board of Education set about reducing grants to teachers in training: there was already serious competition for posts in schools. This had particular implications for women, as did the widespread imposition – by local educational authorities and other employers – of the marriage bar. The increasingly common practice of terminating women's employment when they married was particularly galling in the light of contemporary allegations about higher education being wasted on women. Mabel Tylecote attempted to counter such allegations with carefully calculated evidence.[22] Taking the total of medical women who had graduated from Manchester before 1938, and discounting those who had retired or about whom there was no recent information, she contended that nine-tenths of the remainder were "found to be making use of their professional training, about two-thirds of them on a full-time basis". A significant proportion of those who had married had continued in work, even while bringing up small children.[23]

But medicine was somewhat exceptional in the extent to which it offered scope for at least the most determined of its female practitioners to combine careers with marriage. As employment prospects worsened, many women began to ask themselves whether the cost of a university education, with all the sacrifice that this might entail at home, was really worthwhile. The author of an article on "The English university woman", which appeared in Reading University's magazine *Tamesis* in 1935, was profoundly sceptical. She observed that:

> In England there is still prejudice against choosing women for responsible posts; there is still precedence given to male applicants because they are "bread-earners", the woman's independence, talent and progress is crushed. The married woman with the greater understanding, energy and joy that come from a full sexual life is in most cases banned from the schools and discouraged in the medical profession.[24]

"There is certainly not much encouragement for a woman to study," she concluded, and:

> Yet there are insufficient husbands to go round; poligamy [*sic*] is

unlawful and dependence on parents intolerable. The woman
student is in a dilemma.[25]

In 1943 "Bruce Truscot" published a detailed account of British
universities other than Oxford and Cambridge entitled *Redbrick university*. This was widely read, and two years later the same author was
encouraged to produce a supplementary volume entitled *Redbrick
and these vital days,* in which he contemplated the future of "the university system" in the light of contemporary educational policies.[26] In
this second volume he confessed that "several correspondents" had
taken him "reproachfully to task for having said nothing about Redbrick's treatment of women", an omission that he conceded to have
been unpardonable.[27] The problem, he insisted, was confined to the
staff. Undergraduates, whether men or women, were treated "with
perfect equity".[28] The reader of the foregoing chapters may marvel at
such complacency. But what follows is more interesting. "It is only
when a woman becomes a lecturer," continues Truscot, "that she be-
gins to wonder if she is really wanted."

There were very few women on the staff lists of most universities,
Truscot conceded, and provision for their accommodation and comfort was "quite inadequate". At least until recently, the position of
married women had been made "extremely difficult". Women's prospects of promotion were meagre or non-existent. It was common for
a woman to be called in as *chargée d'affaires*, to shoulder the practical
burden of running a department, but once a new head was appointed,
she would "fade out of the picture", being relegated to a subordinate
position without any improvement in status or salary.[29] "One hesi-
tates, then," concluded Truscot,

> before recommending a woman, however brilliant (and in the
> Arts faculties of modern universities the best students are gener-
> ally women) to embrace a university career.
>
> "What are my prospects?" inquires a First Class woman
> graduand after beating all the men of her year.
>
> "Well," one replies, "you *may* get a post; though, other things
> being equal, a man will probably be preferred to you. If you do
> get one, you will have about £5 per week, with microscopical in-
> crements, and, at the end of five or six years (assuming that you
> keep your post) you will have reached about £6 per week. By the
> time you are forty, you should be earning £400 a year, but it is
> most unlikely that you will go farther. There is little chance of

your moving from one university to another or of your ever becoming a departmental head. So, if you have any material ambitions, apply for some other sort of job: women are better
elsewhere unless they have private means, love the work for the
work's sake alone or intend to seek an early escape in marriage."[30]

There is little to quibble with here, although the same cannot be
said of Truscot's explanation of the reasons for this situation, or of the
remedies he proffered for it. While admitting that traces of prejudice
did still exist, he blamed women themselves for their lack of progress.
After all, male academics were reasonable beings and "thoughtless-
ness", even more than prejudice, characterized their attitudes to their
female colleagues. So while it was disappointing that women had
been so poorly treated in the universities, it was even more disappointing

that they had made no efforts to get themselves treated better.
... A determined and unanimous series of attacks by the combined body of university women teachers would probably win a
comparatively easy victory.[31]

One wonders whether Truscot had ever even heard of the British
Federation of University Women. It is not so much that women's experiences were consciously edited out of history, rather that a whole
dimension of women's separate experiences, history and traditions
had never been fully visible to male observers.

In the context of the controversy that divided Oxford over the
question of the Limitation Statute in the 1920s, the *Sheffield Evening
News* published an article headed "Girl students in the universities:
should their numbers be limited?". The editor had canvassed "a
number of Vice-Chancellors elsewhere in Britain" to elicit their views
on the subject. Most of those quoted were *against* the idea of setting a
ceiling on the proportion of women students.[32] Sir Alfred Ewing,
from Edinburgh, argued that the advantages of admitting women out-
weighed the disadvantages. The proportion of female students might
be high in Edinburgh, but their presence had in "no way altered the
character of the teaching", nor could he detect any "trace of any tendency towards feminine government".[33]

This state of affairs, wholly satisfactory to Sir Alfred Ewing and
many men in the universities, was increasingly disturbing to academic
women and to other feminist observers. In August 1941, Lady Shena

Simon wrote a review of Mabel Tylecote's book on the history of women at Manchester University for *The Woman Citizen*, which was published by the Manchester and Salford Women Citizen's Association.[34] She observed that reading the book had prompted her to muse on a number of important questions. Was it a good thing that the pattern of higher education should be so entirely shaped by men? Were the values set before university students, by professors and lecturers – still overwhelmingly masculine – the values that women can and should accept?[35]

For Lady Simon, who had been much influenced by her reading of Virginia Woolf's *Three guineas* a short while previously, there were many aspects of higher education in Britain that gave cause for disquiet. Could universities be said to provide the best education for citizenship? To what extent did they provide opportunities for young people of intelligence and talent, of either sex, to work towards a more generous vision of social justice both at home and in the wider world? These questions were appropriate in 1941, and they are equally appropriate today.

Notes

1. E. W. Vincent & P. Hinton, *The University of Birmingham, its history and significance* (Birmingham, 1947), p. 203.
2. V. Woolf, *Three guineas* (London, 1938), illustration facing p. 43.
3. Vincent & Hinton, *The University of Birmingham*, p. 171.
4. *Ibid.*, pp. 172, 174.
5. R. McWilliams-Tullberg, *Women at Cambridge, a men's university, though of a mixed type* (London, 1975), illustration facing p. 161.
6. A. Phillips (ed.), *A Newnham anthology* (Cambridge, 1979), illustration between pp. 50 and 51, pp. 150–51; see also T. E. B. Howarth, *Cambridge between two wars* (London, 1978), p. 42.
7. Howarth, *Cambridge between two wars*, p. 42; McWilliams-Tullberg, *Women at Cambridge*, p. 195.
8. *Report of Royal Commission on Oxford and Cambridge Universities*, (Asquith Commission) 1922, Cmd. 1588, p. 173.
9. J. Wells, "Statement of support for limitation statute", July 1927 (limitation of numbers file, archives, Somerville College).
10. *Ibid.*
11. E. Huws-Jones, *Margery Fry, the essential amateur* (Oxford, 1966), p. 147.
12. V. Brittain, *The women at Oxford, a fragment of history* (London, 1960), p. 172.

13. "Birmingham University Guild of Undergraduates, 1901–51", 30 June 1951 (8/vi/2/15, university collection, Heslop Room, Birmingham University). The women presidents were Miss Pither, Miss Boone and Miss Bristol.

14. I. Brooksbank, "Bingles and bicycles", *Oxford Today* 3(2), p. 35, 1991.

15. Quoted by L. Moore in *Bajanellas and semilinas: Aberdeen University and the education of women, 1860–1920* (Aberdeen, 1991), p. 116.

16. *Ibid.*, p. 135.

17. "Boanerges", "I don't like women!", *The Student* (22 October 1929), p. 29.

18. Correspondence, Dr P. Sheavyn to Miss F. Melville, 22 February 1924 (DC 233/2/6/2/17, archives, Glasgow University).

19. Correspondence, Frances Melville to Phoebe Sheavyn, 15 March 1924 (archives, Glasgow University).

20. *Ibid.*

21. *Ibid.*

22. M. Tylecote, *The education of women at Manchester University, 1883–1933* (Manchester, 1943), p. 120.

23. *Ibid.*, pp. 121–2.

24. "B. P.", "The English university woman", *Tamesis* XXXIV(1), p. 21, 1935.

25. *Ibid.*, p. 20.

26. "Bruce Truscot" (Prof. E. Allison Peers), *Redbrick university* (London, 1943), and *Redbrick and these vital days* (London, 1945).

27. "Truscot", *Redbrick and these vital days*, p. 80.

28. *Ibid.*

29. *Ibid.*, pp. 82–4.

30. *Ibid.*, p. 84.

31. *Ibid.*, p. 85.

32. "Girl students in the universities: should their numbers be limited?" *Sheffield Evening News* (29 October 1927). Press cuttings in the registry, Sheffield University. (I am indebted to Peter Linacre for this reference.)

33. *Ibid.*

34. Filed with reviews of Tylecote's book (Box 4, file 4 of Mabel Tylecote collection, Manchester University).

35. *Ibid.*

Appendix I

Numbers of full-time students (men and women) in British universities, 1900–1901 and 1910–11

	1900–1901		1910–1911	
	Men	Women	Men	Women
Birmingham	238	93	519	288
Bristol	209	127	448	216
Cambridge	2830	296	3822	396
Durham	166	16	219	16
Leeds	494	86	550	110
Liverpool	411	70	661	258
London				
King's College	262	12	414	90
LSE	32	16	117	49
UCL	295	167	512	162
Manchester	738	123	881	276
Nottingham Univ. College	137	90	135	107
Oxford	2537	239	3114	328
Reading	33	73	128	117
Sheffield	90	6	203	81
Southampton Univ. College	133	62	153	75
Wales				
Aberystwyth	266	208	262	192
Bangor	179	100	229	95
Cardiff	333	167	408	189
Scotland				
Aberdeen	362	29	379	107
Edinburgh	2,119	235	2,331	580
Glasgow	1,575	346	1,967	670
St Andrews & Dundee	242	109	292	242

Extracted from *Returns of the University Grants Committee*.
Report for period 1929–30 to 1934–35.
Note: these figures are not comprehensive.

Appendix II

Numbers of full-time students (men and women) in British universities, 1920–21 and 1934–5

	1920–1921		1934–1935	
	Men	Women	Men	Women
Birmingham	1,354	455	1,072	450
Bristol	912	328	692	316
Cambridge	4759	428	5328	507
Durham	198	44	387	113
Leeds	1,288	322	1,250	368
Liverpool	1,766	548	1,605	535
London				
King's College	880	285	1,178	548
LSE	491	203	617	294
UCL	1,064	579	1,348	795
Manchester	1,425	581	1,734	634
Nottingham Univ. College	650	126	512	138
Oxford	3663	542	3953	876
Reading	214	335	293	322
Sheffield	751	196	643	133
Southampton Univ. College	198	145	273	102
Wales				
Aberystwyth	778	310	583	245
Bangor	410	190	456	142
Cardiff	763	298	929	363
Scotland				
Aberdeen	1,122	533	846	361
Edinburgh	3,084	1,078	2,437	915
Glasgow	3,396	1,122	3,241	1,149
St Andrews & Dundee	485	292	571	312

Extracted from *Returns of the University Grants Committee.*
Report for period 1929–30 to 1934–5.
Note: these figures are not comprehensive.

Appendix III

Students and residence, 1937–8

	Men	Women	Total	Halls/hostels		Lodgings		Home	
England									
Birmingham	991	413	1404	men:	90	men:	48	men:	53
				women:	102	women:	56	women:	255
Bristol	665	332	997	men:	181	men:	151	men:	333
				women:	177	women:	23	women:	132
Durham	352	84	436	men:	340	men:	7	men:	5
				women:	83	women:	1	women:	0
Leeds	1340	397	1737	men:	193	men:	346	men:	801
				women:	173	women:	52	women:	172
Liverpool	1589	465	2054	men:	104	men:	390	men:	1095
				women:	109	women:	30	women:	326
London									
King's Coll.	1128	435	1563	men:	118	men:	409	men:	601
				women:	95	women:	98	women:	242
LSE	574	384	958	men:	14	men:	381	men:	179
				women:	23	women:	174	women:	187
UCL	1376	707	2043	men:	77	men:	680	men:	619
				women:	85	women:	253	women:	369
Manchester	1564	516	2080	men:	239	men:	193	men:	1132
				women:	196	women:	22	women:	298
Reading	300	277	577	men:	207	men:	52	men:	41
				women:	234	women:	3	women:	40
Sheffield	637	134	771	men:	108	men:	147	men:	382
				women:	48	women:	3	women:	83
Wales									
Aberystwyth	490	220	710	men:	0	men:	445	men:	45
				women:	182	women:	0	women:	38
Bangor	395	117	512	men:	85	men:	222	men:	88
				women:	87	women:	0	women:	30
Cardiff	722	314	1036	men:	31	men:	212	men:	479
				women:	106	women:	24	women:	184

	Men	Women	Total	Halls/hostels		Lodgings		Home	
Scotland									
Aberdeen	796	349	1145	men:	0	men:	430	men:	366
				women:	0	women:	232	women:	117
Edinburgh	2346	828	3174	men:	198	men:	1085	men:	1063
				women:	237	women:	199	women:	392
Glasgow	3132	1007	4139	men:	123	men:	615	men:	2394
				women:	53	women:	155	women:	799
St Andrews &									
Dundee	559	326	885	men:	117	men:	233	men:	209
				women:	159	women:	72	women:	95
Great Britain									
Total	37890	11299	49189	men:	8124	men:	14190	men:	15576
				women:	4314	women:	2163	women:	4822
Per cent	77.0	23.0	100	**men:**	**21.4**	**men:**	**37.5**	**men:**	**41.1**
				women:	**38.2**	**women:**	**19.1**	**women:**	**42.7**

Extracted from the *Returns of the University Grants Committee, 1937–38.*

Appendix IV

The duties of the Warden of University Hall
From Frances Melville's Memorandum to the University Court of St Andrews, August 1909.

1. The Warden has full charge of the students in residence, and has to promote their general interests, maintaining order and discipline according to University Regulations and approved Hall Rules.
2. The Warden has to guide students of the Hall in all educational matters. She has to make all arrangements for private or extra tuition, and has to approve the courses of students who enter the Hall to pursue special non-graduand study at the University.
3. The Warden is responsible for the management, upkeep, and expenditure of the Hall and its auxiliary residences.
4. The Warden conducts all the correspondence concerning the Hall and students in residence.

Under the first heading it is the duty of the Warden to pay attention to the conduct of students, their health, their work, and their social life. She has to arrange with the housekeeper general lines of diet, the hours and arrangements for meals. She has to note each day if the students are all in good health. She has to consult the entry-book each morning after breakfast, and if there are absentees from the first meal, she visits them in their rooms and calls in medical attendance when required. She has to note overwork and slack work, and advise in both cases. She takes an advisory part in the athletics of the students, with charge of the Women Students' Pavilion, and interests herself in their different Societies and in the Women Students' Union (on the Governing Board and House Committee of which she sits, *ex officio*). She has to decide what entertainments shall be given in the Hall, and to what entertainments students may go, granting permission in each separate case. She has to act as hostess for students in the Hall, and ac-

company students to evening and other entertainments when necessary. She has to preside at Hall Meetings, and with the co-operation of
the Senior Student and House Committee guide the internal "policy"
of the Hall. Then there also comes under this heading what the Warden has to consider with regard to the moral welfare of the students.
She has to exert herself to be on such terms with her students that a
strong public opinion in favour of order, decorum, punctuality, and
fulfilment of duties is maintained. She has to deal with disorder, slack-
ness, unpunctuality, deviation from rules, etc. This part of her work,
which makes many claims, does not lend itself to particularization.

The second heading means that the Warden has to guide students in
educational matters and plan suitable courses of study for every student under her care, after daily contact has given her some insight into
the character and capabilities of each, individually. Of these courses a
complete record has to be kept for reference. This also involves giving
advice to intending students before actually coming into residence, to
parents who wish their daughters to enter upon a University Course,
and to teachers who are preparing pupils for the University. These aspects of the advisory function are even more important in the case of
women students than of men, as women have fewer openings at their
command in the end, and their degree has to be more directly concentrated on their future work. They also, as a rule, are allowed less
money than men to prepare for professions and occupations. Therefore the Warden has to bring her experience of education and her
knowledge of women's work to help students both in their choice of
studies and of after professions.

The Warden has, further, to advise students when private or extra
tuition is required in any subject. She has to find suitable tutors and
arrange hours and terms with them. During the Winter Session, e.g.,
extra and private tuition in various subjects, arranged by the Warden,
is going on every day, for the most part in the Hall itself. The Warden
has, moreover, not only to advise but to approve of courses of study
planned by non-graduand University students resident in the Hall,
and insist that the class examinations shall be taken by these students.
Before this was included amongst the Warden's duties, such non-
graduand students were under no control as regards their work, with
the result that one or two both wasted their time and set a bad example to the other Hall students. This danger has been removed by
putting the above jurisdiction in the Warden's hands, and some satis-

factory work has been done by occasional non-graduand students working on lines that have been approved by the Warden.

For the proper discharge of all these advisory duties, as well as her administrative duties as head of a women's College Hall, the Warden must not only have academic experience, but must also keep herself constantly in touch with educational movements and ideas.

Under the third heading the Warden authorizes, and is responsible for, every outlay involved in the management, upkeep, and expenditure. All accounts and vouchers in connection with these have to pass through her hands. She checks all accounts and sends them to the Factor each month. She is finally responsible for every part of the organisation, for the repair and furnishing of the houses, the keeping of the grounds, and the housekeeping. She arranges with the housekeeper as to the number of servants to be employed, the wages to be given, and is consulted before the dismissal of any servant. The housekeeper relieves the Warden of domestic details such as catering, supervision of cookery, serving of meals, care of rooms, actual sick nursing, engaging of servants, ordering their daily work, and supervising them.

Fourthly, the correspondence concerning the Hall and the students in residence includes, in addition to all business communications that have to do with management, the giving of information and issuing of papers to students' parents or guardians, private and public persons. It includes the advertising of the Hall, the making of memoranda, and reports, the drawing up and issuing of prospectuses and papers that keep the Hall in public notice.

These are the principal duties of the Warden of University Hall, which may fairly occupy her time and thoughts.

Reproduced by courtesy of the University of St Andrews.

ᴥ

Select bibliography

I. Archives

1. University collections (university libraries & halls of residence)

Note: Harold Silver & S. John Teague, *The history of British universities, 1800–1969: a bibliography* (Society for Research in Higher Education, 1970) is an indispensable starting point for anyone beginning work on university history. The list which follows should be regarded as supplementary, and as drawing attention to material of particular interest to those concerned with the history of women.

Birmingham
Lodge collection (Heslop Room)
University House collection
Department of Education reports on women students, 1929–45
Papers and correspondence of Senior Tutor to Women Students, 1926–47
Memoir and obituaries of Constance Naden
Student handbooks
Staff appointment ledger
Guild of Undergraduates Yearbook, Jubilee Pamphlet, etc.
Staff Social Club minute book, 1922–3
Mason College Magazine 1883–1900
The Mermaid, 1904–

Bristol
Council minutes (relating to appointment of Lady Tutor, 1899)
Professor Tyndall, "Recollections of sixty years of academic life in Bristol", typescript, 1958
M. F. Pease, "Some reminiscences of University College, Bristol", typescript, 1942

M. F. Pease, "Account of the Marshalls' years at Bristol, 1877–1883, by Mary
  Paley Marshall, notes from memory", manuscript, 1943.
Mrs Barrell, "Reminiscences, 1890–", manuscript, n.d.
Helen Wodehouse, correspondence
Mary Staveley, correspondence
Catherine Winkworth Scholarship Fund, minute book
Minutes of day training college
Minutes of secondary training department
Hostel committee minute book
Press cuttings book
Report of Men Lecturers' Committee, 1909
Calendars, prospectuses
Minutes of Women's Literary Society, 1898–1905
The Magnet, 1898–1900
Bristol University College Gazette, 1908–10
The Bristol Nonesuch

Cambridge

Girton College
Girton College register, 1869–1946
Helen Wodehouse papers
JCR records, including senior students' minute books
Appeals files
Clubs and societies minute books
Obituaries and biographical notices
Eileen Power file
Alice Zimmern file
Centenary scrapbook 1869–1969
Helen Blackburn collection
The Girton Review 1882–1969

Newnham College
Newnham College register, vols I–III, 1871–1971
Memorials and obituaries files
SRC minute book, 1914–26
Press cuttings on admission of women to Cambridge University 1918–22
Minutes of Debating Society, 1900–1904
Margaret Tuke, typescript "Autobiographical notes"
College roll letter, 1880–
Thersites, 1909–37

Durham

University Library (Palace Green)
Papers relating to Women Students' Association (later Women's Union Society), and minute books, 1899–
Women's Sports Association minute books
St Hild's College university students' minute books, 1920–
Phyllis Heatley, "History of the NE division of university women, 1923–73", typescript, 1975
The Sphinx, 1905–22
Calendars
The Durham University Journal, 1898–
Durham University Women's Society minute books, 1934–

St Mary's College
Printed newsletters, reports
List of past and present students, 1929
The Dove
St Mary's College songbook (n.d.)

Leeds

University Library
Yorkshire College, Senate minutes, 1884–
Committee books, 1910–13 (including committees on day training college, women's hostels)
Women Day Students' Association minute books, 1932–
Weetwood Hall file (rules, prospectuses)
Debating Society minute book, 1929
Storm Jamieson, "Recollections", typescript
Correspondence, Michael Sadler to Mrs Redman-King
Obituaries and notices, Irene Manton, Lady Ogilvie
Calendars

Central Filing Office
Files on: Hannah Robertson, Tutor of Women Students and Mistress of Method, 1904–21; Alice Silcox, Dean of Women Students, 1922–31; D. M. Hibgame, Tutor of Women Students, 1931–47.

Liverpool
Minutes and reports of Council
Memorial from local headmistresses about women on staff, 1911 (in Council minutes)
Report of committee to consider proportion of women on staff, 1910–11 (in Council minutes)

Reminiscences of past students (Edna Rideout, Winifred Jones, Enid Hamer, Phyllis Hamilton)
Margaret Miller, copies of correspondence
Calendars, prospectuses
University Hall papers: executive committee reports, correspondence, student house committee minute books, portraits, photographs, *The Phoenix*
Grace Chisholm Young papers
Emma Holt, obituaries, tributes
The Sphinx, 1893–

London

King's College
Records of Ladies' Department, later King's College for Women:
  Minute books
  Warden's letters
  General and policy files
  Applications and testimonials for post of Vice-Principal, 1907
  Reports and memoranda
  Out correspondence of Warden concerning establishment of home science course
  Memoranda and reports relating to Haldane Commission
  Correspondence concerning amalgamation of King's College and King's College for Women, 1912–15
  Annual reports of Delegacy
  Syllabi and prospectuses
  Scrapbooks
  File on establishment of hostel for women students in Bayswater
King's College (Ladies' Department) Magazine, 1896–1914
King's College Records:
  Calendars
  Union handbooks
  King's College Review, 1899–
  King's College women's common room committee minute books, 1920–39
Queen Elizabeth College records

London School of Economics
Papers, prospectuses, calendars and summary programmes
College miscellanea
Report by Miss E. A. H. Pearson on openings for university women . . . with special reference to graduates of LSE (May 1924)
Students' Union minute books
Scholarships files: Shaw studentships; B. L. Hutchins studentship
Clare Market Review, 1905–
LSE register, 1895–1932 (London, 1934)

University College

A. Manuscript room

Bellot collection:

  Documents and memoranda

  Typescript and manuscript reminiscences

  Papers relating to women's fund

  Material on student societies

Prospectuses of Ladies' Educational Association

College archive collection:

  Prospectuses

  Calendars

  Records of student societies

  Minutes of Women's Debating Society

  Union records

  Personnel files

  Papers relating to death of Rosa Morison and the position of the Lady Superintendent

University College Gazette

UCL Union magazine

B. Records office

Records of Women's Union Society

Transcript of proceedings of extraordinary general meeting held on 18 July 1883
  (in relation to applications of Annie Besant and Alice Bradlaugh)

Margaret Murray file

Manchester

University Library (Main Building)

Archives of Owens College, the Victoria University, and the Victorian University
of Manchester, including:

  Ashburne Hall papers

  Student registers, department for women

  Declaration books

  Class registers (women, 1898–1901)

  Miscellaneous material (uncatalogued) relating to the education of women

  E. C. Wilson, correspondence

  Department of Education papers, 1890–1911

  Manuscript reminiscences of the early days of the women's department,
    written for Mabel Tylecote

The Iris, 1887–1894 (magazine of the women's department)

The Serpent, 1917–

John Rylands Library, Deansgate
Mabel Tylecote collection

Ashburne Hall archives
Reports, papers, correspondence
Ashburne Hall Chronicle, 1898–
Photograph album, 1900–1049
Press cuttings book, 1883–7
House committee minutes
Yggdrasill, 1901–

Nottingham

University Library
Papers from town clerk's and registrar's departments
Calendars, prospectuses
Prospectus for Florence Boot Hall of Residence, 1930s
Edith Becket papers and notes for history of Nottingham University College
Printed advertisement for "Lady Warden of the Women's Hostel", 1914
Papers relating to proposal for course of training for teachers of domestic
  science, 1935
Papers relating to Revis Foundation and Scholarships, 1925/6–31
The Gong, 1896–
Press cutting, "Women's place in university life" from *The Nottingham Journal*,
  9 July 1928

Florence Boot Hall archives
Papers, prospectuses, photographs
"CHS", "*Plus ça change, plus c'est la meme chose*", unpublished typescript, life
  in Florence Boot Hall between the wars

Oxford

Somerville College
Somerville College register, 1879–1938
Maitland file
Discipline file
Royal Commission file
Limitation of numbers file

Reading
Edith Morley, "Looking before and after: reminiscences of a working life",
  typescript, *c.* 1946
Vice-Chancellor's correspondence with Edith Morley and W. G. de Burgh in

connection with professorships in English
Vice-Chancellor's papers relating to discipline, halls of residence, and on
    questions relating to women students, 1917–43
Lady Selbourne, correspondence, 1931, in relation to proportion of women on
    Council
Files from registry in relation to discipline, 1928–49
Women's Hall committee minutes, 1924–5
Advisory committee on domestic economy, minutes 1916–35
Papers relating to diploma in domestic subjects
Foundation collection: Students' Union minute books
Lady Stenton collection: books and correspondence
Tamesis
Reading University College Review

Sheffield
Chapman collection:
    Prospectuses and press notices relating to St Peter's (Mason-Fenn) Memorial
        Hall
    Papers and prospectuses relating to halls of residence and hostels for women
        students, 1882–
    Notes on the position of women students, 1929–52
    Items relating to Tutorship for women students, 1924
    Papers relating to diploma in domestic science, 1910–13
    Items relating to first woman to sit on University Council, 1935
Council minutes
Press cuttings collection
Executive committee minutes, board of management of halls, 1931–
Floreamus
Registry: papers and press cuttings relating to women students and members of
    staff

Southampton
Central and departmental records
Papers relating to hall of residence for women students (Bevois Mount Hostel)
Calendars, student handbooks
Annie Trout, papers and memorabilia
Staff contracts book, 1900–1929
Junior Staff Association minute books from 1930
Student reminiscences: correspondence, scrapbooks, albums of photographs

University of Wales

Aberystwyth

Lady Stamp (née Olive Marsh): "Life at Aberystwyth and Alexandra Hall at the end of the nineteenth century . . . being extracts from the letters of Lady Stamp, 1898–1900" (unpublished typescript)
Calendars
Prospectuses
Reports submitted to Court of Governors
University College of Wales Magazine
The Dragon
Alexandra Hall archives: pamphlets and prospectuses; memoranda on discipline; Wardens' correspondence; press cuttings; photographs

Bangor

Dilys Glynne Jones (née Lloyd Davies): letters from Newnham College, Cambridge, 1877–8; correspondence
Discipline book, 1906–32
Minutes of day training committee, 1894–
Press cuttings
Material relating to "Bangor controversy" of 1892–4, including minutes of Senate enquiry, 1892, pamphlets and press cuttings
Calendars
Student handbooks
The North Wales Chronicle

Cardiff

Archives in Aberdare Hall:
  Register of students, 1885–97
  Record of entrants, 1903–14
  Prospectuses
  Printed reports
  Minutes of Ladies' Hall Committee
  House committee minute books
  Minutes of general meetings
  Correspondence with Board of Education
  Memorandum submitted to Senate on compulsory residence, 1919

Scotland

Edinburgh

Papers relating to Edinburgh Ladies' Educational Association (later Edinburgh Association for the University Education of Women)
Minutes of University Court
Calendars, prospectuses, student handbooks

File with miscellaneous items on women staff and students
Minutes of Association for Provision of Hostels for Women Students, 1913–
Minutes of Women's Representative Committee, 1895– ; (later Women's
  Committee of Student Representative Council)
Masson Hall papers:
  Subscription leaflets
  Prospectuses, pamphlets
  Minutes of executive committee
  Annual reports and abstracts of accounts
  Boxes of unclassified material including Warden's memoranda, correspond-
    ence
  Scrapbook and photographs
Note on Pfeiffer bequest
The University of Edinburgh Journal
The Student

Glasgow

Minutes of University Court: report on committee on negotiations with
  Muirhead Trustees, 1893; memorial for Queen Margaret College committee
  (on conflict with Mrs Elder) 1896
Minutes of Senate: petition from women students, 1904
Calendars, student handbooks
Collection of pamphlets on the higher education of women
Papers relating to Glasgow Association for Higher Education for Women
Papers relating to Glasgow Association of University Women, 1901–41 (later the
  Glasgow division of the British Federation of University Women)
Notes on hostels for women students, 1907
Queen Margaret College collection:
  Mrs Elder's correspondence with university on the question of separate classes
    for women
  QMC Literary and Debating Society minutes, 1899–1905
  Various college societies, papers and minute books
  Queen Margaret Hall: regulations and discussion about discipline
  Correspondence between Frances Melville and Phoebe Sheavyn, 1924
  Photographs
Pass It On (Magazine of Women's Education Union, 1935)
Jus Suffragii Alumnae (1909)
The College Courant

St Andrews

Minutes of Senate, including:
  Petitions from ladies for instruction
  Report on will of Sir William Taylour Thomson and bequest to assist women to
    study for medical profession, 1883
  Motion on supervision of lady students, 1895

Report of committee on supervision of lady students, 1896
Minutes of University Court, 1913 (re suffrage summer school in University
    Hall)
University calendars
Women Students' Union: minute book 1912–13; accounts, 1902–17
Minutes of women students' reading room committee, 1894–9
Minute book of Town Students' Association, 1925–33
University Hall archives:
    Miss Dobson's scrapbook
    Louisa Lumsden's "Story of University Hall", 1910
    Wardens' files
    Correspondence on suffrage summer school (Dobson file)
    Accounts and press cuttings
    Applications for wardenship, 1936
    Frances Melville's notes on finance, 1907
    Frances Melville's memorandum on duties of Warden
College Echoes
The Alumnus Chronicle

2. Modern Records Centre (University of Warwick)

Clara Collet: papers and correspondence; "Diary of a young assistant mistress,
    1878–1885" (includes reference to her experiences as a student of University
    College London, resident in College Hall)
Association of Assistant Mistresses, annual reports from 1885
Association of Headmistresses, committee minutes, conference reports (includes
    Report on the supervision of university girl students, 1912)
Association of University Teachers: records and correspondence, minutes of
    Council, 1919–75
Association of University Women Teachers: annual report, 1917–18, with list of
    members

3. The British Federation of University Women

Note: In 1992 the BFUW became the British Federation of Women Graduates,
moving from Crosby Hall to premises in Battersea Park Road.

Minute books, 1909–
Committee on International Relationships, minute books
Minute books, Manchester branch, 1922–
Academic subcommittee minute books
Education committee minutes
Public affairs committee minutes
Local association files

Executive committee correspondence
Files on equal pay, married women teachers
Fellowships files (including Rose Sidgwick Memorial Fellowship)
Crosby Hall appeal leaflets
Business and university committee correspondence
Scrapbooks of press cuttings
BFUW *Newssheet* (from 1937, *The University Women's Review*)
Annual reports
1931 survey, *Position of women on the teaching staff of British universities*, questionnaires, returns, etc.
1937 survey, *Economic status of gainfully employed university women*, (various papers)
1932 Edinburgh conference, International Federation of University Women, papers, publicity material and correspondence

4. *The University Women's Club (Audley Square)*

Minutes of annual general meetings, 1883–
Minutes of house committee meetings
General committee minutes
Candidates books
Subscription book, 1920–26
Grace Thornton album, "Some distinguished members"

5. *The Public Records Office*

University Grants Committee: returns from 1919
Reports and annual surveys
Reports of subcommittees
Education files on universities and university colleges
Endowment files, universities and university colleges
Files on grants to training colleges and university departments of education
Awards and scholarships files – material on state scholarships, 1919–

6. *Gilchrist Educational Trust*

Minutes and accounts from 1874
Papers, reports, pamphlets

II. Parliamentary papers

Report of commissioners appointed to consider the draft charter for the proposed Gresham University in London, 1893–4 (the Gresham Report, C 7259 xxxi, 807).

Reports from university colleges participating in the grant of £15,000 made by Parliament for university colleges in Great Britain, 1894–1913/4 (1894: C 7459 vol. 66, 1914: Cd. 8137 vol. 19)

Returns from universities and university colleges in receipt of Treasury grant, 1919–20 (1921, vol. 26, Cmd. 1265, p. 605)

Board of Education interim report of consultative committee on scholarships for higher education, 1916 (Cd. 8291, vol. viii)

Report of Royal Commission on university education in London (Haldane Commission):

    First report, 1910, Cd. 5165, xxiii, 639
    Evidence, appendices and index, 1910 Cd. 5166, xxiii, 643
    Second report, 1911, Cd. 5527, xx, 1
    Evidence, appendices, 1911, Cd. 5528, xx, 5
    Third report, 1911, Cd. 5910, xx, 453
    Evidence, appendices, 1911, Cd. 5911, xx, 452
    Fourth report, 1912–13, Cd. 6015, xxii, 581
    Fifth report, 1912–13, Cd. 6015, xxii, 587
    Appendix to fifth report, 1912–13, Cd. 6312, xxii, 591
    Final report, 1913, Cd. 6717, x1, 297
    Evidence, appendices, index, 1913, Cd. 6718, x1, 543

Report of Royal Commission on Oxford and Cambridge universities, 1922 (Asquith Commission, Cmd. 1588, x, 27)

III. Theses

Berman, J. W. *A sense of achievement: the significance of higher education for British women, 1890–1930* (PhD thesis, State University of New York at Buffalo, 1982).

Cohen, E. G. *An investigation into the early development of the training of schoolmistresses in the late nineteenth and early twentieth centuries, with special reference to the faculty of education in University College, Cardiff* (MEd thesis, University of Wales, 1977).

Davies, P. A. *The women students at University College, Cardiff, 1883–1933* (MEd thesis, University of Wales, 1983).

Gibert, J. S. *Women at the English civic universities, 1880–1920* (PhD thesis, University of North Carolina at Chapel Hill, 1988).

Hamilton, S. *Women and the Scottish universities c. 1869–1939: a social history*

(PhD thesis, University of Edinburgh, 1987).

Lemoine, S. *The North of England Council for Promoting the Higher Education of Women* (MA thesis, University of Manchester, 1968).

Logan, C. *Women at Glasgow University: determination or predetermination?* (MA dissertation, University of Glasgow, 1986).

Perrone, F. *University teaching as a profession for women in Oxford, Cambridge and London, 1870–1930* (DPhil thesis, University of Oxford, 1991).

Scobie, K. *Women at Glasgow University in the 1920s and 1930s* (MA dissertation, University of Glasgow, 1986).

Simon, J. *Shena Simon, Feminist and Educationist* (typescript, for private circulation, 1986).

Sommerkorn, I. *On the position of women in the university teaching profession in England: an interview study of 100 women teachers* (PhD thesis, London School of Economics, 1967).

Weston, D. *Clio's daughters, change and continuity: the question of the role of women academics in the "old" and "new" women's history* (MA thesis, Thames Polytechnic, 1987).

Wills, S. R. *The social and economic aspects of higher education for women between 1844 and 1870, with special reference to the North of England Council* (MA thesis, University of London, 1951).

Woodgate, D. A. *Ashburne Hall, Manchester, 1899–1924, the first 25 years: the construction of a history of student life in a university women's hall of residence* (BA dissertation, University of Manchester, 1994).

IV. Published sources, pre-1945

A. Pamphlets and articles

[Aberdare], *Aberdare Hall, 1885–1935* (Cardiff, 1936).

Anstruther, E., Ladies' Clubs. *The Nineteenth Century* XLV, 1899, pp. 598–611.

Burton, K., *A memoir of Mrs Crudelius* (Edinburgh, 1879).

Busk, H., *Short history of Bedford College (for women)* (London: Jubilee Publication, 1899).

Carthew, A. G. E., *The University Women's Club: extracts from fifty years of minute books, 1886–1936* (1st edn 1937; Eastbourne, 1985).

Collier, A., Social origins of a sample of entrants to Glasgow University. *Sociological Review* XXX, 1938, pp. 161–277.

Crump, P., Women students at the University of Manchester. *Journal of Careers* (November), 1928, pp. 28–30.

Donaldson, R. E. D., Women students at the universities: no. V, Durham. *Journal of Careers* (January), 1930, pp. 36–38.

Fitch, J. G. Women and the universities. *Contemporary Review* 58, 1890, pp. 240–55.

Gordon, A. The after careers of university educated women. *The Nineteenth Century* 37, 1895, pp. 955–60.

[Hope Hogg], *Mary Hope Hogg, 1863–1936* (memorial pamphlet) (Manchester, 1936).

Hutchins, B. L., Higher education and marriage. *The Englishwoman* 18, 1913, pp. 257–64.

Jex-Blake, S., *Medical education of women: a comprehensive summary of present facilities* (Edinburgh, 1888).

Knight, W., *A history of the LLA examination and diploma for women and of the university hall for women students at the University of St Andrews* (Dundee, 1896).

Maudsley, H., Sex in mind and education. *Fortnightly Review* XV, 1874, pp. 466–83.

Melville, F., The preparation of girls for university. *The Secondary School Journal* (8 June), 1915, pp. 40–42.

Melville, F., *University education for women in Scotland; its effects on social and intellectual life* (St Andrews, 1902).

Melville, F., The university education of women in the twentieth century. *The Educational News* (10 August), 1901, pp. 551–2.

Murray, D., *Miss Janet Ann Galloway and the higher education of women in Glasgow* (Glasgow, 1914).

Neville, E. H., This misdemeanour of marriage. *The Universities Review* VI(1), 1933, pp. 5–8.

Rackstraw, M., *Masson Hall, retrospect and forecast* (Edinburgh, 1931).

Robertson, C. G., The provincial universities. *Sociological Review* 31, 1939, pp. 248–59.

Sheavyn, P., *Higher education for women in Great Britain.* (London, *c.* 1924).

Shepherd, N., Women in the university: fifty years, 1892–1942. *Aberdeen University Review* XXIX, 1941–2, pp. 171–81.

Shuttleworth, Lord, *Pioneering work in education: The Gilchrist Educational Trust* (Cambridge, 1930).

Sidgwick, Mrs. H., *Health statistics of women students of Cambridge and Oxford and of their sisters* (Cambridge, 1890).

Smedley Maclean, I., *A short account of the British Federation of University Women* (London, 1935).

Thorburn, J. *Female education from a physiological point of view* (Manchester, 1884).

Tuke, M., Women students in the universities. *Contemporary Review* 133, 1928, pp. 71–7.

Wilson, E. C., *In memoriam, Alice Drayton Greenwood, 1862–1935* (privately printed, 1935).

Zimmern, A., Lady students at Cambridge. *London Society* (May), 1882, pp. 494–9.

Zimmern, A., Women at the universities. *Leisure Hour* (August), 1898, pp. 433–42.

Zimmern, A., Women in European universities. *Forum* (April), 1895, pp. 187–99.

B. Books

Becket, E. M., *The University College of Nottingham* (Nottingham, 1928).
Bellot, H. Hale, *University College London, 1826–1926* (London, 1926).
Bremner, C. S., *Education of girls and women in Great Britain* (London, 1897).
Brittain, V., *The dark tide* (London, 1923).
Brodie, D. M., *Women's University Settlement, 1887–1937* (London, 1937).
[Cashmore] *Hilda Cashmore, 1876–1943* (Gloucester, privately printed, 1943).
Collet, C., *Educated working women: essays on the economic position of women workers in the middle classes* (London, 1902).
Compton Burnett, I. *Dolores* (Edinburgh & London, 1911).
"Dane, Clemence" (Winifred Ashton), *Regiment of women* (London, 1917).
Davies, E., *Women in the universities of England and Scotland* (Cambridge, 1896).
Dawson, W. H. (ed.), *Yearbook of the universities of the Empire (of the Commonwealth)* (London, annually from 1914 (except 1941–6)).
[Directory], *The directory of women teachers and other women engaged in higher and secondary education* (London, 1913, 1914, 1925, 1927).
Edinburgh University Women's Union, *Atalanta's Garland, being the book of the Edinburgh University Women's Union* (Edinburgh, 1926).
Ellis, G. S. M., *The poor student and the university* (London, 1925).
Gardner, A., *A short history of Newnham College, Cambridge* (Cambridge, 1921).
Grier, L., *The life of Winifred Mercier* (Oxford, 1937).
Haldane, C., *Motherhood and its enemies* (London, 1927).
Harrison, J., *Reminiscences of a student's life* (London, 1925).
Hearnshaw, F. J. C., *The centenary history of King's College London, 1828–1928* (London, 1929).
Hogben, L. (ed.), *Political arithmetic* (London, 1938).
Horner, I. B., *Alice M. Cooke: a memoir* (Manchester, 1940).
Hughes, W. R., *Constance Naden: a memoir* (London & Birmingham, 1890).
[Hutchinson's] *Hutchinson's woman's Who's Who* (London, 1934).
Lee, J., *This great journey* (New York & Toronto, 1942).
Lehmann, R., *Dusty answer* (London, 1927).
Lodge, Sir O., Preface to *The position of woman: actual and ideal . . . papers delivered in Edinburgh in 1911 with a preface by Sir Oliver Lodge* (London, 1911).
Logan Turner, A., *History of the University of Edinburgh, 1883–1933* (Edinburgh, 1933).
Lumsden, L. I., *Yellow leaves: memories of a long life* (Edinburgh & London, 1933).
Milne Rae, L., *Ladies in debate, being a history of the Ladies' Edinburgh Debating*

Society, 1865–1935 (Edinburgh, 1936).

Morgan, I., *The college by the sea: University College of Wales, Aberystwyth* (Aberystwyth, 1928).

Morley, E. (ed.), *Women workers in seven professions* (London, 1914).

Oakeley, H., *History and progress* (London, 1923).

Oakeley, H., *My adventures in education* (London, 1939).

Pascoe, C., *Schools for girls and colleges for women: a handbook of female education* (London, 1879).

Pfeiffer, E., *Women and work: an essay* (London, 1888).

Redlich, M., *Cheap return; portrait of an educated young woman* (London, 1934).

Rich, R. W., *The training of teachers in England and Wales during the nineteenth century* (Cambridge, 1933).

Riddell, Lord, *Dame Louisa Aldrich Blake* (London, n.d.).

Roberts, R. D., *Education in the nineteenth century* (Cambridge, 1901).

Rogers, A. M. A., *Degrees by degrees* (Oxford, 1938).

Sayers, D., *Gaudy night* (London, 1935).

Shaen, M. J., *Memorials of two sisters, Susanna and Catherine Winkworth . . . edited by their niece* (London, 1908).

Simon, B., *A student's view of the universities* (London, 1943).

Starkie, E., *A lady's child* (London, 1941).

Stephen, B., *Emily Davies and Girton College* (London, 1927).

Stephen, B., *Girton College, 1869–1932* (Cambridge, 1933).

Stronach, A., *A Newnham friendship* (London, 1901).

"Travers, Graham" (Margaret G. Todd), *Mona Maclean, medical student* (Edinburgh & London, 1892).

"Truscot, B." (E. Allison Peers), *Redbrick and these vital days* (London, 1945).

"Truscot, B." (E. Allison Peers), *Redbrick university* (London, 1943).

Tuke, M., *A history of Bedford College for Women, 1849–1937* (Oxford, 1939).

Tylecote, M., *The education of women at Manchester University, 1883–1933* (Manchester, 1941).

Tylecote, M., *Votiva tabella: a memorial volume of St Andrews University in connection with its quincentenary festival* (St Andrews, 1911).

Whiting, C. E., *The University of Durham, 1832–1932* (London, 1932).

Wilson, E. C., *Catherine Isabella Dodd, 1860–1932, a memorial sketch* (London, 1936).

Winstanley, D. A., *Early Victorian Cambridge* (Cambridge, 1940).

Woolf, V., *A room of one's own* (London, 1928).

Woolf, V., *Three guineas* (London, 1938).

V. Published sources, post-1945

A. Pamphlets and articles

Acker, S., Women, the other academics. *British Journal of Sociology of Education* 1(1), 1980, pp. 81–91.

Alexander, W., *First ladies of medicine: the origins, education and destination of the early women medical graduates of Glasgow University* (Glasgow, 1987).

Allan, A., *University bodies: a survey of inter and supra university bodies and their records* (Chippenham, 1990).

Anderson, Dame K., *Women and the universities: a changing pattern* (London, 1963).

Banks, J. A. & O. Banks, The Bradlaugh–Besant trial and the English newspapers. *Population Studies* 8, 1954–5, pp. 22–33.

Batho, E., *A lamp of friendship, 1918–1968: a short history of the International Federation of University Women* (Eastbourne, 1968).

Berg, M., The first women economic historians. *Economic History Review* XLV(2), 1992, pp. 308–29.

Boog Watson, E., *The Edinburgh Association for the University Education of Women, 1867–1967* (privately printed, n.d.).

Boog Watson, W. N., The first eight ladies. *University of Edinburgh Journal* 23, 1970, pp. 227–34.

Boog Watson, W. N., The story of the Women Students' Union. *University of Edinburgh Journal* 24, 1970, pp. 186–92.

Bowie-Menzler, M., *Founders of Crosby Hall* (London, 1981).

Brooksbank, I., Bingles and bicycles. *Oxford Today* 3(2), 1991, pp. 34–5.

Butcher, E. E., *Clifton Hill House: the first phase, 1909–1959* (no publisher, n.d.).

Callender, B., *Education in the melting pot* (Norwich, n.d., c.1972).

Cambridge University Women's Action Group, *Forty years on . . . report on the numbers and status of academic women in the University of Cambridge* (Cambridge, 1988).

Carter, S. B., Academic women revisited: an empirical study of changing patterns in women's employment as college and university faculty, 1890–1963. *Journal of Social History* 14(4), 1981, pp. 675–99.

Catto, I. (ed.), *"No spirits and precious few women": Edinburgh University Union, 1889–1989* (Edinburgh, 1989).

Checkland, O., *Queen Margaret Union, 1890–1980: women in the University of Glasgow* (Glasgow, 1980).

Ellis, E. L. (ed.), *Alexandra Hall, 1896–1986* (Aberystwyth, 1986).

Fletcher, J. & C. Upton, Monastic enclave or open society? A consideration of the role of women in the life of an Oxford college community in the early Tudor period. *History of Education* 16(1), 1987, pp. 1–9.

Gibby, C. W., Academic Durham in 1926. *The Durham University Journal* (December), 1986, pp. 1–6.

SELECT BIBLIOGRAPHY

Gilchrist, M., Some early recollections of the Queen Margaret Medical School. *Surgo* (March), 1948.

Goodbody, M., *Five daughters in search of learning: the Sturge family, 1820–1944* (Bristol, 1986).

Hamilton, S., Interviewing the middle class: women graduates of the Scottish universities, c. 1900–1935. *Oral History* 10(2), 1982, pp. 58–67.

Harding, J. N. (ed.), *Aberdare Hall, 1885–1985* (Cardiff, 1986).

Hargreaves, J., "Playing like gentlemen while behaving like ladies": contradictory features of the formative years of women's sport. *British Journal of Sports History* II, 1985, pp. 40–52.

Harte, N. B., *The admission of women to University College, London, a centenary lecture* (London, 1979).

Herbertson, B., *The Pfeiffer bequest and the education of women: a centenary review* (Cambridge, printed for private circulation, 1993).

Hird, M. (ed.), *Doves and dons: a history of St Mary's College, Durham* (Durham, 1982).

Howarth, J. & M. Curthoys, The political economy of women's higher education in late nineteenth and early twentieth century Britain. *Historical Research* 60(142), 1987, pp. 208–31.

Hughes, M. W. (ed.), *Ashburne Hall: the first fifty years, 1899–1949* (Manchester, 1949).

Jenkins, I., The Yorkshire Ladies' Council of Education, 1871–91. *Publications of the Thoresby Society Miscellany* 16(124), 1978, pp. 27–71.

Jones, J. & J. Castle, Women in UK universities, 1920–1980. *Studies in Higher Education* 11(3), 1986, pp. 289–97.

Kendall, C. M., Higher education and the emergence of the professional woman in Glasgow, c. 1890–1914. *History of Universities* X, 1991, pp. 199–223.

Laurence, M., Anecdotage, 1927–31. *University of Edinburgh Journal* 28, 1977, pp. 126–9.

Lonsdale, K., Women in science: reminiscences and reflections. *Impact of Science on Society* 20, 1970, pp. 46–59.

Love, R., "Alice in Eugenics-land": feminism and eugenics in the scientific careers of Alice Lee and Ethel Elderton. *Annals of Science* 36, 1979, pp. 145–58.

Mackinnon, A., Male heads on female shoulders? New questions for the history of women's higher education. *History of Education Review* 19(2), 1990, pp. 36–47.

Melville, F., Queen Margaret College. *The College Courant* (Whitsun), 1949, pp. 99–107.

Moore, L., Aberdeen and the higher education of women, 1868–1877. *Aberdeen University Review* 163, 1980, pp. 280–303.

Moore, L. The Aberdeen Ladies' Educational Association, 1877–1883. *Northern Scotland* 3, (1977–80), pp. 123–57.

Musgrove, F., Middle class education and employment in the nineteenth century. *Economic History Review* 12, 1959, pp. 99–111.

Park, A., Women, men, and the academic hierarchy: exploring the relationship between rank and sex. *Oxford Review of Education* **18**(3), 1992, pp. 227–39.

Perrone, F., Women academics in England, 1870–1930. *History of Universities* XII, 1993, pp. 339–67.

Phare, E. E., From Devon to Cambridge, 1926: or, mentioned with derision. *The Cambridge Review* (26 February), 1982, pp. 144–9.

Pope, R. D. & M. G. Verbeke, Ladies' educational organisations in England, 1865–1885. *Paedagogica Historica* **16**(2), 1976, pp. 336–61.

Robertson, A., Catherine I. Dodd and innovation in teacher training, 1892–1905. *History of Education Society Bulletin* (Spring),1991, pp. 32–41.

Smart, R. N., Literate ladies – a fifty year experiment. *Alumnus Chronicle* (St Andrews, June, 1968), pp. 21–31.

Sondheimer, J., *History of the British Federation of University Women, 1907–1957* (London, 1957).

Spurling, A., *Report of the women in higher education research project, 1988–90* (King's College, Cambridge, 1990).

Stanier, M. B., The old order: an undergraduate in the 1920s. *University of Edinburgh Journal* **23**, 1968, pp. 157–9.

Thomas, J. B., The day training college: a Victorian innovation in teacher training. *British Journal of Teacher Education* **4**(3), 1978, pp. 249–61.

Thomas, N. B., Students, staff and curriculum in a day training college: a case study of University College, Cardiff, 1890–1914. *Paedagogica Historica* **2**(25), 1985, pp. 281–96.

Thomas, J. B., University College, Bristol: pioneering teacher training for women. *History of Education* **17**(1), 1988, pp. 55–70.

Thornton, G., *Conversation piece: an introduction to the ladies in the dining room* (London, University Women's Club, 1985).

University Hall Association (Liverpool), *University Hall, fiftieth anniversary bulletin* (Liverpool, 1952).

Vicinus, M., "One life to stand beside me": emotional conflicts in first generation college women in England. *Feminist Studies* **8**, 1982, pp. 603–27.

Walton, A., Attitudes to women scientists. *Chemistry in Britain* (May), 1985, pp. 461–5.

Wilkie, H., Steps which led to the appointment of a woman superintendent of studies. *University of Edinburgh Journal* **25**, 1971, pp. 136–9.

B. Books

Abir-am, P. G. & D. Outram (eds), *Uneasy careers and intimate lives: women in science, 1789–1979* (Rutgers University Press, 1987).

Acker, S. & D. Warren Piper, *Is higher education fair to women?* (Guildford, 1984).

Anderson, R. D., *Education and opportunity in Victorian Scotland: schools and universities* (Oxford, 1983).

Anderson, R. D., *The student community at Aberdeen, 1860–1939* (Aberdeen,

1988).

Anderson, R. D., *Universities and elites in Britain since 1800* (Basingstoke, 1992).

Anning, S. T. & W. K. J. Walls, *A history of the Leeds School of Medicine: one and a half centuries, 1831–1981* (Leeds, 1982).

Anning, S. T., *The history of medicine in Leeds* (Leeds, 1980).

Armytage, W. H. G., *Civic universities: aspects of a British tradition* (London, 1955).

Benjamin, M. (ed.), *Science and sensibility, gender and scientific enquiry in England, 1780–1945* (Oxford, 1991).

Benstock, S. (ed.), *The private self: theory and practice of women's autobiographical writings* (London, 1988).

Bernard, J., *Academic women* (Pennsylvania, 1964).

Bettenson, E. M., *The University of Newcastle-upon-Tyne, a historical introduction, 1834–1931* (Newcastle, 1971).

Beveridge, J., *An epic of Clare Market: birth and early days of the London School of Economics* (London, 1960).

Beveridge, Lord, *The London School of Economics and its problems, 1919–1937* (London, 1960).

Bingham, C., *The history of Royal Holloway College, 1886–1986* (London, 1987).

Blake, C., *The charge of the parasols: women's entry to the medical profession* (London, 1990).

Bradburn, E., *Dr Dora Esther Yates: an appreciation* (Liverpool, 1975).

Brittain, V., *The women at Oxford: a fragment of history* (London, 1960).

Bryson, E., *Look back in wonder* (1st edn 1966; Dundee, 1980).

Burstyn, J. N., *Victorian education and the ideal of womanhood* (Rutgers University Press, 1984).

Bussey, G. & M. Tims, *Pioneers for peace: Women's International League for Peace and Freedom, 1915–65* (London, 1965).

Butler, E. M., *Paper boats* (London, 1959).

Caine, S., *The history of the foundation of the London School of Economics and Political Science* (London, 1963).

Callan, H. & S. Ardener (eds), *The incorporated wife* (London, 1984).

Campbell, P. D. A., *A short history of the Durham Union Society* (Durham, 1952).

Carleton, D., *A university for Bristol: an informal history in text and pictures* (Bristol, 1984).

Carter, I., *Ancient cultures of conceit: British university fiction in the post-war years* (London, 1990).

Chapman, A. W., *The story of a modern university: a history of the University of Sheffield* (Oxford, 1955).

Cheesewright, M., *Mirror to a mermaid: pictorial reminiscences of Mason College and the University of Birmingham, 1875–1975* (Birmingham, 1975).

Chrimes, S. B. (ed.), *The University College of South Wales and Monmouthshire: a centenary history, 1883–1983* (Cardiff, 1983).

Clifford, G. J. (ed.), *Lone voyagers: academic women in co-educational institu-*

274

tions, 1870–1937 (New York, 1989).

Copping, A. M., *The story of College Hall* (London, 1974).

Cottle, B. & J. Sherborne, *The life of a university* (Bristol, 1957).

Deem, R. (ed.), *Schooling for women's work* (London, 1980).

Delamont, S., *Knowledgeable women: structuralism and the reproduction of elites* (London, 1989).

Delamont, S. & L. Duffin (eds), *The nineteenth-century woman: her cultural and physical world* (London, 1978).

Donaldson, G., *Four centuries: Edinburgh University life, 1583–1983* (Edinburgh, 1983).

Dyhouse, C., *Girls growing up in late Victorian and Edwardian England* (London, 1981).

Ellis, E. L., *The University College of Wales, Aberystwyth, 1872–1972* (Cardiff, 1972).

Evans, J., *Prelude and fugue: an autobiography* (London, 1964).

Evans, W. G., *Education and female emancipation: the Welsh experience, 1847–1914* (Cardiff, 1990).

Faderman, L., *Surpassing the love of men: romantic friendship and love between women from the Renaissance to the present* (London, 1982).

Gordon, L. D., *Gender and higher education in the progressive era* (New Haven, 1990).

Gosden, P. H. & A. J. Taylor (eds), *Studies in the history of a university, 1874–1974* (Leeds, 1975).

Grier, L., *Achievement in education: the work of Michael Ernest Sadler, 1885–1935* (London, 1952).

Griffin, P. (ed.), *St Hugh's: one hundred years of women's education in Oxford* (Oxford, 1986).

Hall, R. A., *Science for industry: a short history of the Imperial College of Science and Technology and its antecedents* (London, 1982).

Halsey, A. & M. Trow, *The British academics* (London, 1971).

Hansard Society, *Women at the top: the report of the Hansard Society Commission* (London, 1990).

Harrison, B. (ed.), *The history of the University of Oxford*, vol. VIII, *the twentieth century* (Oxford, 1994).

Heilbrun, C., *Writing a woman's life* (London, 1988).

Higonnet, M. R. et al. (eds), *Behind the lines: gender and the two world wars* (New Haven, 1987).

Holt, J. C., *The University of Reading, the first fifty years* (Reading, 1977).

Horowitz, Helen Lefkowitz, *Alma Mater: design and experience in the women's colleges from their nineteenth-century beginnings to the 1930s* (New York, 1984).

Horowitz, Helen Lefkowitz, *Campus life* (Chicago, 1987).

Hubback, J., *Wives who went to college* (London, 1957).

Hughes, B. & S. Ahern, *Redbrick and bluestockings: women at Victoria, 1899–1993* (Wellington, 1993).

275

Hunt, F. (ed.), *Lessons for life: the schooling of girls and women, 1850–1950* (Oxford, 1987).

Huws-Jones, E., *Margery Fry, the essential amateur* (London, 1966).

Huxley, E., *Love among the daughters* (London, 1968).

Janssen, R. M., *The first hundred years: Egyptology at University College, London, 1892–1992* (London, 1992).

Jarausch, K. H., *The transformation of higher learning, 1860–1930* (Chicago, 1983).

Jeffreys, S., *The spinster and her enemies: feminism and sexuality, 1880–1930* (London, 1985).

Jepson, N., *The beginnings of English university adult education: policy and problems* (London, 1973).

Jones, D. R., *The origins of civic universities: Manchester, Leeds and Liverpool* (London, 1988).

Jones, G., & M. Quinn (eds), *Fountains of praise: University College Cardiff, 1883–1983* (Cardiff, 1983).

Judd, D., *Alison Uttley, the life of a country child, 1884–1976* (London, 1986).

Kamm, J., *Hope deferred: girls' education in English history* (London, 1965).

Kanter, R. M., *Men and women of the corporation.* (USA: Basic Books, 1977).

Kelly, T., *For advancement of learning: the University of Liverpool, 1881–1981* (Liverpool, 1981).

Kingsley Kent, S., *Making peace: the reconstruction of gender in interwar Britain* (Princeton, 1993).

Lansbury, C., *The old brown dog: women, workers and vivisection in Edwardian England* (Wisconsin, 1985).

Lawrence, A., *St Hild's College, 1858–1958* (Darlington, 1958).

Lennox, G. R., *Echoes from the hills* (Devon, 1978).

Leonardi, S. J., *Dangerous by degrees: women at Oxford and the Somerville College novelists* (New Brunswick & London, 1989).

London Feminist History Group (eds), *The sexual dynamics of history* (London, 1983).

McCrone, K., *Sport and the physical emancipation of English women, 1870–1914* (London, 1988).

Mackenzie, N. & J. Mackenzie (eds), *All the good things in life, the diary of Beatrice Webb*, vol II, *1892–1905* (London, 1983).

McLaren, A., *Birth control in nineteenth-century England* (London, 1978).

Macqueen, J. & S. Taylor (eds), *University and community: essays to mark the centenary of the founding of University College Bristol* (Bristol, 1976).

McWilliams-Tullberg, R., *Women at Cambridge: a men's university, though of a mixed type* (London, 1975).

Mangan, J. A., *Athleticism in the Victorian and Edwardian public school: the emergence and consolidation of an educational ideology* (Cambridge, 1981).

Mangan, J. A. & R. J. Park (eds), *From "fair sex" to feminism. Sport and the socialisation of women in the industrial and post-industrial eras* (London, 1987).

Marsh, N., *The history of Queen Elizabeth College* (London, 1986).

Marshall, M. Paley, *What I remember* (Cambridge, 1947).

Martindale, L., *A woman surgeon* (London, 1951).

Moore, L., *Bajanellas and semilinas: Aberdeen University and the education of women, 1860–1920* (Aberdeen, 1991).

Muller, D., F. Ringer, & B. Simon (eds), *The rise of the modern educational system: structural change and social reproduction* (Cambridge, 1987).

Murray, M., *My first hundred years* (London, 1963).

Nethercott, A., *The first five lives of Annie Besant* (London, 1961).

Oldfield, S. (ed.), *This working-day world: women's lives and culture(s) in Britain, 1914–45* (London, 1994).

Peck, W., *A little learning, or a Victorian childhood* (London, 1952).

Pedersen, J. S., *The reform of girls' secondary and higher education in Victorian England: a study of elites and educational change* (New York & London, 1987).

Perkin, H. J., *Key profession* (London, 1969).

Phillips, A. (ed.), *A Newnham anthology* (Cambridge, 1979).

Proctor, Mortimer, *The English university novel* (Berkeley & Los Angeles, 1957).

Rayner, M. E., *The centenary history of St Hilda's College, Oxford* (Oxford, 1993).

Richardson, J., *Enid Starkie* (London, 1973).

Rossiter, M., *Women scientists in America: struggles and strategies to 1940* (Baltimore, 1982).

Rothblatt, S., *The revolution of the dons* (Cambridge, 1968).

Rubinstein, W. D., *Men of property: the very wealthy in Britain since the Industrial Revolution* (London, 1981).

Sanderson, M., *The universities and British industry 1850–1970* (London, 1972).

Shafe, M., *University education in Dundee, 1881–1981: a pictorial history* (Dundee, 1982).

Shimmin, A. N., *The University of Leeds: the first half-century* (Cambridge, 1954).

Silver, H. & S. J. Teague, *The history of British universities 1800–1969, (excluding Oxford and Cambridge) a bibliography* (London, 1970).

Simmons, J., *Leicester and its university* (Leicester, 1963).

Slater, S. D. & D. A. Dow, *The Victoria Infirmary of Glasgow, 1890–1990: a centenary history* (Glasgow, 1990).

Solomon, B. Miller, *In the company of educated women* (New Haven, 1985).

Sondheimer, J., *Castle Adamant in Hampstead: a history of Westfield College, 1882–1982* (London, 1983).

Stacey, J., S. Béreaud, & J. Daniels (eds), *And Jill came tumbling after: sexism in American education* (New York, 1974).

Stocks, M., *My commonplace book* (London, 1970).

Temple Patterson, A., *The University of Southampton: a centenary history of the evolution and development of the University of Southampton, 1862–1962* (Southampton, 1962).

Thomas, J. B. (ed.), *British universities and teacher education: a century of change*

(Lewes, 1990).

Thompson, F. M. L. (ed.), *The University of London and the world of learning, 1836–1986* (London & Ronceverte, 1990).

Tudor, H., *St Cuthbert's Society, 1888–1988* (Durham, 1988).

Vicinus, M., *Independent women: work and community for single women, 1850–1920* (London, 1985).

Vincent, E. W. & P. Hinton, *The University of Birmingham, its history and significance* (Birmingham, 1947).

Walters, D., *The Oxford Union, playground of power* (London, 1984).

Wheeler, Sir Mortimer, *The British Academy, 1949–1968* (Oxford, 1970).

Williams, J. Gwynn, *The University College of North Wales: foundations, 1884–1927* (Cardiff, 1985).

Wood, A. C., *A history of the University College Nottingham, 1881–1948* (Oxford, 1953).

Wootton, B., *In a world I never made* (London, 1967).

Index

day training college 19
and degrees for women 158
disciplinary proecedures at Somerville
     214
and equal opportunities 1, 2, 4
Local Examinations 14
Somerville College 161–2
undergraduates and local women 56
women students 239–40, 241
  chaperonage of 192–3
  costs for 28
  marriages 24

Pares, Bernard 166
Pearson, Karl 145, 149, 150
Pease, Marian 22, 58–9, 65, 136
Pechey, Edith 28
Peck, Winifred 24
Penrose, Emily 44, 214
Perkin, Harold 149
Perrone, Fernanda 6, 138, 161
Perry, Sir Cooper 147
Pethick-Lawrence, Emmeline 166
Petrie, Flinders 148, 149, 155
Petrie, Mary 207
Pfeiffer, Emily (neé Davis) 97–8, 192
Phare, Elsie (later Duncan-Jones) 83–4,
     162–3
Phillips, Marion 142
Pick, Marion 142
Pinchbeck, Ivy 146
Pioneer, The 172
Plumer, Eleanor 47, 205
Powell, Dilys 214
Power, Eileen 143, 146–7, 176, 224
professors
  wives of 57–8, 71, 94, 227
  women 137, 138, 140, 142, 150
  Edith Morley 159–61

Rackstraw, Marjorie 81–2, 110, 116,
     216, 217
Radford, G. H. 169–70
Radice, Alice (neé Murray) 146
Rae, Lettice Milne 209
"rag weeks" 211–13
Rankine, John 43
Rathbone, Eleanor 144, 164
Rathbone, Mrs Hugh 99
Raymont, Mr 136–7
Reading University
  boat racing 202–3

Edith Morley at 140, 156–61
and equal opportunities 3
halls and hostels 93
male students' misdeeds 214–15
and marriages of women students 25
sexual division among students 225–6
social distinctions among students 120
Tamesis magazine 190, 214, 243
Reichel (Principal of Bangor College)
     104–5, 194–5
Reid, Elizabeth 38
Rendel, Margherita 6, 138, 139
research, grants and sponsorship 141–7
Rideout, Edna 35
Riesman, David 153
Roberts, Laura 21, 40
Robertson, Hannah 76–7, 136
Romer, Sir Robert 69
Room of one's own, A (Woolf) 1–2, 37
Rossiter, Margaret 40
Rowntree, Seebohm 222
Royal Holloway College 38, 44, 45, 121,
     135, 140, 173, 203
Rubinstein, W. D. 37

Sadler, Michael 76–8, 79
St Andrews University
  College Echoes and the admission of
     women students 197–8
  Elizabeth Macdonald (Bryson) at 26–7
  hall of residence 94
  "Lady Literate in Arts" certificate (LLA)
     12, 13, 171
  Lady Superintendent 70
  scholarships 29
  student magazine 197–8, 199
  and teacher education 18
  tuition fees 27
  Warden of hall of residence 105–6
  women students
    medical students 44
    proportion of 17
  and women's suffrage 218, 219, 220
salaries
  headmistresses' 149–50
  lady superintendents 100
  wardens 108, 148–9
  women tutors 78
  women university teachers 148–50,
     244–5
Sargeant, Joan 82
Schofield, Marjorie (neé Woodward) 24